Book 5 – Fixed Income, Derivatives, and Alternative Investments

D0520971

SCHWESERNOTES™ 2013 CFA LEVEL I BOOK 5: FIXED INCOME, DERIVATIVES, AND ALTERNATIVE INVESTMENTS

©2012 Kaplan, Inc. All rights reserved.

Published in 2012 by Kaplan Schweser.

Printed in the United States of America.

ISBN: 978-1-4277-4265-0 / 1-4277-4265-0

PPN: 3200-2848

Reading Assignments and Learning Outcome Statements

The following material is a review of the Fixed Income, Derivatives, and Alternative Investments principles designed to address the learning outcome statements set forth by CFA Institute.

Study Session 15

Reading Assignments

Equity and Fixed Income, CFA Program 2013 Curriculum, Volume 5 (CFA Institute, 2012)

Study Session 16

Reading Assignments

Equity and Fixed Income, CFA Program 2013 Curriculum, Volume 5 (CFA Institute, 2012)

Study Session 17

Reading Assignments

Derivatives and Alternative Investments, CFA Program 2013 Curriculum, Volume 6 (CFA Institute, 2012)

Study Session 18

Reading Assignments

Derivatives and Alternative Investments, CFA Program 2013 Curriculum, Volume 6 (CFA Institute, 2012)

LEARNING OUTCOME STATEMENTS (LOS)

The CFA Institute Learning Outcome Statements are listed below. These are repeated in each topic review; however, the order may have been changed in order to get a better fit with the flow of the review.

STUDY SESSION 15

The topical coverage corresponds with the following CFA Institute assigned reading:

52. **Features of Debt Securities**
    The candidate should be able to:
    a. explain the purposes of a bond's indenture and describe affirmative and negative covenants. (page 11)
    b. describe the basic features of a bond, the various coupon rate structures, and the structure of floating-rate securities. (page 12)
    c. define accrued interest, full price, and clean price. (page 14)
    d. explain the provisions for redemption and retirement of bonds. (page 14)
    e. identify common options embedded in a bond issue, explain the importance of embedded options, and identify whether an option benefits the issuer or the bondholder. (page 16)
    f. describe methods used by institutional investors in the bond market to finance the purchase of a security (i.e., margin buying and repurchase agreements). (page 17)

The topical coverage corresponds with the following CFA Institute assigned reading:

53. **Risks Associated with Investing in Bonds**
    The candidate should be able to:
    a. explain the risks associated with investing in bonds. (page 25)
    b. identify the relations among a bond's coupon rate, the yield required by the market, and the bond's price relative to par value (i.e., discount, premium, or equal to par). (page 27)
    c. explain how a bond maturity, coupon, embedded options and yield level affect its interest rate risk. (page 27)
    d. identify the relation of the price of a callable bond to the price of an option-free bond and the price of the embedded call option. (page 29)
    e. explain the interest rate risk of a floating-rate security and why its price may differ from par value. (page 29)
    f. calculate and interpret the duration and dollar duration of a bond. (page 30)
    g. describe yield-curve risk and explain why duration does not account for yield-curve risk. (page 32)
    h. explain the disadvantages of a callable or prepayable security to an investor. (page 34)
    i. identify the factors that affect the reinvestment risk of a security and explain why prepayable amortizing securities expose investors to greater reinvestment risk than nonamortizing securities. (page 34)
    j. describe types of credit risk and the meaning and role of credit ratings. (page 35)
    k. explain liquidity risk and why it might be important to investors even if they expect to hold a security to the maturity date. (page 36)

l. describe the exchange rate risk an investor faces when a bond makes payments in a foreign currency. (page 37)

m. explain inflation risk. (page 37)

n. explain how yield volatility affects the price of a bond with an embedded option and how changes in volatility affect the value of a callable bond and a putable bond. (page 37)

o. describe sovereign risk and types of event risk. (page 38)

The topical coverage corresponds with the following CFA Institute assigned reading:

54. Overview of Bond Sectors and Instruments

The candidate should be able to:

a. describe features, credit risk characteristics, and distribution methods for government securities. (page 46)

b. describe the types of securities issued by the U.S. Department of the Treasury (e.g., bills, notes, bonds, and inflation protection securities), and distinguish between on-the-run and off-the-run Treasury securities. (page 47)

c. describe how stripped Treasury securities are created and distinguish between coupon strips and principal strips. (page 49)

d. describe the types and characteristics of securities issued by U.S. federal agencies. (page 49)

e. describe the types and characteristics of mortgage-backed securities and explain the cash flow and prepayment risk for each type. (page 50)

f. explain the motivation for creating a collateralized mortgage obligation. (page 52)

g. describe the types of securities issued by municipalities in the United States and distinguish between tax-backed debt and revenue bonds. (page 53)

h. describe the characteristics and motivation for the various types of debt issued by corporations (including corporate bonds, medium-term notes, structured notes, commercial paper, negotiable CDs, and bankers acceptances). (page 55)

i. define an asset-backed security, describe the role of a special purpose vehicle in an asset-backed security's transaction, state the motivation for a corporation to issue an asset-backed security, and describe the types of external credit enhancements for asset-backed securities. (page 59)

j. describe collateralized debt obligations. (page 60)

k. describe the mechanisms available for placing bonds in the primary market and distinguish between the primary and secondary markets for bonds. (page 61)

The topical coverage corresponds with the following CFA Institute assigned reading:

55. Understanding Yield Spreads

The candidate should be able to:

a. identify the interest rate policy tools available to a central bank. (page 69)

b. describe a yield curve and the various shapes of the yield curve. (page 70)

c. explain the basic theories of the term structure of interest rates and describe the implications of each theory for the shape of the yield curve. (page 71)

d. define a spot rate. (page 73)

e. calculate and compare yield spread measures. (page 74)

f. describe credit spreads and relationships between credit spreads and economic conditions. (page 75)

g. describe how embedded options affect yield spreads. (page 76)

h. explain how liquidity and issue-size affects the yield spread of a bond relative to other similar securities. (page 76)

i.   calculate the after-tax yield of a taxable security and the tax-equivalent yield of a tax-exempt security. (page 77)

j.   define LIBOR and explain its importance to funded investors who borrow short term. (page 78)

STUDY SESSION 16

The topical coverage corresponds with the following CFA Institute assigned reading:

56. **Introduction to the Valuation of Debt Securities**
    The candidate should be able to:
    a.   explain steps in the bond valuation process. (page 87)
    b.   describe types of bonds for which estimating the expected cash flows is difficult. (page 87)
    c.   calculate the value of a bond (coupon and zero-coupon). (page 88)
    d.   explain how the price of a bond changes if the discount rate changes and as the bond approaches its maturity date. (page 91)
    e.   calculate the change in value of a bond given a change in its discount rate. (page 92)
    f.   explain and demonstrate the use of the arbitrage-free valuation approach and describe how a dealer can generate an arbitrage profit if a bond is mispriced. (page 94)

The topical coverage corresponds with the following CFA Institute assigned reading:

57. **Yield Measures, Spot Rates, and Forward Rates**
    The candidate should be able to:
    a.   describe the sources of return from investing in a bond. (page 101)
    b.   calculate and interpret traditional yield measures for fixed-rate bonds and explain their limitations and assumptions. (page 101)
    c.   explain the reinvestment assumption implicit in calculating yield to maturity and describe the factors that affect reinvestment risk. (page 108)
    d.   calculate and interpret the bond equivalent yield of an annual-pay bond and the annual-pay yield of a semiannual-pay bond. (page 110)
    e.   describe the calculation of the theoretical Treasury spot rate curve and calculate the value of a bond using spot rates. (page 111)
    f.   explain nominal, zero-volatility, and option-adjusted spreads and the relations among these spreads and option cost. (page 115)
    g.   explain a forward rate and calculate spot rates from forward rates, forward rates from spot rates, and the value of a bond using forward rates. (page 118)

The topical coverage corresponds with the following CFA Institute assigned reading:

58. **Introduction to the Measurement of Interest Rate Risk**
    The candidate should be able to:
    a.   distinguish between the full valuation approach (the scenario analysis approach) and the duration/convexity approach for measuring interest rate risk, and explain the advantage of using the full valuation approach. (page 134)
    b.   describe the price volatility characteristics for option-free, callable, prepayable, and putable bonds when interest rates change. (page 136)
    c.   describe positive convexity and negative convexity, and their relation to bond price and yield. (page 136)

d. calculate and interpret the effective duration of a bond, given information about how the bond's price will increase and decrease for given changes in interest rates. (page 139)

e. calculate the approximate percentage price change for a bond, given the bond's effective duration and a specified change in yield. (page 141)

f. distinguish among the alternative definitions of duration and explain why effective duration is the most appropriate measure of interest rate risk for bonds with embedded options. (page 142)

g. calculate the duration of a portfolio, given the duration of the bonds comprising the portfolio, and explain the limitations of portfolio duration. (page 144)

h. describe the convexity measure of a bond and estimate a bond's percentage price change, given the bond's duration and convexity and a specified change in interest rates. (page 145)

i. distinguish between modified convexity and effective convexity. (page 147)

j. calculate the price value of a basis point (PVBP), and explain its relationship to duration. (page 147)

k. describe the impact of yield volatility on the interest rate risk of a bond. (page 148)

The topical coverage corresponds with the following CFA Institute assigned reading:
59. **Fundamentals of Credit Analysis**
The candidate should be able to:

a. describe credit risk and credit-related risks affecting corporate bonds. (page 157)

b. describe seniority rankings of corporate debt and explain the potential violation of the priority of claims in a bankruptcy proceeding. (page 158)

c. distinguish between corporate issuer credit ratings and issue credit ratings and describe the rating agency practice of "notching". (page 159)

d. explain risks in relying on ratings from credit rating agencies. (page 160)

e. explain the components of traditional credit analysis. (page 161)

f. calculate and interpret financial ratios used in credit analysis. (page 163)

g. evaluate the credit quality of a corporate bond issuer and a bond of that issuer, given key financial ratios for the issuer and the industry. (page 167)

h. describe factors that influence the level and volatility of yield spreads. (page 169)

i. calculate the return impact of spread changes. (page 169)

j. explain special considerations when evaluating the credit of high yield, sovereign, and municipal debt issuers and issues. (page 172)

STUDY SESSION 17

The topical coverage corresponds with the following CFA Institute assigned reading:
60. **Derivative Markets and Instruments**
The candidate should be able to:

a. define a derivative and distinguish between exchange-traded and over-the-counter derivatives. (page 191)

b. contrast forward commitments and contingent claims. (page 191)

c. define forward contracts, futures contracts, options (calls and puts), and swaps and compare their basic characteristics. (page 192)

d. describe purposes of and controversies related to derivative markets. (page 192)

e. explain arbitrage and the role it plays in determining prices and promoting market efficiency. (page 193)

The topical coverage corresponds with the following CFA Institute assigned reading:

61. **Forward Markets and Contracts**

The candidate should be able to:

a. explain delivery/settlement and default risk for both long and short positions in a forward contract. (page 197)

b. describe the procedures for settling a forward contract at expiration, and how termination prior to expiration can affect credit risk. (page 198)

c. distinguish between a dealer and an end user of a forward contract. (page 199)

d. describe the characteristics of equity forward contracts and forward contracts on zero-coupon and coupon bonds. (page 200)

e. describe the characteristics of the Eurodollar time deposit market, and define LIBOR and Euribor. (page 202)

f. describe forward rate agreements (FRAs) and calculate the gain/loss on a FRA. (page 203)

g. calculate and interpret the payoff of a FRA and explain each of the component terms of the payoff formula. (page 203)

h. describe the characteristics of currency forward contracts. (page 205)

The topical coverage corresponds with the following CFA Institute assigned reading:

62. **Futures Markets and Contracts**

The candidate should be able to:

a. describe the characteristics of futures contracts. (page 213)

b. compare futures contracts and forward contracts. (page 213)

c. distinguish between margin in the securities markets and margin in the futures markets, and explain the role of initial margin, maintenance margin, variation margin, and settlement in futures trading. (page 214)

d. describe price limits and the process of marking to market, and calculate and interpret the margin balance, given the previous day's balance and the change in the futures price. (page 216)

e. describe how a futures contract can be terminated at or prior to expiration. (page 218)

f. describe the characteristics of the following types of futures contracts. Treasury bill, Eurodollar, Treasury bond, stock index, and currency. (page 219)

The topical coverage corresponds with the following CFA Institute assigned reading:

63. **Option Markets and Contracts**

The candidate should be able to:

a. describe call and put options. (page 226)

b. distinguish between European and American options. (page 227)

c. define the concept of moneyness of an option. (page 228)

d. compare exchange-traded options and over-the-counter options. (page 229)

e. identify the types of options in terms of the underlying instruments. (page 229)

f. compare interest rate options with forward rate agreements (FRAs). (page 230)

g. define interest rate caps, floors, and collars. (page 231)

h. calculate and interpret option payoffs and explain how interest rate options differ from other types of options. (page 233)

i. define intrinsic value and time value, and explain their relationship. (page 234)

j. determine the minimum and maximum values of European options and American options. (page 237)

k. calculate and interpret the lowest prices of European and American calls and puts based on the rules for minimum values and lower bounds. (page 238)

l.   explain how option prices are affected by the exercise price and the time to expiration. (page 242)

m. explain put–call parity for European options, and explain how put–call parity is related to arbitrage and the construction of synthetic options. (page 243)

n.   explain how cash flows on the underlying asset affect put–call parity and the lower bounds of option prices. (page 245)

o.   determine the directional effect of an interest rate change or volatility change on an option's price. (page 246)

The topical coverage corresponds with the following CFA Institute assigned reading:

64. Swap Markets and Contracts
The candidate should be able to:

a.   describe the characteristics of swap contracts and explain how swaps are terminated. (page 255)

b.   describe, calculate, and interpret the payments of currency swaps, plain vanilla interest rate swaps, and equity swaps. (page 256)

The topical coverage corresponds with the following CFA Institute assigned reading:

65. Risk Management Applications of Option Strategies
The candidate should be able to:

a.   determine the value at expiration, the profit, maximum profit, maximum loss, breakeven underlying price at expiration, and payoff graph of the strategies of buying and selling calls and puts and determine the potential outcomes for investors using these strategies. (page 268)

b.   determine the value at expiration, profit, maximum profit, maximum loss, breakeven underlying price at expiration, and payoff graph of a covered call strategy and a protective put strategy, and explain the risk management application of each strategy. (page 272)

STUDY SESSION 18

The topical coverage corresponds with the following CFA Institute assigned reading:

66. Introduction to Alternative Investments
The candidate should be able to:

a.   compare alternative investments with traditional investments. (page 278)

b.   describe categories of alternative investments. (page 278)

c.   describe potential benefits of alternative investments in the context of portfolio management. (page 279)

d.   describe hedge funds, private equity, real estate, commodities, and other alternative investments, including, as applicable, strategies, sub-categories, potential benefits and risks, fee structures, and due diligence. (page 280)

e.   describe issues in valuing, and calculating returns on, hedge funds, private equity, real estate, and commodities. (page 280)

f.   describe, calculate, and interpret management and incentive fees and net-of-fees returns to hedge funds. (page 292)

g.   describe risk management of alternative investments. (page 294)

The topical coverage corresponds with the following CFA Institute assigned reading:

67. Investing in Commodities

The candidate should be able to:

a. explain the relationship between spot prices and expected future prices in terms of contango and backwardation. (page 303)

b. describe the sources of return and risk for a commodity investment and the effect on a portfolio of adding an allocation to commodities. (page 304)

c. explain why a commodity index strategy is generally considered an active investment. (page 305)

The following is a review of the Analysis of Fixed Income Investments principles designed to address the learning outcome statements set forth by CFA Institute. This topic is also covered in:

FEATURES OF DEBT SECURITIES

Study Session 15

EXAM FOCUS

Fixed income securities, historically, were promises to pay a stream of semiannual payments for a given number of years and then repay the loan amount at the maturity date. The contract between the borrower and the lender (the indenture) can really be designed to have any payment stream or pattern that the parties agree to. Types of contracts that are used frequently have specific names, and there is no shortage of those (for you to learn) here.

You should pay special attention to how the periodic payments are determined (fixed, floating, and variants of these) and to how/when the principal is repaid (calls, puts, sinking funds, amortization, and prepayments). These features all affect the value of the securities and will come up again when you learn how to value these securities and compare their risks, both at Level I and Level II.

LOS 52.a: Explain the purposes of a bond's indenture and describe affirmative and negative covenants.

CFA® Program Curriculum, Volume 5, page 294

The contract that specifies all the rights and obligations of the issuer and the owners of a fixed income security is called the **bond indenture.** The indenture defines the obligations of and restrictions on the borrower and forms the basis for all future transactions between the bondholder and the issuer. These contract provisions are known as *covenants* and include both *negative covenants* (prohibitions on the borrower) and *affirmative covenants* (actions that the borrower promises to perform) sections.

Negative covenants include restrictions on asset sales (the company can't sell assets that have been pledged as collateral), negative pledge of collateral (the company can't claim that the same assets back several debt issues simultaneously), and restrictions on additional borrowings (the company can't borrow additional money unless certain financial conditions are met).

Affirmative covenants include the maintenance of certain financial ratios and the timely payment of principal and interest. For example, the borrower might promise to maintain the company's current ratio at a value of two or higher. If this value of the current ratio is not maintained, then the bonds could be considered to be in (technical) default.

LOS 52.b: Describe the basic features of a bond, the various coupon rate structures, and the structure of floating-rate securities.

CFA® Program Curriculum, Volume 5, page 295

A *straight* (option-free) bond is the simplest case. Consider a Treasury bond that has a 6% **coupon** and **matures** five years from today in the amount of $1,000. This bond is a promise by the **issuer** (the U.S. Treasury) to pay 6% of the $1,000 **par value** (i.e., $60) each year for five years and to repay the $1,000 five years from today.

With Treasury bonds and almost all U.S. corporate bonds, the annual interest is paid in two semiannual installments. Therefore, this bond will make nine coupon payments (one every six months) of $30 and a final payment of $1,030 (the par value plus the final coupon payment) at the end of five years. This stream of payments is fixed when the bonds are issued and does not change over the life of the bond.

Note that each semiannual coupon is one-half the coupon rate (which is always expressed as an annual rate) times the par value, which is sometimes called the *face value* or *maturity value*. An 8% Treasury note with a face value of $100,000 will make a coupon payment of $4,000 every six months and a final payment of $104,000 at maturity.

A U.S. Treasury bond is denominated (of course) in U.S. dollars. Bonds can be issued in other currencies as well. The **currency denomination** of a bond issued by the Mexican government will likely be Mexican pesos. Bonds can be issued that promise to make payments in any currency.

Coupon Rate Structures: Zero-Coupon Bonds, Step-Up Notes, Deferred-Coupon Bonds

Zero-coupon bonds are bonds that do not pay periodic interest. They pay the par value at maturity and the interest results from the fact that zero-coupon bonds are initially sold at a price below par value (i.e., they are sold at a significant *discount to par value*). Sometimes we will call debt securities with no explicit interest payments *pure discount securities*.

Step-up notes have coupon rates that increase over time at a specified rate. The increase may take place one or more times during the life of the issue.

Deferred-coupon bonds carry coupons, but the initial coupon payments are deferred for some period. The coupon payments accrue, at a compound rate, over the deferral period and are paid as a lump sum at the end of that period. After the initial deferment period has passed, these bonds pay regular coupon interest for the rest of the life of the issue (to maturity).

Floating-Rate Securities

Floating-rate securities are bonds for which the coupon interest payments over the life of the security vary based on a specified interest rate or index. For example, if market interest rates are moving up, the coupons on straight floaters will rise as well. In essence, these bonds have coupons that are reset periodically (normally every 3, 6, or 12 months) based on prevailing market interest rates.

The most common procedure for setting the coupon rates on floating-rate securities is one which starts with a *reference rate* (e.g., the rate on certain U.S. Treasury securities or the London Interbank Offered Rate [LIBOR]) and then adds or subtracts a stated *margin* to or from that reference rate. The quoted margin may also vary over time according to a schedule that is stated in the indenture. The schedule is often referred to as the *coupon formula*. Thus, to find the new coupon rate, you would use the following coupon formula:

new coupon rate = reference rate $\pm$ quoted margin

Just as with a fixed-coupon bond, a semiannual coupon payment will be one-half the (annual) coupon *rate*.

An **inverse floater** is a floating-rate security with a coupon formula that actually increases the coupon rate when a reference interest rate decreases, and vice versa. A coupon formula such as coupon rate = 12% – reference rate accomplishes this.

Some floating-rate securities have coupon formulas based on inflation and are referred to as **inflation-indexed bonds**. A bond with a coupon formula of 3% + annual change in the Consumer Price Index is an example of such an inflation-linked security.

The parties to the bond contract can limit their exposure to extreme fluctuations in the reference rate by placing upper and lower limits on the coupon rate. The upper limit, which is called a **cap**, puts a maximum on the interest rate paid by the borrower/ issuer. The lower limit, called a **floor**, puts a minimum on the periodic coupon interest payments received by the lender/security owner. When both limits are present simultaneously, the combination is called a **collar**.

Consider a floating-rate security (floater) with a coupon rate at issuance of 5%, a 7% cap, and a 3% floor. If the coupon rate (reference rate plus the margin) rises above 7%, the borrower will pay (lender will receive) only 7% for as long as the coupon rate, according to the formula, remains at or above 7%. If the coupon rate falls below 3%, the borrower will pay 3% for as long as the coupon rate, according to the formula, remains at or below 3%.

LOS 52.c: Define accrued interest, full price, and clean price.

CFA® Program Curriculum, Volume 5, page 301

When a bond trades between coupon dates, the seller is entitled to receive any interest earned from the previous coupon date through the date of the sale. This is known as **accrued interest** and is an amount that is payable by the buyer (new owner) of the bond. The new owner of the bond will receive all of the next coupon payment and will then recover any accrued interest paid on the date of purchase. The accrued interest is calculated as the fraction of the coupon period that has passed times the coupon.

In the United States, the convention is for the bond buyer to pay any accrued interest to the bond seller. The amount that the buyer pays to the seller is the agreed-upon price of the bond (the **clean price**) plus any accrued interest. In the United States, bonds trade with the next coupon attached, which is termed *cum coupon*. A bond traded without the right to the next coupon is said to be trading *ex-coupon*. The total amount paid, including accrued interest, is known as the **full** (or **dirty**) **price** of the bond. The full price = clean price + accrued interest.

If the issuer of the bond is in default (i.e., has not made periodic obligatory coupon payments), the bond will trade without accrued interest, and it is said to be trading *flat*.

LOS 52.d: Explain the provisions for redemption and retirement of bonds.

CFA® Program Curriculum, Volume 5, page 301

The redemption provisions for a bond refer to how, when, and under what circumstances the principal will be repaid.

Coupon Treasury bonds and most corporate bonds are **nonamortizing**; that is, they pay only interest until maturity, at which time the entire par or face value is repaid. This repayment structure is referred to as a *bullet bond* or *bullet maturity*. Alternatively, the bond terms may specify that the principal be repaid through a series of payments over time or all at once prior to maturity, at the option of either the bondholder or the issuer (putable and callable bonds).

Amortizing securities make periodic *interest and principal* payments over the life of the bond. A conventional mortgage is an example of an amortizing loan; the payments are all equal, and each payment consists of the periodic interest payment and the repayment of a portion of the original principal. For a fully amortizing loan, the final (level) payment at maturity retires the last remaining principal on the loan (e.g., a typical automobile loan).

Prepayment options give the issuer/borrower the right to accelerate the principal repayment on a loan. These options are present in mortgages and other amortizing loans. Amortizing loans require a series of equal payments that cover the periodic interest and reduce the outstanding principal each time a payment is made. When a person gets a home mortgage or an automobile loan, she often has the right to prepay it at any time, in whole or in part. If the borrower sells the home or auto, she is required to pay the loan off in full. The significance of a prepayment option to an investor in a mortgage or mortgage-backed security is that there is additional uncertainty about the cash flows to be received compared to a security that does not permit prepayment.

Call provisions give the issuer the right (but not the obligation) to retire all or a part of an issue prior to maturity. If the bonds are called, the bondholders have no choice but to surrender their bonds for the call price because the bonds quit paying interest when they are called. Call features give the issuer the opportunity to replace higher-than-market coupon bonds with lower-coupon issues.

Typically, there is a period of years after issuance during which the bonds cannot be called. This is termed the period of *call protection* because the bondholder is protected from a call over this period. After the period (if any) of call protection has passed, the bonds are referred to as *currently callable*.

There may be several call dates specified in the indenture, each with a lower call price. Customarily, when a bond is called on the first permissible call date, the call price is above the par value. If the bonds are not called entirely or not called at all, the call price declines over time according to a schedule. For example, a call schedule may specify that a 20-year bond can be called after five years at a price of 110 (110% of par), with the call price declining to 105 after ten years and 100 in the 15th year.

Nonrefundable bonds prohibit the call of an issue using the proceeds from a lower coupon bond issue. Thus, a bond may be callable but not refundable. A bond that is *noncallable* has absolute protection against a call prior to maturity. In contrast, a callable but *nonrefundable* bond can be called for any reason other than refunding.

When bonds are called through a call option or through the provisions of a sinking fund, the bonds are said to be **redeemed**. If a lower coupon issue is sold to provide the funds to call the bonds, the bonds are said to be **refunded**.

Sinking fund provisions provide for the repayment of principal through a series of payments over the life of the issue. For example, a 20-year issue with a face amount of $300 million may require that the issuer retire $20 million of the principal every year beginning in the sixth year. This can be accomplished in one of two ways—*cash* or *delivery*:

- *Cash payment.* The issuer may deposit the required cash amount annually with the issue's trustee who will then retire the applicable proportion of bonds (1/15 in this example) by using a selection method such as a lottery. The bonds selected by the trustee are typically retired at par.
- *Delivery of securities.* The issuer may purchase bonds with a total par value equal to the amount that is to be retired in that year in the market and deliver them to the trustee who will retire them.

If the bonds are trading below par value, delivery of bonds purchased in the open market is the less expensive alternative. If the bonds are trading above the par value, delivering cash to the trustee to retire the bonds at par is the less expensive way to satisfy the sinking fund requirement.

An **accelerated sinking fund provision** allows the issuer the choice of retiring more than the amount of bonds specified in the sinking fund requirement. As an example, the issuer may be required to redeem $5 million par value of bonds each year but may choose to retire up to $10 million par value of the issue.

Regular and Special Redemption Prices

When bonds are redeemed under the call provisions specified in the bond indenture, these are known as regular redemptions, and the call prices are referred to as **regular redemption prices.** However, when bonds are redeemed to comply with a sinking fund provision or because of a property sale mandated by government authority, the redemption prices (typically par value) are referred to as **special redemption prices.** Asset sales may be forced by a regulatory authority (e.g., the forced divestiture of an operating division by antitrust authorities or through a governmental unit's right of eminent domain). Examples of sales forced through the government's right of eminent domain would be a forced sale of privately held land for erection of electric utility lines or for construction of a freeway.

LOS 52.e: Identify common options embedded in a bond issue, explain the importance of embedded options, and identify whether an option benefits the issuer or the bondholder.

CFA® Program Curriculum, Volume 5, page 302

The following are examples of *embedded options*, embedded in the sense that they are an integral part of the bond contract and are not a separate security. Some embedded options are exercisable at the option of the issuer of the bond, and some are exercisable at the option of the purchaser of the bond.

Security owner options. In the following cases, the option embedded in the fixed-income security is an option granted to the security holder (lender) and gives additional value to the security, compared to an otherwise-identical straight (option-free) security.

1. A *conversion option* grants the holder of a bond the right to convert the bond into a fixed number of common shares of the issuer. This choice/option has value for the bondholder. An exchange option is similar but allows conversion of the bond into a security other than the common stock of the issuer.

2. *Put provisions* give bondholders the right to sell (put) the bond to the issuer at a specified price prior to maturity. The put price is generally par if the bonds were originally issued at or close to par. If interest rates have risen and/or the creditworthiness of the issuer has deteriorated so that the market price of such bonds has fallen below par, the bondholder may choose to exercise the put option and require the issuer to redeem the bonds at the put price.

3. *Floors* set a minimum on the coupon rate for a floating-rate bond, a bond with a coupon rate that changes each period based on a reference rate, usually a short-term rate such as LIBOR or the T-bill rate.

Security issuer options. In these cases, the embedded option is exercisable at the option of the issuer of the fixed income security. Securities where the issuer chooses whether to exercise the embedded option will be priced less (or with a higher coupon) than otherwise identical securities that do not contain such an option.

1. *Call provisions* give the bond issuer the right to redeem (pay off) the issue prior to maturity. The details of a call feature are covered later in this topic review.

2. *Prepayment options* are included in many amortizing securities, such as those backed by mortgages or car loans. A prepayment option gives the borrower/issuer the right to prepay the loan balance prior to maturity, in whole or in part, without penalty. Loans may be prepaid for a variety of reasons, such as the refinancing of a mortgage due to a drop in interest rates or the sale of a home prior to its loan maturity date.

3. *Accelerated sinking fund provisions* are embedded options held by the issuer that allow the issuer to (annually) retire a larger proportion of the issue than is required by the sinking fund provision, up to a specified limit.

4. *Caps* set a maximum on the coupon rate for a floating-rate bond, a bond with a coupon rate that changes each period based on a reference rate, usually a short-term rate such as LIBOR or the T-bill rate.

> *Professor's Note: Caps and floors do not need to be "exercised" by the issuer or bondholder. They are considered embedded options because a cap is equivalent to a series of interest rate call options and a floor is equivalent to a series of interest rate put options. This will be explained further in our topic review of Option Markets and Contracts in the Study Session covering derivatives.*

To summarize, the following embedded options favor the issuer/borrower: (1) the right to call the issue, (2) an accelerated sinking fund provision, (3) a prepayment option, and (4) a cap on the floating coupon rate that limits the amount of interest payable by the borrower/issuer. Bonds with these options will tend to have higher market yields since bondholders will require a premium relative to otherwise identical option-free bonds.

The following embedded options favor the *bondholders*: (1) conversion provisions, (2) a floor that guarantees a minimum interest payment to the bondholder, and (3) a put option. The market yields on bonds with these options will tend to be lower than otherwise identical option-free bonds since bondholders will find these options attractive.

LOS 52.f: Describe methods used by institutional investors in the bond market to finance the purchase of a security (i.e., margin buying and repurchase agreements).

CFA® Program Curriculum, Volume 5, page 308

Margin buying involves borrowing funds from a broker or a bank to purchase securities where the securities themselves are the collateral for the margin loan. The margin amount (percentage of the bonds' value) is regulated by the Federal Reserve in the United States, under the Securities and Exchange Act of 1934.

A **repurchase (repo) agreement** is an arrangement by which an institution sells a security with a commitment to buy it back at a later date at a specified (higher) price. The *repurchase price* is greater than the selling price and accounts for the interest charged by the buyer, who is, in effect, lending funds to the seller. The interest rate implied by the two prices is called the *repo rate*, which is the annualized percentage difference between the two prices. A repurchase agreement for one day is called an *overnight repo*, and an agreement covering a longer period is called a *term repo*. The interest cost of a *repo* is customarily less than the rate a bank or brokerage would charge on a margin loan.

Most bond-dealer financing is achieved through repurchase agreements rather than through margin loans. Repurchase agreements are not regulated by the Federal Reserve, and the collateral position of the lender/buyer in a repo is better in the event of bankruptcy of the dealer, since the security is owned by the lender. The lender has only the obligation to sell it back at the price specified in the repurchase agreement, rather than simply having a claim against the assets of the dealer for the margin loan amount.

KEY CONCEPTS

LOS 52.a
A bond's indenture contains the obligations, rights, and any options available to the issuer or buyer of a bond.

Covenants are the specific conditions of the obligation:
- Affirmative covenants specify actions that the borrower/issuer must perform.
- Negative covenants prohibit certain actions by the borrower/issuer.

LOS 52.b
Bonds have the following features:
- Maturity—the term of the loan agreement.
- Par value (face value)—the principal amount of the fixed income security that the bond issuer promises to pay the bondholders over the life of the bond.
- Coupon rate—the rate used to determine the periodic interest to be paid on the principal amount. Interest can be paid annually or semiannually, depending on the terms. Coupon rates may be fixed or variable.

Types of coupon rate structures:
- Option-free (straight) bonds pay periodic interest and repay the par value at maturity.
- Zero-coupon bonds pay no explicit periodic interest and are sold at a discount to par value.
- Step-up notes have a coupon rate that increases over time according to a specified schedule.
- Deferred-coupon bonds initially make no coupon payments (they are deferred for a period of time). At the end of the deferral period, the accrued (compound) interest is paid, and the bonds then make regular coupon payments until maturity.
- A floating (variable) rate bond has a coupon formula that is based on a reference rate (usually LIBOR) and a quoted margin. A cap is a maximum coupon rate the issuer must pay, and a floor is a minimum coupon rate the bondholder will receive on any coupon date.

LOS 52.c
Accrued interest is the interest earned since the last coupon payment date and is paid by a bond buyer to a bond seller.

Clean price is the quoted price of the bond without accrued interest.

Full price refers to the quoted price plus any accrued interest.

LOS 52.d

Bond retirement (payoff) provisions:

- Amortizing securities make periodic payments that include both interest and principal payments so that the entire principal is paid off with the last payment unless prepayment occurs.
- A prepayment option is contained in some amortizing debt and allows the borrower to pay off principal at any time prior to maturity, in whole or in part.
- Sinking fund provisions require that a part of a bond issue be retired at specified dates, typically annually.
- Call provisions enable the borrower (issuer) to buy back the bonds from the investors (redeem them) at a call price(s) specified in the bond indenture.
- Callable but nonrefundable bonds can be called prior to maturity, but their redemption cannot be funded by the issuance of bonds with a lower coupon rate.

LOS 52.e

Embedded options that benefit the issuer reduce the bond's value (increase the yield) to a bond purchaser. Examples are:

- Call provisions.
- Accelerated sinking fund provisions.
- Caps (maximum interest rates) on floating-rate bonds.

Embedded options that benefit bondholders increase the bond's value (decrease the yield) to a bond purchaser. Examples are:

- Conversion options (the option of bondholders to convert their bonds into shares of the bond issuer's common stock).
- Put options (the option of bondholders to return their bonds to the issuer at a predetermined price).
- Floors (minimum interest rates) on floating-rate bonds.

LOS 52.f

Institutions can finance secondary market bond purchases by margin buying (borrowing some of the purchase price, using the securities as collateral) or, more commonly, by repurchase (repo) agreements, an arrangement in which an institution sells a security with a promise to buy it back at an agreed-upon higher price at a specified date in the future.

CONCEPT CHECKERS

1. A bond's indenture:
    A. contains its covenants.
    B. is the same as a debenture.
    C. relates only to its interest and principal payments.

2. A bond has a par value of $5,000 and a coupon rate of 8.5% payable semiannually. What is the dollar amount of the semiannual coupon payment?
    A. $212.50.
    B. $238.33.
    C. $425.00.

3. From the perspective of the bondholder, which of the following pairs of options would add value to a straight (option-free) bond?
    A. Call option and conversion option.
    B. Put option and conversion option.
    C. Prepayment option and put option.

4. A 10-year bond pays no interest for three years, then pays $229.25, followed by payments of $35 semiannually for seven years and an additional $1,000 at maturity. This bond is a:
    A. step-up bond.
    B. zero-coupon bond.
    C. deferred-coupon bond.

5. Consider a $1 million semiannual-pay, floating-rate issue where the rate is reset on January 1 and July 1 each year. The reference rate is 6-month LIBOR, and the stated margin is +1.25%. If 6-month LIBOR is 6.5% on July 1, what will the next semiannual coupon be on this issue?
    A. $38,750.
    B. $65,000.
    C. $77,500.

6. Which of the following statements is *most accurate* with regard to floating-rate issues that have caps and floors?
    A. A cap is an advantage to the bondholder, while a floor is an advantage to the issuer.
    B. A floor is an advantage to the bondholder, while a cap is an advantage to the issuer.
    C. A floor is an advantage to both the issuer and the bondholder, while a cap is a disadvantage to both the issuer and the bondholder.

7. An investor paid a full price of $1,059.04 each for 100 bonds. The purchase was between coupon dates, and accrued interest was $23.54 per bond. What is each bond's clean price?
    A. $1,000.00.
    B. $1,035.50.
    C. $1,082.58.

8. Which of the following statements is *most accurate* with regard to a call provision?
    A. A call provision will benefit the issuer in times of declining interest rates.
    B. A callable bond will trade at a higher price than an identical noncallable bond.
    C. A nonrefundable bond provides more protection to the bondholder than a noncallable bond.

9. Which of the following *most accurately* describes the maximum price for a currently callable bond?
    A. Its par value.
    B. The call price.
    C. The present value of its par value.

Use the following information to answer Questions 10 and 11.

Consider $1,000,000 par value, 10-year, 6.5% coupon bonds issued on January 1, 2005. The bonds are callable and there is a sinking fund provision. The market rate for similar bonds is currently 5.7%. The main points of the prospectus are summarized as follows:

Call dates and prices:

*   2005 through 2009: 103.
*   After January 1, 2010: 102.

Additional information:

*   The bonds are non-refundable.
*   The sinking fund provision requires that the company redeem $100,000 of the principal amount each year. Bonds called under the terms of the sinking fund provision will be redeemed at par.
*   The credit rating of the bonds is currently the same as at issuance.

10. Using only the preceding information, Gould should conclude that:
    A. the bonds do not have call protection.
    B. the bonds were issued at and currently trade at a premium.
    C. given current rates, the bonds will likely be called and new bonds issued.

11. Which of the following statements about the sinking fund provisions for these bonds is *most accurate*?
    A. An investor would benefit from having his bonds called under the provision of the sinking fund.
    B. An investor will receive a premium if the bond is redeemed prior to maturity under the provision of the sinking fund.
    C. The bonds do not have an accelerated sinking fund provision.

12. An investor buying bonds on margin:
    A. must pay interest on a loan.
    B. is not restricted by government regulation of margin lending.
    C. actually lends the bonds to a bank or brokerage house.

13. Which of the following is *least likely* a provision for the early retirement of debt by the issuer?
    A. A conversion option.
    B. A call option.
    C. A sinking fund.

14. A mortgage is *least likely*:
    A. a collateralized loan.
    B. subject to early retirement.
    C. characterized by highly predictable cash flows.

Study Session 15

ANSWERS – CONCEPT CHECKERS

1. **A** An indenture is the contract between the company and its bondholders and contains the bond's covenants.

2. **A** The annual interest is 8.5% of the $5,000 par value, or $425. Each semiannual payment is one-half of that, or $212.50.

3. **B** A put option and a conversion option have positive value to the bondholder. The other options favor the issuer and result in a lower value than a straight bond.

4. **C** This pattern describes a deferred-coupon bond. The first payment of $229.25 is the value of the accrued coupon payments for the first three years.

5. **A** The coupon rate is 6.5 + 1.25 = 7.75. The semiannual coupon payment equals (0.5)(0.0775)($1,000,000) = $38,750.

6. **B** A cap is a maximum on the coupon rate and is advantageous to the issuer. A floor is a minimum on the coupon rate and is, therefore, advantageous to the bondholder.

7. **B** The full price includes accrued interest, while the clean price does not. Therefore, the clean price is 1,059.04 – 23.54 = $1,035.50.

8. **A** A call provision gives the bond issuer the right to call the bond at a price specified in the bond indenture. A bond issuer may want to call a bond if interest rates have decreased so that borrowing costs can be decreased by replacing the bond with a lower coupon issue.

9. **B** Whenever the price of the bond increases above the strike price stipulated on the call option, it will be optimal for the issuer to call the bond. So theoretically, the price of a currently callable bond should never rise above its call price.

10. **A** The bonds are callable in 2005, indicating that there is no period of call protection. We have no information about the pricing of the bonds at issuance. The company may not *refund* the bonds (i.e., they cannot call the bonds with the proceeds of a new debt offering at the currently lower market yield).

11. **C** The sinking fund provision does not provide for an acceleration of the sinking fund redemptions. With rates currently below the coupon rate, the bonds will be trading at a premium to par value. Thus, a sinking fund call at par would not benefit a bondholder.

12. **A** Margin loans require the payment of interest, and the rate is typically higher than funding costs when repurchase agreements are used.

13. **A** A conversion option allows bondholders to exchange their bonds for common stock. The option is held by the boldholder, not the issuer.

14. **C** A mortgage can typically be retired early in whole or in part (a prepayment option), and this makes the cash flows difficult to predict with any accuracy.

The following is a review of the Analysis of Fixed Income Investments principles designed to address the learning outcome statements set forth by CFA Institute. This topic is also covered in:

RISKS ASSOCIATED WITH INVESTING IN BONDS

Study Session 15

EXAM FOCUS

This topic review introduces various sources of risk that investors are exposed to when investing in fixed income securities. The key word here is "introduces." The most important source of risk, interest rate risk, has its own full topic review in Study Session 16 and is more fully developed after the material on the valuation of fixed income securities. Prepayment risk has its own topic review at Level II, and credit risk and reinvestment risk are revisited to a significant extent in other parts of the Level I curriculum. In this review, we present some working definitions of the risk measures and identify the factors that will affect these risks. To avoid unnecessary repetition, some of the material is abbreviated here, but be assured that your understanding of this material will be complete by the time you work through this Study Session and the one that follows.

LOS 53.a: Explain the risks associated with investing in bonds.

CFA® Program Curriculum, Volume 5, page 320

Interest rate risk refers to the effect of changes in the prevailing market rate of interest on bond values. When interest rates rise, bond values fall. This is the source of interest rate risk which is approximated by a measure called **duration**.

Yield curve risk arises from the possibility of changes in the shape of the yield curve (which shows the relation between bond yields and maturity). While duration is a useful measure of interest rate risk for equal changes in yield at every maturity (parallel changes in the yield curve), changes in the shape of the yield curve mean that yields change by different amounts for bonds with different maturities.

Call risk arises from the fact that when interest rates fall, a callable bond investor's principal may be returned and must be reinvested at the new lower rates. Certainly bonds that are not callable have no call risk, and call protection reduces call risk. When interest rates are more volatile, callable bonds have relatively more call risk because of an increased probability of yields falling to a level where the bonds will be called.

Prepayment risk is similar to call risk. Prepayments are principal repayments in excess of those required on amortizing loans, such as residential mortgages. If rates fall, causing prepayments to increase, an investor must reinvest these prepayments at the new lower rate. Just as with call risk, an increase in interest rate volatility increases prepayment risk.

Reinvestment risk refers to the fact that when market rates fall, the cash flows (both interest and principal) from fixed-income securities must be reinvested at lower rates, reducing the returns an investor will earn. Note that reinvestment risk is related to call risk and prepayment risk. In both of these cases, it is the reinvestment of principal cash flows at lower rates than were expected that negatively impacts the investor. Coupon bonds that contain neither call nor prepayment provisions will also be subject to reinvestment risk, because the coupon interest payments must be reinvested as they are received.

Note that investors can be faced with a choice between reinvestment risk and price risk. A noncallable zero-coupon bond has no reinvestment risk over its life because there are no cash flows to reinvest, but a zero-coupon bond (as we will cover shortly) has more interest rate risk than a coupon bond of the same maturity. Therefore, the coupon bond will have more reinvestment risk and less price risk.

Credit risk is the risk that the creditworthiness of a fixed-income security's issuer will deteriorate, increasing the required return and decreasing the security's value.

Liquidity risk has to do with the risk that the sale of a fixed-income security must be made at a price less than fair market value because of a lack of liquidity for a particular issue. Treasury bonds have excellent liquidity, so selling a few million dollars worth at the prevailing market price can be easily and quickly accomplished. At the other end of the liquidity spectrum, a valuable painting, collectible antique automobile, or unique and expensive home may be quite difficult to sell quickly at fair-market value. Since investors prefer more liquidity to less, a decrease in a security's liquidity will decrease its price, as the required yield will be higher.

Exchange-rate risk arises from the uncertainty about the value of foreign currency cash flows to an investor in terms of his home-country currency. While a U.S. Treasury bill (T-bill) may be considered quite low risk or even risk-free to a U.S.-based investor, the value of the T-bill to a European investor will be reduced by a depreciation of the U.S. dollar's value relative to the euro.

Inflation risk might be better described as *unexpected* inflation risk and even more descriptively as purchasing-power risk. While a $10,000 zero-coupon Treasury bond can provide a payment of $10,000 in the future with near certainty, there is uncertainty about the amount of goods and services that $10,000 will buy at the future date. This uncertainty about the amount of goods and services that a security's cash flows will purchase is referred to here as inflation risk.

Volatility risk is present for fixed-income securities that have embedded options, such as call options, prepayment options, or put options. Changes in interest rate volatility affect the value of these options and, thus, affect the values of securities with embedded options.

Event risk encompasses the risks outside the risks of financial markets, such as the risks posed by natural disasters and corporate takeovers.

Sovereign risk is essentially the credit risk of a sovereign bond issued by a country other than the investor's home country.

LOS 53.b: Identify the relations among a bond's coupon rate, the yield required by the market, and the bond's price relative to par value (i.e., discount, premium, or equal to par).

CFA® Program Curriculum, Volume 5, page 320

When the coupon rate on a bond is equal to its market yield, the bond will trade at its **par value**. When issued, the coupon rate on bonds is typically set at or near the prevailing market yield on similar bonds so that the bonds trade initially at or near their par value. If the yield required in the market for the bond subsequently rises, the price of the bond will fall and it will trade at a **discount** to (below) its par value. The required yield can increase because interest rates have increased, because the extra yield investors require to compensate for the bond's risk has increased, or because the risk of the bond has increased since it was issued. Conversely, if the required yield falls, the bond price will increase and the bond will trade at a **premium** to (above) its par value.

The relation is illustrated in Figure 1.

Figure 1: Market Yield vs. Bond Value for an 8% Coupon Bond

 Professor's Note: This is a crucial concept and the reasons underlying this relation will be clear after you cover the material on bond valuation methods in the next Study Session.

LOS 53.c: Explain how a bond maturity, coupon, embedded options and yield level affect its interest rate risk.

CFA® Program Curriculum, Volume 5, page 322

Interest rate risk, as we are using it here, refers to the sensitivity of a bond's value to changes in market interest rates/yields. Remember that there is an inverse relationship between yield and bond prices—when yields increase, bond prices decrease. The term we use for the measure of interest rate risk is **duration**, which gives us a good approximation of a bond's change in price for a given change in yield.

Professor's Note: This is a very important concept. Notice that the terms "interest rate risk," "interest rate sensitivity," and "duration" are used interchangeably.

We introduce this concept by simply looking at how a bond's maturity and coupon affect its price sensitivity to interest rate changes.

- If two bonds are identical except for maturity, the one with the longer maturity has the greater duration because it will have a greater percentage change in value for a given change in yield.
- For two otherwise identical bonds, the one with the higher coupon rate has the lower duration. The price of the bond with the higher coupon rate will change less for a given change in yield than the price of the lower coupon bond will.

The presence of embedded options also affects the sensitivity of a bond's value to interest rate changes (its duration). Prices of putable and callable bonds will react differently to changes in yield than the prices of straight (option-free) bonds will.

- A call feature limits the upside price movement of a bond when interest rates decline; loosely speaking, the bond price will not rise above the call price. This leads to the conclusion that the value of a callable bond will be less sensitive to interest rate changes than an otherwise identical option-free bond.
- A put feature limits the downside price movement of a bond when interest rates rise; loosely speaking, the bond price will not fall below the put price. This leads to the conclusion that the value of a putable bond will be less sensitive to interest rate changes than an otherwise identical option-free bond.

The relations we have developed so far are summarized in Figure 2.

Figure 2: Bond Characteristics and Interest Rate Risk

Characteristic	Interest Rate Risk	Duration
Maturity up	Interest rate risk up	Duration up
Coupon up	Interest rate risk down	Duration down
Add a call	Interest rate risk down	Duration down
Add a put	Interest rate risk down	Duration down

Professor's Note: We have examined several factors that affect interest rate risk, but only maturity is positively related to interest rate risk (longer maturity, higher duration). To remember this, note that the words "maturity" and "duration" both have to do with time. The other factors, coupon rate, yield, and the presence of puts and calls, are all negatively related to interest rate risk (duration). Higher coupons, higher yields, and embedded options all decrease interest rate sensitivity (duration).

LOS 53.d: Identify the relation of the price of a callable bond to the price of an option-free bond and the price of the embedded call option.

CFA® Program Curriculum, Volume 5, page 322

As we noted earlier, a call option favors the issuer and decreases the value of a callable bond relative to an otherwise identical option-free bond. The issuer owns the call. Essentially, when you purchase a callable bond, you have purchased an option-free bond but have given a call option to the issuer. The value of the callable bond is less than the value of an option-free bond by an amount equal to the value of the call option.

This relation can be shown as:

callable bond value = value of option-free bond – value of embedded call option

Figure 3 shows this relationship. The value of the call option is greater at lower yields so that as the yield falls, the difference in price between a straight bond and a callable bond increases.

Figure 3: Price-Yield Curves for Callable and Noncallable Bonds

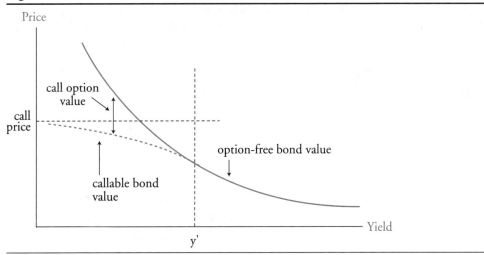

LOS 53.e: Explain the interest rate risk of a floating-rate security and why its price may differ from par value.

CFA® Program Curriculum, Volume 5, page 324

Recall that floating-rate securities have a coupon rate that floats, in that it is periodically reset based on a market-determined reference rate. The objective of the resetting mechanism is to bring the coupon rate in line with the current market yield so the bond sells at or near its par value. This will make the price of a floating-rate security much less sensitive to changes in market yields than a fixed-coupon bond of equal maturity. That's the point of a floating-rate security, less interest rate risk.

Between coupon dates, there is a time lag between any change in market yield and a change in the coupon rate (which happens on the next *reset* date). The longer the time period between the two dates, the greater the amount of potential bond price fluctuation. In general, we can say that the longer (shorter) the reset period, the greater (less) the interest rate risk of a floating-rate security at any reset date.

As long as the required margin above the reference rate exactly compensates for the bond's risk, the price of a floating-rate security will return to par at each reset date. For this reason, the interest rate risk of a floating-rate security is very small as the reset date approaches.

There are two primary reasons that a bond's price may differ from par at its coupon reset date. The presence of a **cap** (maximum coupon rate) can increase the interest rate risk of a floating-rate security. If the reference rate increases enough that the cap rate is reached, further increases in market yields will decrease the floater's price. When the market yield is above its capped coupon rate, a floating-rate security will trade at a discount. To the extent that the cap fixes the coupon rate on the floater, its price sensitivity to changes in market yield will be increased. This is sometimes referred to as **cap risk**.

A floater's price can also differ from par due to the fact that the margin is fixed at issuance. Consider a firm that has issued floating-rate debt with a coupon formula of LIBOR + 2%. This 2% margin should reflect the credit risk and liquidity risk of the security. If the firm's creditworthiness improves, the floater is less risky and will trade at a premium to par. Even if the firm's creditworthiness remains constant, a change in the market's required yield premium for the firm's risk level will cause the value of the floater to differ from par.

LOS 53.f: Calculate and interpret the duration and dollar duration of a bond.

CFA® Program Curriculum, Volume 5, page 326

By now you know that duration is a measure of the price sensitivity of a security to changes in yield. Specifically, it can be interpreted as an approximation of the *percentage* change in the security price for a 1% change in yield. We can also interpret duration as the *ratio* of the percentage change in price to the change in yield in percent.

This relation is:

$$\text{duration} = -\frac{\text{percentage change in bond price}}{\text{yield change in percent}}$$

When calculating the direction of the price change, remember that yields and prices are inversely related. If you are given a rate decrease, your result should indicate a price increase. Also note that the duration of a zero-coupon bond is approximately equal to its years to maturity, and the duration of a floater is equal to the fraction of a year until the next reset date.

Let's consider some numerical examples.

> **Example: Approximate price change when yields increase**
>
> If a bond has a duration of 5 and the yield increases from 7% to 8%, calculate the approximate percentage change in the bond price.
>
> **Answer:**
>
> –5 × 1% = –5%, or a 5% decrease in price. Because the yield increased, the price decreased.

> **Example: Approximate price change when yields decrease**
>
> A bond has a duration of 7.2. If the yield decreases from 8.3% to 7.9%, calculate the approximate percentage change in the bond price.
>
> **Answer:**
>
> –7.2 × (–0.4%) = 2.88%. Here the yield decreased and the price increased.

The formula for what we just did (because duration is always expressed as a positive number and because of the negative relation between yield and price) is:

> percentage price change = –duration × (yield change in %)

Sometimes the interest rate risk of a bond or portfolio is expressed as its **dollar duration**, which is simply the approximate price change in dollars in response to a change in yield of 100 basis points (1%). With a duration of 5.2 and a bond market value of $1.2 million, we can calculate the dollar duration as 5.2% × $1.2 million = $62,400.

Now let's do it in reverse and calculate the duration from the change in yield and the *percentage* change in the bond's price.

> **Example: Calculating duration given a yield increase**
>
> If a bond's yield rises from 7% to 8% and its price falls 5%, calculate the duration.
>
> **Answer:**
>
> $$\text{duration} = -\frac{\text{percentage change in price}}{\text{change in yield}} = -\frac{-5.0\%}{+1.0\%} = 5$$

Example: Calculating duration given a yield decrease

If a bond's yield decreases by 0.1% and its price increases by 1.5%, calculate its duration.

Answer:

$$\text{duration} = -\frac{\text{percentage change in price}}{\text{change in yield}} = -\frac{1.5\%}{-0.1\%} = 15$$

 Professor's Note: Because bond price changes for yield increases and for yield decreases are typically different, duration is typically calculated using an average of the price changes for an increase and for a decrease in yield. In a subsequent reading on interest rate risk we cover this calculation of "effective duration." Here we simply illustrate the basic concept of duration as the approximate percentage price change for a change in yield of 1%.

Example: Calculating the new price of a bond

A bond is currently trading at $1,034.50, has a yield of 7.38%, and has a duration of 8.5. If the yield rises to 7.77%, calculate the new price of the bond.

Answer:

The change in yield is 7.77% – 7.38% = 0.39%.

The approximate price change is –8.5 × 0.39% = –3.315%.

Since the yield *increased*, the price will decrease by this *percentage*.

The new price is (1 – 0.03315) × $1,034.50 = $1,000.21.

LOS 53.g: Describe yield-curve risk and explain why duration does not account for yield-curve risk.

CFA® Program Curriculum, Volume 5, page 327

The duration for a portfolio of bonds has the same interpretation as for a single bond; it is the approximate percentage change in *portfolio* value for a 1% change in yields. Duration for a portfolio measures the sensitivity of a portfolio's value to an equal change in yield for all the bonds in the portfolio.

A graph of the relationship between maturity and yield is known as a **yield curve**. The yield curve can have any shape: upward sloping, downward sloping, flat, or some combination of these slopes. Changing yield curve shapes lead to **yield curve risk**, the interest rate risk of a portfolio of bonds that is not captured by the duration measure.

In Figure 4, we illustrate two ways that the yield curve might shift when interest rates increase, a parallel shift and a non-parallel shift.

Figure 4: Yield Curve Shifts

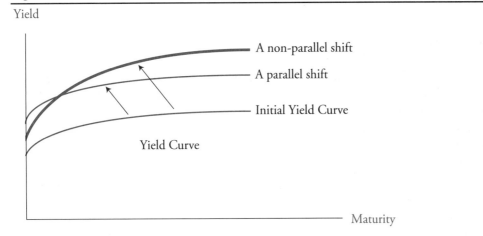

The duration of a bond portfolio can be calculated from the individual bond durations and the proportions of the total portfolio value invested in each of the bonds. That is, the portfolio duration is a market-weighted average of the individual bond's durations. If the yields on all the bonds in the portfolio change by the same absolute percent amount, we term that a **parallel shift**. Portfolio duration is an approximation of the price sensitivity of a portfolio to parallel shifts of the yield curve.

For a non-parallel shift in the yield curve, the yields on different bonds in a portfolio can change by different amounts, and duration alone cannot capture the effect of a yield change on the value of the portfolio. This risk of decreases in portfolio value from changes in the shape of the yield curve (i.e., from non-parallel shifts in the yield curve) is termed yield curve risk.

Considering the non-parallel yield curve shift in Figure 4, the yield on short maturity bonds has increased by a small amount, and they will have experienced only a small decrease in value as a consequence. Long maturity bonds have experienced a significant increase in yield and significant decreases in value as a result. Duration can be a poor approximation of the sensitivity of the value of a bond portfolio to non-parallel shifts in the yield curve.

To estimate the impact of non-parallel shifts, bond portfolio managers calculate **key rate durations**, which measure the sensitivity of the portfolio's value to changes in yields for specific maturities (or portions of the yield curve). Key rate duration is described in detail at Level II.

LOS 53.h: Explain the disadvantages of a callable or prepayable security to an investor.

CFA® Program Curriculum, Volume 5, page 331

Compared to an option-free bond, bonds with call provisions and securities with prepayment options offer a much less certain cash flow stream. This uncertainty about the timing of cash flows is one disadvantage of callable and prepayable securities.

A second disadvantage stems from the fact that the call of a bond and increased prepayments of amortizing securities are both more probable when interest rates have decreased. The disadvantage here is that more principal (all of the principal, in the case of a call) is returned when the opportunities for reinvestment of these principal repayments are less attractive. When rates are low, you get more principal back that must be reinvested at the new lower rates. When rates rise and opportunities for reinvestment are better, less principal is likely to be returned early.

A third disadvantage is that the potential price appreciation of callable and prepayable securities from decreases in market yields is less than that of option-free securities of like maturity. For a currently callable bond, the call price puts an upper limit on the bond's price appreciation. While there is no equivalent price limit on a prepayable security, the effect of the prepayment option operates similarly to a call feature and reduces the appreciation potential of the securities in response to falling market yields.

Overall, the risks of early return of principal and the related uncertainty about the yields at which funds can be reinvested are termed *call risk* and *prepayment risk*, respectively.

LOS 53.i: Identify the factors that affect the reinvestment risk of a security and explain why prepayable amortizing securities expose investors to greater reinvestment risk than nonamortizing securities.

CFA® Program Curriculum, Volume 5, page 331

As noted in our earlier discussion of reinvestment risk, cash flows prior to stated maturity from coupon interest payments, bond calls, principal payments on amortizing securities, and prepayments all subject security holders to reinvestment risk. Remember, a lower coupon increases duration (interest rate risk) but decreases reinvestment risk compared to an otherwise identical higher coupon issue.

A security has *more* reinvestment risk under the following conditions:

- The coupon is higher so that interest cash flows are higher.
- It has a call feature.
- It is an amortizing security.
- It contains a prepayment option.

As noted earlier, when interest rates decline, there is an increased probability of the early return of principal for prepayable securities. The early return of principal increases the amount that must be reinvested at lower prevailing rates. With prepayable securities, the uncertainty about the bondholder's return due to early return of principal and the prevailing reinvestment rates when it is returned (i.e., reinvestment risk) is greater.

LOS 53.j: Describe types of credit risk and the meaning and role of credit ratings.

CFA® Program Curriculum, Volume 5, page 332

A bond's *rating* is used to indicate its relative probability of default, which is the probability of its issuer not making timely interest and principal payments as promised in the bond indenture. A bond rating of AA is an indication that the expected probability of default over the life of the bond is less than that of an A rated bond, which has a lower expected probability of default than a BBB (triple B) rated bond, and so on through the lower ratings. We can say that lower-rated bonds have more **default risk**, the risk that a bond will fail to make promised/scheduled payments (either interest payments or principal payments). Because investors prefer less risk of default, a lower-rated issue must promise a higher yield to compensate investors for taking on a greater probability of default.

The difference between the yield on a Treasury security, which is assumed to be default risk-free, and the yield on a similar maturity bond with a lower rating is termed the **credit spread**.

> yield on a risky bond = yield on a default-free bond + credit spread

Credit spread risk refers to the fact that the default risk premium required in the market for a given rating can increase, even while the yield on Treasury securities of similar maturity remains unchanged. An increase in this credit spread increases the required yield and decreases the price of a bond.

Downgrade risk is the risk that a credit rating agency will lower a bond's rating. The resulting increase in the yield required by investors will lead to a decrease in the price of the bond. A rating increase is termed an **upgrade** and will have the opposite effect, decreasing the required yield and increasing the price.

Rating agencies give bonds ratings which are meant to give bond purchasers an indication of the risk of default. While the ratings are primarily based on the financial strength of the company, different bonds of the same company can have slightly different ratings depending on differences in collateral or differences in the priority of the bondholders' claim (e.g., junior or subordinated bonds may get lower ratings than senior bonds). Bond ratings are not absolute measures of default risk, but rather give an indication of the relative probability of default across the range of companies and bonds.

For ratings given by Standard and Poor's Corporation, a bond rated AAA (triple-A) has been judged to have the least risk of failing to make its promised interest and principal payments (defaulting) over its life. Bonds with greater risk of defaulting on promised payments have lower ratings such as AA (double-A), A (single-A), BBB, BB, and so on. U.S. Treasury securities and a small number of corporate bonds receive an AAA rating.

Pluses and minuses are used to indicate differences in default risk within categories, with AA+ a better rating than AA, which is better than AA-. Bonds rated AAA through BBB are considered *investment grade* and bonds rated BB and below are considered speculative and sometimes termed *junk bonds* or, more positively, *high-yield bonds*. Bonds rated CCC, CC, and C are highly speculative and bonds rated D are currently in default. Moody's Investor Services, Inc., another prominent issuer of bond ratings, classifies bonds similarly but uses Aa1 as S&P uses AA+, Aa2 as AA, Aa3 as AA-, and so on. Bonds with lower ratings carry higher promised yields in the market because investors exposed to more default risk require a higher promised return to compensate them for bearing greater default risk.

LOS 53.k: Explain liquidity risk and why it might be important to investors even if they expect to hold a security to the maturity date.

CFA® Program Curriculum, Volume 5, page 336

We described liquidity earlier and noted that investors prefer more liquidity to less. This means that investors will require a higher yield for less liquid securities, other things equal. The difference between the price that dealers are willing to pay for a security (the bid) and the price at which dealers are willing to sell a security (the ask) is called the **bid-ask spread**. The bid-ask spread is an indication of the liquidity of the market for a security. If trading activity in a particular security declines, the bid-ask spread will widen (increase), and the issue is considered to be less liquid.

If investors are planning to sell a security prior to maturity, a decrease in liquidity will increase the bid-ask spread, lead to a lower sale price, and can decrease the returns on the position. Even if an investor plans to hold the security until maturity rather than trade it, poor liquidity can have adverse consequences stemming from the need to periodically assign current values to portfolio securities. This periodic valuation is referred to as **marking-to-market**. When a security has little liquidity, the variation in dealers' bid prices or the absence of dealer bids altogether makes valuation difficult and may require that a valuation model or pricing service be used to establish current value. If this value is low, institutional investors may be hurt in two situations.

1. Institutional investors may need to mark their holdings to market to determine their portfolio's value for periodic reporting and performance measurement purposes. If the market is illiquid, the prevailing market price may misstate the true value of the security and can reduce returns/performance.

2. Marking-to-market is also necessary with repurchase agreements to ensure that the collateral value is adequate to support the funds being borrowed. A lower valuation can lead to a higher cost of funds and decreasing portfolio returns.

> *Professor's Note: CFA Institute seems to use "low liquidity" and "high liquidity risk" interchangeably. I believe you can treat these (liquidity and liquidity risk) as the same concept on the exam, although you should remember that low liquidity means high liquidity risk.*

LOS 53.l: Describe the exchange rate risk an investor faces when a bond makes payments in a foreign currency.

CFA® Program Curriculum, Volume 5, page 338

If a U.S. investor purchases a bond that makes payments in a foreign currency, dollar returns on the investment will depend on the exchange rate between the dollar and the foreign currency. A depreciation (decrease in value) of the foreign currency will reduce the returns to a dollar-based investor. **Exchange rate risk** is the risk that the actual cash flows from the investment may be worth less in domestic currency than was expected when the bond was purchased.

LOS 53.m: Explain inflation risk.

CFA® Program Curriculum, Volume 5, page 338

Inflation risk refers to the possibility that prices of goods and services in general will increase more than expected. Because fixed-coupon bonds pay a constant periodic stream of interest income, an increasing price level decreases the amount of real goods and services that bond payments will purchase. For this reason, inflation risk is sometimes referred to as purchasing power risk. When expected inflation increases, the resulting increase in nominal rates and required yields will decrease the values of previously issued fixed-income securities.

LOS 53.n: Explain how yield volatility affects the price of a bond with an embedded option and how changes in volatility affect the value of a callable bond and a putable bond.

CFA® Program Curriculum, Volume 5, page 339

Without any volatility in interest rates, a call provision and a put provision have little value, if any, assuming no changes in credit quality that affect market values. In general, an increase in the yield/price volatility of a bond increases the values of both put options and call options.

We already saw that the value of a callable bond is less than the value of an otherwise-identical option-free (straight) bond by the value of the call option because the call option is retained by the issuer, not owned by the bondholder. The relation is:

value of a callable bond = value of an option-free bond − value of the call

An increase in yield volatility increases the value of the call option and decreases the market value of a callable bond.

A put option is owned by the bondholder, and the price relation can be described by:

value of a putable bond = value of an option-free bond + value of the put

An increase in yield volatility increases the value of the put option and increases the value of a putable bond.

Therefore, we conclude that increases in interest rate volatility affect the prices of callable bonds and putable bonds in opposite ways. **Volatility risk** for callable bonds is the risk that volatility will increase, and volatility risk for putable bonds is the risk that volatility will decrease.

LOS 53.o: Describe sovereign risk and types of event risk.

CFA® Program Curriculum, Volume 5, page 339

Event risk occurs when something significant happens to a company (or segment of the market) that has a sudden and substantial impact on its financial condition and on the underlying value of an investment. Event risk, with respect to bonds, can take many forms:

- *Disasters* (e.g., hurricanes, earthquakes, or industrial accidents) impair the ability of a corporation to meet its debt obligations if the disaster reduces cash flow. For example, an insurance company's ability to make debt payments may be affected by property/casualty insurance payments in the event of a disaster.
- *Corporate restructurings* [e.g., spin-offs, leveraged buyouts (LBOs), and mergers] may have an impact on the value of a company's debt obligations by affecting the firm's cash flows and/or the underlying assets that serve as collateral. This may result in bond-rating downgrades and may also affect similar companies in the same industry.
- *Regulatory issues*, such as changes in clean air requirements, may cause companies to incur large cash expenditures to meet new regulations. This may reduce the cash available to bondholders and result in a ratings downgrade. A change in the regulations for some financial institutions prohibiting them from holding certain types of security, such as junk bonds (those rated below BBB), can lead to a volume of sales that decreases prices for the whole sector of the market.

Investors who buy bonds of foreign governments face **sovereign risk**. Just as with credit risk, we can identify three separate reasons that sovereign bond prices may decline.

1. The credit spread for a sovereign bond may increase although its rating has not changed.

2. A sovereign bond's credit rating may decline.

3. A sovereign bond can default.

Price declines in sovereign bonds due to credit events usually result from deterioration in a foreign government's ability to pay interest and principal in the future. This inability to pay typically is the result of poor economic conditions that result in low tax revenues, high government spending, or both. The significant decline in Greek government debt prices in 2009–2010 is an example of such a scenario.

With foreign bonds we must also consider the fact that the foreign government may refuse to pay (repudiate) the debt at some future date. Historically, inability to pay due to poor fiscal policy and poor economic conditions has been the primary cause of sovereign defaults.

KEY CONCEPTS

LOS 53.a
There are many types of risk associated with fixed income securities:
- *Interest rate risk*—uncertainty about bond prices due to changes in market interest rates.
- *Call risk*—the risk that a bond will be called (redeemed) prior to maturity under the terms of the call provision and that the funds must then be reinvested at the then-current (lower) yield.
- *Prepayment risk*—the uncertainty about the amount of bond principal that will be repaid prior to maturity.
- *Yield curve risk*—the risk that changes in the shape of the yield curve will reduce bond values.
- *Credit risk*—includes the risk of default, the risk of a decrease in bond value due to a ratings downgrade, and the risk that the credit spread for a particular rating will increase.
- *Liquidity risk*—the risk that an immediate sale will result in a price below fair value (the prevailing market price).
- *Exchange rate risk*—the risk that the domestic currency value of bond payments in a foreign currency will decrease due to exchange rate changes.
- *Volatility risk*—the risk that changes in expected interest rate volatility will affect the values of bonds with embedded options.
- *Inflation risk*—the risk that inflation will be higher than expected, eroding the purchasing power of the cash flows from a fixed income security.
- *Event risk*—the risk of decreases in a security's value from disasters, corporate restructurings, or regulatory changes that negatively affect the firm.
- *Sovereign risk*—the risk that governments may repudiate debt or not be able to make debt payments in the future.

LOS 53.b
When a bond's coupon rate is less than its market yield, the bond will trade at a discount to its par value.

When a bond's coupon rate is greater than its market yield, the bond will trade at a premium to its par value.

LOS 53.c
The level of a bond's interest rate risk (duration) is:
- Positively related to its maturity.
- Negatively related to its coupon rate.
- Negatively related to its market YTM.
- Less over some ranges for bonds with embedded options.

LOS 53.d
The price of a callable bond equals the price of an identical option-free bond minus the value of the embedded call.

LOS 53.e

Floating-rate bonds have interest rate risk between reset dates, and their prices can differ from their par values, even at reset dates, due to changes in liquidity or in credit risk after they have been issued.

LOS 53.f

The duration of a bond is the approximate percentage price change for a 1% change in yield.

The dollar duration of a bond is the approximate dollar price change for a 1% change in yield.

LOS 53.g

Yield curve risk of a bond portfolio is the risk (in addition to interest rate risk) that the portfolio's value may decrease due to a non-parallel shift in the yield curve (change in its shape).

When yield curve shifts are not parallel, the duration of a bond portfolio does not capture the true price effects because yields on the various bonds in the portfolio may change by different amounts.

LOS 53.h

Disadvantages to an investor of a callable or prepayable security:
* Timing of cash flows is uncertain.
* Principal is most likely to be returned early when interest rates available for reinvestment are low.
* Potential price appreciation is less than that of option-free bonds.

LOS 53.i

A security has more reinvestment risk when it has a higher coupon, is callable, is an amortizing security, or has a prepayment option.

A prepayable amortizing security has greater reinvestment risk because of the probability of accelerated principal payments when interest rates, including reinvestment rates, fall.

LOS 53.j

Credit risk includes:
* Default risk—the probability of default.
* Downgrade risk—the probability of a reduction in the bond rating.
* Credit spread risk—uncertainty about the bond's yield spread to Treasuries based on its bond rating.

Credit ratings are designed to indicate to investors a bond's relative probability of default. Bonds with the lowest probability of default receive ratings of AAA. Bonds rated AA, A, and BBB are also considered investment grade bonds. Speculative or high yield bonds are rated BB or lower.

LOS 53.k

Lack of liquidity can have adverse effects on calculated portfolio values and, therefore, on performance measures for a portfolio. This makes liquidity a concern for a manager even though sale of the bonds is not anticipated.

LOS 53.l

An investor who buys a bond with cash flows denominated in a foreign currency will see the value of the bond decrease if the foreign currency depreciates (the exchange value of the foreign currency declines) relative to the investor's home currency.

LOS 53.m

If inflation increases unexpectedly, the purchasing power of a bond's future cash flows is decreased and bond values fall.

LOS 53.n

Increases in yield volatility increase the value of put and call options embedded in bonds, decreasing the value of a callable bond (because the bondholder is short the call) and increasing the value of putable bonds (because the bondholder is long the put).

LOS 53.o

Event risk encompasses non-financial events that can hurt the value of a bond, including disasters that reduce the issuer's earnings or diminish asset values; takeovers or restructurings that can have negative effects on the priority of bondholders' claims; and changes in regulation that can decrease the issuer's earnings or narrow the market for a particular class of bonds.

Sovereign risk is the possibility that a foreign government will refuse to pay or become unable to repay its debts due to poor economic conditions and government deficit spending.

CONCEPT CHECKERS

1. A bond with a 7.3% yield has a duration of 5.4 and is trading at $985. If the yield decreases to 7.1%, the new bond price is *closest* to:
   A. $974.40.
   B. $995.60.
   C. $1,091.40.

2. If interest rate volatility *increases*, which of the following bonds will experience a price *decrease*?
   A. A callable bond.
   B. A putable bond.
   C. A zero-coupon, option-free bond.

3. A noncallable, AA-rated, 5-year zero-coupon bond with a yield of 6% is *least likely* to have:
   A. interest rate risk.
   B. reinvestment risk.
   C. default risk.

4. The current price of a bond is 102.50. If interest rates change by 0.5%, the value of the bond price changes by 2.50. What is the duration of the bond?
   A. 2.44.
   B. 2.50.
   C. 4.88.

5. Which of the following bonds has the *greatest* interest rate risk?
   A. 5% 10-year callable bond.
   B. 5% 10-year putable bond.
   C. 5% 10-year option-free bond.

6. A floating-rate security will have the greatest duration:
   A. the day before the reset date.
   B. the day after the reset date.
   C. never—floating-rate securities have a duration of zero.

7. The duration of a bond is 5.47, and its current price is $986.30. Which of the following is the *best* estimate of the bond price change if interest rates *increase* by 2%?
   A. −$109.40.
   B. −$107.90.
   C. $109.40.

8. A straight 5% bond has two years remaining to maturity and is priced at $981.67. A callable bond that is the same in every respect as the straight bond, except for the call feature, is priced at $917.60. With the yield curve flat at 6%, what is the value of the embedded call option?
   A. $45.80.
   B. $64.07.
   C. $101.00.

9. A straight 5% coupon bond has two years remaining to maturity and is priced at
    $981.67 ($1,000 par value). A putable bond, which is the same in every respect
    as the straight bond except for the put provision, is priced at 101.76 (percent of
    par value). With the yield curve flat at 6%, what is the value of the embedded
    put option?
    A. $17.60.
    B. $26.77.
    C. $35.93.

10. Which of the following is *least likely* to fall under the heading of event risk with
    respect to fixed-income securities?
    A. A change in rate regulation.
    B. One firm's acquisition by another.
    C. A Federal Reserve decrease in money supply.

11. Which of the following 5-year bonds has the *highest* interest rate risk?
    A. A floating-rate bond.
    B. A zero-coupon bond.
    C. A 5% fixed-coupon bond.

12. An investor is concerned about interest rate risk. Which of the following three
    bonds (similar except for yield and maturity) has the *least* interest rate risk? The
    bond with:
    A. 5% yield and 10-year maturity.
    B. 5% yield and 20-year maturity.
    C. 6% yield and 10-year maturity.

13. Which of the following statements about the risks of bond investing is *most
    accurate*?
    A. A bond rated AAA has no credit risk.
    B. A bond with call protection has volatility risk.
    C. A U.S. Treasury bond has no reinvestment risk.

14. Which of the following securities will have the *least* reinvestment risk for a
    long-term investor?
    A. A 10-year, zero-coupon bond.
    B. A 6-month T-bill.
    C. A 30-year, prepayable amortizing bond.

15. A 2-year, zero-coupon U.S. Treasury note is *least likely* to have:
    A. inflation risk.
    B. currency risk.
    C. volatility risk.

ANSWERS – CONCEPT CHECKERS

1. **B** The percentage price change, based on duration is equal to $-5.4 \times (-0.2\%) = 1.08\%$. The new price is $1.0108 \times 985 = \$995.64$.

2. **A** An increase in volatility will increase the value of the call option and decrease the value of a callable bond. A putable bond will increase in value. The value of option-free bonds will be unaffected.

3. **B** A zero-coupon bond, as a security, has no reinvestment risk because there are no cash flows prior to maturity that must be reinvested. A double-A bond has some (small) default risk. Zero-coupon bonds have the most interest rate risk for a given maturity.

4. **C** The duration is computed as follows:

$$\text{duration} = \frac{\text{percentage change in price}}{\text{change in yield as a decimal}} = \frac{2.50/102.5}{0.005} = \frac{2.44\%}{0.5\%} = 4.88$$

5. **C** Embedded options reduce duration/interest rate risk.

6. **B** The duration of a floating-rate bond is higher the greater the time lag until the next coupon payment/reset date. The greatest duration/interest rate risk is, therefore, immediately after the coupon has been reset.

7. **B** The approximate dollar change in price is computed as follows:

dollar price change = $-5.47 \times 0.02 \times 986.30 = -\$107.90$

8. **B** The option value is the difference between the value of an option-free bond and the corresponding price of the callable bond. Its value is computed as:

call option value = $981.67 - \$917.60 = \$64.07$

9. **C** The value of the embedded put option is the difference between the price of the putable bond and the price of the straight bond. So it is computed as:

option value = $1,017.60 - \$981.67 = \$35.93$

10. **C** Event risk refers to events that can impact a firm's ability to pay its debt obligations that are separate from market risks. The Fed's actions can impact interest rates, but this is a market risk factor, not event risk.

11. **B** The zero-coupon bond will have the greatest duration of any of the three bonds and, as such, will be subject to the greatest interest rate risk.

12. **C** Interest rate risk is *inversely* related to the yield and directly related to maturity. All else equal, the lower the yield, the greater the interest rate risk. All else equal, the longer the maturity, the greater the interest rate risk. This bond has the higher yield and the shorter maturity, and, thus, has the lowest interest rate risk.

13. **B**   A Treasury bond pays semiannual coupon interest and, therefore, has reinvestment risk. A triple-A rated bond can lose its AAA rating, so it has downgrade risk, a component of credit risk. A bond with a call feature has volatility risk even when the call cannot be exercised immediately. The call feature still has value (to the issuer), and its value will be affected by volatility changes.

14. **A**   A 10-year, zero-coupon bond has no cash flows prior to maturity to reinvest while the entire amount invested in 6-month bills must be reinvested twice each year.

15. **C**   It will have inflation (purchasing power) risk. It will have currency risk to non-U.S. dollar investors. Volatility risk only applies to bonds with embedded options.

The following is a review of the Analysis of Fixed Income Investments principles designed to address the learning outcome statements set forth by CFA Institute. This topic is also covered in:

OVERVIEW OF BOND SECTORS AND INSTRUMENTS

Study Session 15

EXAM FOCUS

This review introduces the various types of fixed income securities and a fair amount of terminology relating to fixed income securities. Pay special attention to the mechanics of these securities; that is, how they pay, when they pay, and what they pay. The additional information is nice, but likely not crucial. Try to gain enough understanding of the terms listed in the learning outcome statements so that you will understand them when they are used in a question. Knowing the basics about Treasury securities, mortgage-backed securities, and municipal securities is important as a foundation for much of the material on debt securities that follows, as well as for the more detailed material on fixed income valuation and risk that is contained in the Level II and Level III curriculum.

LOS 54.a: Describe features, credit risk characteristics, and distribution methods for government securities.

CFA® Program Curriculum, Volume 5, page 357

Bonds issued by a country's central government are referred to as **sovereign bonds** or sovereign debt. The sovereign debt of the U.S. government consists of U.S. Treasury securities, which are considered to be essentially free of default risk. The sovereign debt of other countries is considered to have varying degrees of credit risk. Sovereign debt can be issued in a country's own domestic market, another country's foreign bond market, or in the Eurobond market.

Sovereign debt is typically issued in the currency of the issuing country, but can be issued in other currencies as well. Bond rating agencies, such as Standard and Poor's, rate sovereign debt based on its perceived credit risk, often giving different ratings to sovereign debt denominated in the home currency (local currency) and to the sovereign debt of the same country denominated in foreign currency.

Professor's Note: Remember that it is often easier for a country to print currency (expand the money supply) in order to meet obligations denominated in the home currency than it is to exchange the local currency for a fixed amount of foreign currency. Thus, local currency sovereign debt often receives a higher rating than the foreign currency denominated debt of the same country.

There are four primary methods used by central governments to issue sovereign debt.

1. **Regular cycle auction—single price.** Under this method, the debt is auctioned periodically according to a cycle and the highest price (lowest yield) at which the entire issue to be auctioned can be sold is awarded to all bidders. This is the system used by the U.S. Treasury.

2. **Regular cycle auction—multiple price.** Under this method, winning bidders receive the bonds at the price(s) that they bid.

3. An **ad hoc auction system** refers to a method where the central government auctions new securities when it determines market conditions are advantageous.

4. A **tap system** refers to the issuance and auction of bonds identical to previously issued bonds. Under this system, bonds are sold periodically, not according to a regular cycle.

LOS 54.b: Describe the types of securities issued by the U.S. Department of the Treasury (e.g., bills, notes, bonds, and inflation protection securities), and distinguish between on-the-run and off-the-run Treasury securities.

CFA® Program Curriculum, Volume 5, page 358

Treasury securities (Treasuries) are issued by the U.S. Treasury. Because they are backed by the full faith and credit of the U.S. government, they are considered to be free from credit risk (though they're still subject to interest rate/price risk). The Treasury issues three distinct types of securities: (1) bills, (2) notes and bonds, and (3) inflation-protected securities.

Treasury bills (T-bills) have maturities of less than one year and do not make explicit interest payments, paying only the face (par) value at the maturity date. T-bills are sold at a discount to par value and interest is received when the par value is paid at maturity (like zero-coupon bonds). The interest on T-bills is sometimes called *implicit interest* since the interest (difference between the purchase price and the par value) is not made in a separate, explicit payment, as it is on bonds and notes. Securities of this type are known as *pure discount* securities.

- There are *three maturity cycles*: 28, 91, and 182 days, adjustable by one day (up or down) due to holidays. They are also known as 4-week, 3-month, and 6-month T-bills, respectively.
- Periodically, the Treasury also issues *cash management* bills with maturities ranging from a few days to six months to help overcome temporary cash shortages prior to the quarterly receipt of tax payments.

Treasury notes and **Treasury bonds** pay semiannual coupon interest at a rate that is fixed at issuance. Notes have original maturities of 2, 3, 5, and 10 years. Bonds have original maturities of 20 or 30 years.

Prior to 1984, some Treasury bonds were issued that are callable at par five years prior to maturity. The Treasury has not issued callable bonds since 1984.

Treasury bond and note prices in the secondary market are quoted in percent and 32nds of 1% of face value. A quote of 102-5 (sometimes 102:5) is 102% plus $\frac{5}{32}$% of par, which for a $100,000 face value T-bond, translates to a price of:

$$\left[102 + \frac{5}{32}\right]\% \times \$100,000 = 1.0215625 \times \$100,000 = \$102,156.25$$

Since 1997, the U.S. Treasury has issued **Treasury Inflation-Protected Securities** (TIPS). Currently, inflation-protected 5- and 10-year notes and 20-year bonds are offered by the Treasury. TIPS work as follows:

- TIPS make semiannual coupon interest payments at a rate fixed at issuance, just like notes and bonds.
- The par value of TIPS begins at $1,000 and is adjusted semiannually for changes in the Consumer Price Index (CPI). If there is deflation (falling price levels), the adjusted par value is reduced for that period. The fixed coupon rate is paid semiannually as a percentage of the *inflation adjusted par value*.
- Any increase in the par value from the inflation adjustment is taxed as income in the year of the adjustment:

$$\text{TIPS coupon payment} = \text{inflation-adjusted par value} \times \frac{\text{stated coupon rate}}{2}$$

For example, consider a $100,000 par value TIPS with a 3% coupon rate, set at issuance. Six months later, the *annual* rate of inflation (CPI) is 4%. The par value will be increased by one-half of the 4% (i.e., 2%) and will be 1.02 × 100,000 = $102,000.

The first *semiannual* coupon will be one-half of the 3% coupon rate times the inflation adjusted par value: 1.5% × 102,000 = $1,530. Any percentage change in the CPI over the next 6-month period will be used to adjust the par value from $102,000 to a new inflation-adjusted value, which will be multiplied by 1.5% to compute the next coupon payment.

If the adjusted par value (per bond) is greater than $1,000 at maturity, the holder receives the adjusted par value as the maturity payment. If the adjusted par value is less than $1,000 (due to deflation), holders receive $1,000 at maturity as this is the minimum repayment amount.

On-the-Run and Off-the-Run Treasury Securities

Treasury issues are divided into two categories based on their vintage:

1. **On-the-run issues** are the most recently auctioned Treasury issues.

2. **Off-the-run issues** are older issues that have been replaced (as the most traded issue) by a more recently auctioned issue. Issues replaced by several more recent issues are known as *well off-the-run* issues.

The distinction is that the on-the-run issues are more actively traded and therefore more liquid than off-the-run issues. Market prices of on-the-run issues provide better information about current market yields.

LOS 54.c: Describe how stripped Treasury securities are created and distinguish between coupon strips and principal strips.

CFA® Program Curriculum, Volume 5, page 360

Since the U.S. Treasury does not issue zero-coupon notes and bonds, investment bankers began stripping the coupons from Treasuries to create zero-coupon securities of various maturities to meet investor demand. These securities are termed **stripped Treasuries or Treasury strips.** In 1985, the Treasury introduced the Separate Trading of Registered Interest and Principal Securities (STRIPS) program. Under this program, the Treasury issues coupon-bearing notes and bonds as it normally does, but then it allows certain government securities dealers to buy large amounts of these issues, strip the coupons from the principal, repackage the cash flows, and sell them separately as zero-coupon bonds, at discounts to par value.

For example, a 10-year T-note has 20 coupons and one principal payment; these 21 cash flows can be repackaged and sold as 21 different zero-coupon securities. The stripped securities (Treasury strips) are divided into two groups:

1. **Coupon strips** (denoted as ci) refers to strips created from coupon payments stripped from the original security.

2. **Principal strips** refers to bond and note principal payments with the coupons stripped off. Those derived from stripped bonds are denoted bp and those from stripped notes np.

 Professor's Note: While the payments on coupon strips and principal strips with the same maturity date are identical, certain countries treat them differently for tax purposes, and they often trade at slightly different prices.

STRIPS are taxed by the IRS on their implicit interest (movement toward par value), which, for fully taxable investors, results in negative cash flows in years prior to maturity. The Treasury STRIPS program also created a procedure for *reconstituting* Treasury notes and bonds from the individual pieces.

LOS 54.d: Describe the types and characteristics of securities issued by U.S. federal agencies.

CFA® Program Curriculum, Volume 5, page 363

Agency bonds are debt securities issued by various agencies and organizations of the U.S. government, such as the Federal Home Loan Bank (FHLB). Most agency issues are *not* obligations of the U.S. Treasury and technically should not be considered the same as Treasury securities.

Even so, they are very high quality securities that have almost no risk of default.

There are two types of federal agencies:

1. *Federally related institutions,* such as the Government National Mortgage Association (Ginnie Mae) and the Tennessee Valley Authority (TVA), which are owned by the U.S. government and are exempt from Securities and Exchange Commission (SEC) registration. In general, these securities are backed by the full faith and credit of the U.S. government, except in the case of the TVA and Private Export Funding Corporation. Essentially, these securities are free from credit risk.

2. *Government sponsored enterprises* (GSEs) include the Federal Farm Credit System, the Federal Home Loan Bank System, the Federal National Mortgage Association (Fannie Mae), the Federal Home Loan Bank Corporation (Freddie Mac), and the Student Loan Marketing Association (Sallie Mae). These are privately owned, but publicly chartered organizations, and were created by the U.S. Congress. They issue their securities directly in the marketplace and expose investors to some (albeit very little) credit risk.

Debentures are securities that are not backed by collateral (i.e., they are unsecured). GSEs commonly issue debentures. These are of many maturity structures and can be coupon interest paying securities or discount securities (referred to as bills).

LOS 54.e: Describe the types and characteristics of mortgage-backed securities and explain the cash flow and prepayment risk for each type.

CFA® Program Curriculum, Volume 5, page 364

Mortgage-backed securities (MBSs) are backed (secured) by pools of mortgage loans, which not only provide *collateral* but also the *cash flows* to service the debt. A mortgage-backed security is any security where the collateral for the issued security is a pool of mortgages.

The cash flows from a mortgage are different from the cash flows of a coupon bond. Mortgage loans are amortizing loans in that they make a series of equal payments consisting of the periodic interest on the outstanding principal and a partial repayment of the principal amount. Residential real estate mortgages are typically for 30 years and consist of 360 equal monthly payments. In the early years, the greater portion of the payment is interest, and the final payment, after 30 years, is almost all principal.

 Professor's Note: Amortizing loans and amortization schedules are covered in the Study Session on Quantitative Methods.

The Government National Mortgage Association (GNMA), the Federal National Mortgage Association (FNMA), and the Federal Home Loan Mortgage Corporation

(FHLMC) all issue mortgage-backed securities. All three are sponsored by the U.S. government and they are known now by the names Ginnie Mae, Fannie Mae, and Freddie Mac. Each purchases mortgages from lenders to provide funds for mortgage loans. The agencies issue three types of mortgage-backed securities: mortgage passthrough securities, collateralized mortgage obligations, and stripped mortgage-backed securities. This process of combining many similar debt obligations as the collateral for issuing securities is called *securitization*. The primary reason for mortgage securitization is to increase the debt's attractiveness to investors and to decrease investor required rates of return, increasing the availability of funds for home mortgages.

There are three types of cash flows from a mortgage: (1) periodic interest, (2) scheduled repayments of principal, and (3) principal repayments in excess of scheduled principal payments. Borrowers (issuers of mortgages) typically have the right to pay additional principal amounts without penalty, reducing the outstanding principal amount and thereby reducing future interest cash flows. If the borrower sells the property backing the mortgage, the entire principal amount is repaid at one time. Because the borrower can accelerate principal repayment, the owner of a mortgage has *prepayment risk*. Prepayment risk is similar to call risk except that prepayments may be part of or all of the outstanding principal amount. (Partial prepayment of remaining principal is called *curtailment*.) This, in turn, subjects the mortgage holder to reinvestment risk, as principal may be repaid when yields for reinvestment are low.

Ginnie Mae, Fannie Mae, and Freddie Mac all guarantee the timely payment of scheduled interest and principal payments from their mortgage-backed securities. They are able to do this because they only purchase or underwrite loans that conform to certain standards regarding borrower credit ratings, loan size, and the ratio of each loan to the value of the property securing it.

A **mortgage passthrough security** passes the payments made on a pool of mortgages through proportionally to each security holder. A holder of a mortgage passthrough security that owns a 1% portion of the issue will receive a 1% share of all the monthly cash flows from all the mortgages, after a small percentage fee for administration is deducted. Each monthly payment consists of interest, scheduled principal payments, and prepayments of principal in excess of the scheduled amount. Since each holder receives a percentage of all cash flows, a mortgage passthrough security has prepayment risk as a single mortgage would, but there is some diversification benefit from the pooling of hundreds or thousands of mortgages. Since prepayments tend to accelerate when interest rates fall, due to the refinancing and early payoff of existing mortgage loans, security holders can expect to receive greater principal payments when mortgage rates have decreased since the mortgages in the pool were issued.

Collateralized mortgage obligations (CMOs) are created from mortgage passthrough certificates and referred to as derivative mortgage-backed securities, since they are derived from a simpler MBS structure. CMOs have a more complex structure than mortgage passthroughs. A CMO issue has different **tranches**, each of which has a different type of claim to the cash flows from the pool of mortgages (i.e., their claims are not just a proportional claim on the total cash flows from the pool).

Professor's Note: Tranche is from the French word for "slice." In finance, when a security issue consists of different classes of securities with differing claims and especially with differing risks, the different classes of securities are called tranches. You will likely run into this term only in reference to the different classes of securities that make up a CMO.

An example of a simple *sequential* CMO structure with three tranches will help to illustrate a CMO structure. Assume that three tranches are created out of a passthrough security. Let's call them Tranches I, II, and III. They receive interest on the basis of their outstanding par values. The following are the details of the payments to each of the three tranches.

1. Tranche I (the *short*-term segment of the issue) receives net interest on outstanding principal and all of the principal payments from the mortgage pool until it is completely paid off.

2. Tranche II (the *intermediate*-term) receives its share of net interest and starts receiving all of the principal payments after Tranche I has been completely paid off. Prior to that, it only receives interest payments.

3. Tranche III (the *long*-term) receives monthly net interest and starts receiving all principal repayments after Tranches I and II have been completely paid off. Prior to that, it only receives interest payments.

Tranche I has the shortest expected maturity and may appeal to an investor with a preference for securities with a shorter time horizon, who previously could not participate in the mortgage-backed securities market. Other structures, with prepayments primarily affecting only some of the tranches, are used to redistribute prepayment risk. The tranches with less prepayment risk will become more attractive to some investors. Investors better able to bear prepayment risk will find the tranches with higher prepayment risk attractive.

Stripped mortgage-backed securities are either the principal or interest portions of a mortgage passthrough security. Prepayments affect the values of interest-only (IO) strips and principal-only (PO) strips differently. The holder of a principal-only strip will gain from prepayments because the face value of the security is received sooner rather than later. The holder of an interest-only strip will receive less total payments when prepayment rates are higher since interest is only paid on the outstanding principal amount, which is decreased by prepayments.

LOS 54.f: Explain the motivation for creating a collateralized mortgage obligation.

CFA® Program Curriculum, Volume 5, page 369

The **motivation for creating CMOs** is to *redistribute the prepayment risk* inherent in mortgage passthrough securities and/or *create securities with various maturity ranges*. The CMO structure takes the cash flows from the mortgage pool and, in a simple structure, allocates any principal payments (both scheduled payments and prepayments) sequentially over time to holders of different CMO tranches, rather than equally to all security holders. Creating a CMO does not alter the *overall* risk of prepayment, it redistributes prepayment risk.

As a general rule, CMOs are created to satisfy a broader range of investor risk/return preferences—making investing in mortgage-backed securities more appealing to a wider audience and decreasing overall borrowing costs.

LOS 54.g: Describe the types of securities issued by municipalities in the United States and distinguish between tax-backed debt and revenue bonds.

CFA® Program Curriculum, Volume 5, page 371

Debt securities issued by state and local governments in the United States are known as *municipal bonds* (or *munis* for short). *Municipal bonds* are issued by states, counties, cities, and other political subdivisions (e.g., school, water, or sewer districts). These bonds are often issued as *serial bonds*, that is, a larger issue is divided into a series of smaller issues, each with its own maturity date and coupon rate.

Municipal bonds are often referred to as *tax-exempt* or *tax-free* bonds, since the coupon interest is exempt from federal income taxes. Note that, while interest income may be tax free, realized capital gains are not. They are subject to normal capital gains taxes at the federal level. However, not all municipal bonds are tax exempt; some are taxable:

- *Tax exempt.* Different states tax municipal securities differently; the vast majority of states treat *their own bonds* (i.e., those issued within the state) as tax exempt, but consider the interest income earned on out-of-state bonds as fully taxable. Thus, the interest income earned on most in-state bonds held by a resident of that state is free from *both* state and federal income tax. Such bonds are referred to as *double tax free*.
- *Taxable.* A municipal bond must meet certain federal standards in order to qualify for the tax-exempt status. If they don't, the bonds are considered taxable and the *interest income on these bonds is subject to federal income tax* (they could still be exempt from state taxes). *Taxable municipal bonds are the exception* rather than the rule, as most municipal issues are exempt from federal taxes.

An opinion as to the tax-exempt status of the bonds, typically by a well-respected law firm specializing in municipal bond issues, is provided to purchasers when the bonds are issued.

Tax-Backed Debt and Revenue Bonds

Tax-backed bonds, also called general obligation (GO) bonds, are backed by the full faith, credit, and *taxing power* of the issuer. Tax-backed debt is issued by school districts, towns, cities, counties, states, and special districts, and include the following types:

- *Limited tax GO debt* is subject to a statutory limit on taxes that may be raised to pay off the obligation.
- *Unlimited tax GO debt*, the most common type of GO bond, is secured by the full faith and credit of the borrower and backed by its unlimited taxing authority, which includes the ability to impose individual income tax, sales tax, property tax, and corporate tax. This is the more secure form of GO.

- *Double-barreled bonds*, a special class of GOs, are backed not only by the issuing authority's taxing power, but also by additional resources that could include fees, grants, and special charges that fall outside the general fund.
- *Appropriation-backed obligations* are also known as *moral obligation bonds.* States sometimes act as a back up source of funds for issuers during times of shortfall. However, the state's obligation is not legally binding, but is a "moral obligation." The state may appropriate funds from its general fund. This *moral pledge* enhances the security of such bonds.
- Debt supported by *public credit enhancement* programs possess a guarantee by the state or federal government, which is a legally enforceable contract and is used normally to assist the state's school system.

Revenue bonds are supported only through revenues generated by projects that are funded with the help of the original bond issue. For example, revenue bonds can be issued to fund transportation systems, housing projects, higher education, health care, sports arenas, harbors, and ports. These bonds fall outside GO debt limits and do not require voter approval.

The distinction between a general obligation and a revenue bond is important for a bondholder, because the issuer of a revenue bond is obligated to pay principal and interest *only if a sufficient level of revenue is generated* by the project. If the funds aren't there, the issuer does not make payments on the bond. In contrast, general obligation bonds are required to be serviced in a timely fashion irrespective of the level of tax income generated by the municipality. At issuance, revenue bonds typically involve more risk than general obligation bonds and, therefore, provide higher yields.

Insured Bonds and Prefunded Bonds

Insured bonds carry the guarantee of a third party that all principal and interest payments will be made in a timely manner. The third-party guarantee (insurance) typically cannot be canceled; it is good for the life of the bond. There are several firms that specialize in providing insurance for municipal bond issues. Municipal bond insurance results in higher ratings, which reduces the required yield and improves the liquidity of the bonds. Insured bonds are especially common in the revenue bond market, but the general obligation bonds of smaller municipal issuers are often insured to broaden their appeal to investors.

Prefunded bonds are bonds for which Treasury securities have been purchased and placed in a special escrow account in an amount sufficient to make all the remaining required bond payments. The Treasury securities' income and principal payments must be sufficient to fund the municipal bond's required payments until maturity or through the first call date. Bonds that are prefunded have little or no credit risk and are likely to receive a rating of AAA.

LOS 54.h: Describe the characteristics and motivation for the various types of debt issued by corporations (including corporate bonds, medium-term notes, structured notes, commercial paper, negotiable CDs, and bankers acceptances).

CFA® Program Curriculum, Volume 5, page 375

Rating Agencies and Credit Ratings

Rating agencies, such as Moody's and S&P, rate specific debt issues of corporations. Some of the factors they consider are quantitative, but many are qualitative. Even quantitative factors can be somewhat subjective. The ratings are issued to indicate the relative probability that all promised payments on the debt will be made over the life of the security and, therefore, must be forward looking. Ratings on long-term bonds will consider factors that may come into play over at least one full economic cycle.

Some of the *firm-specific* factors considered are:

- Past repayment history.
- Quality of management, ability to adapt to changing conditions.
- The industry outlook and firm strategy.
- Overall debt level of the firm.
- Operating cash flow, ability to service debt.
- Other sources of liquidity (cash, salable assets).
- Competitive position, regulatory environment, and union contracts/history.
- Financial management and controls.
- Susceptibility to event risk and political risk.

Some factors *specific to a particular debt issue* are:

- Priority of the claim being rated.
- Value/quality of any collateral pledged to secure the debt.
- The covenants of the debt issue.
- Any guarantees or obligations for parent company support.

 Professor's Note: It may help to remember the primary factors as all Cs: Character of the issuer, Capacity to repay, the Collateral provided, and the Covenants of the debt issue.

Secured Debt, Unsecured Debt, and Credit Enhancements for Corporate Bonds

Secured debt is backed by the pledge of assets/collateral, which can take the following forms:

- *Personal property* (e.g., machinery, vehicles, patents).
- *Real property* (e.g., land and buildings).
- *Financial assets* (e.g., stocks, bonds, notes). These assets are marked to market from time to time to monitor their liquidation values. Covenants may require a pledge of more assets if values are insufficient. Bonds backed by financial assets are called *collateral trust bonds.*

In all of these cases, the bondholder holds a lien on the pledged property. In the case of default, the lien holder can sell the property and use the proceeds to satisfy the obligations of the borrower. In most cases of default, some mutual agreement will be reached for a new structure, but the bondholders' claim on the pledged assets significantly strengthens their position in renegotiation.

Unsecured debt is not backed by any pledge of specific collateral. Unsecured bonds are referred to as *debentures*. They represent a general claim on any assets of the issuer that have not been pledged to secure other debt. If pledged assets generate funds upon liquidation in excess of the obligation, then these excess funds are available for satisfying the claims of unsecured debt holders. *Subordinated debentures* have claims that are satisfied after (subordinate to) the claims of *senior debt*.

Credit enhancements are the guarantees of others that the corporate debt obligation will be paid in a timely manner. Typically, they take one of the following forms:

- *Third-party* guarantees that the debt obligations will be met. Often, parent companies guarantee the loans of their affiliates and subsidiaries.
- *Letters of credit* are issued by banks and guarantee that the bank will advance the funds to service the corporation's debt.
- *Bond insurance* can be obtained from firms that specialize in providing it.

When analyzing credit-enhanced debt, analysts should focus on the financial strength of both the corporation issuing the debt and the financial strength of the party providing credit enhancement. The protection to the bond holder is no better than the promise of the entity offering the credit enhancement. A decrease in the creditworthiness of the guarantor (enhancer) can lead to a rating downgrade of the debt issue.

Medium-Term Notes

 Professor's Note: Be careful here. Medium-term notes are not necessarily medium-term or notes!

Corporate bond issues typically (1) are sold all at once, (2) are sold on a firm-commitment basis whereby an underwriting syndicate guarantees the sale of the whole issue, and (3) consist of bonds with a single coupon rate and maturity.

Medium-term notes (MTNs) differ from a regular corporate bond offering in all of these characteristics.

MTNs are registered under SEC Rule 415 (*shelf registration*) which means that they need not be sold all at once. Once registered, such securities can be "placed on the shelf" and sold in the market over time at the discretion of the issuer. MTNs are sold over time, with each sale satisfying some minimum dollar amount set by the issuer, typically $1 million and up.

MTNs are issued in various maturities, ranging from nine months to periods as long as 100 years. Issuers provide *maturity ranges* (e.g., 18 months to two years) for MTNs that they wish to sell and provide yield quotes for those ranges, typically as a spread to comparable maturity Treasury issues. Investors interested in purchasing the notes make an offer to the issuer's agent, specifying the face value and an exact maturity within one of the ranges offered. The agent then confirms the issuer's willingness to sell those MTNs and effects the transaction.

The offering is done by the issuer's agent on a *best-efforts* basis. There is no firm commitment on the agent's part to sell a specific amount of bonds.

MTNs can have fixed or floating-rate coupons, can be denominated in any currency, and can have special features, such as calls, caps, floors, and non-interest rate indexed coupons. The notes issued can be combined with derivative instruments to create the special features that an investor requires. The combination of the derivative and notes is called a *structured security*.

Structured Notes

A **structured note** is a debt security created when the issuer combines a typical bond or note with a derivative. This is done to create a security that has special appeal to some institutional investors. The targeted institutional investors face restrictions on the types of securities they can purchase. Structured securities allow them to avoid these restrictions. As with any innovative debt security, the motivation to issue them is to lower overall borrowing costs.

As an example, consider an institutional investor that is prohibited from owning equity or derivative securities. An issuer could create a structured note where the periodic coupon payments were based on the performance of an equity security or an equity index. This structured note would still be a debt security, but would produce returns closer to holding the equity index itself. The mechanics of creating this security would be to issue a debt security and combine it with an *equity swap*. An equity swap is a derivative that requires the payment of a fixed rate of interest (the coupon rate on the bond here), and pays its owner the rate of return on the equity or equity index each period. By combining the bond with the equity swap, a structured note is created that pays the percentage rate of return on the equity semiannually instead of paying a fixed coupon payment.

Types of structured medium-term notes include:

- *Step-up notes*—Coupon rate increases over time on a preset schedule.
- *Inverse floaters*—Coupon rate increases when the reference rate decreases and decreases when the reference rate increases.
- *Deleveraged floaters*—Coupon rate equals a fraction of the reference rate plus a constant margin.
- *Dual-indexed floaters*—Coupon rate is based on the difference between two reference rates.
- *Range notes*—Coupon rate equals the reference rate if the reference rate falls within a specified range, or zero if the reference rate falls outside that range.
- *Index amortizing notes*—Coupon rate is fixed but some principal is repaid before maturity, with the amount of principal prepaid based on the level of the reference rate.

We will cover equity swaps, interest rate swaps, and other derivatives commonly used to create structured notes in a subsequent study session. For our purposes here, it is sufficient that you understand that structured notes are created by combining regular debt with derivative securities to make a "debt security" that allows certain institutional investors to get around restrictions they face and thereby reduce the borrowing costs of the company creating the structured note.

Commercial Paper: Directly-Placed and Dealer-Placed Paper

Commercial paper is a short-term, unsecured debt instrument used by corporations to borrow money at rates lower than bank rates. Commercial paper is issued with maturities of 270 days or less, since debt securities with maturities of 270 days or less are exempt from SEC registration. It is issued with maturities as short as two days, with most issues being in the 2-day to 90-day range.

Similar to T-bills, commercial paper is typically issued as a pure discount security and makes a single payment equal to the face value at maturity. There is no active secondary market in commercial paper, and most buyers hold commercial paper until maturity.

Commercial paper is generally issued by corporations with relatively strong credit and the proceeds are often used to finance credit given to the firm's customers or to finance inventories. Finance subsidiaries of manufacturing firms issue commercial paper to fund customers' purchases of the parent company's products. Issuers often keep unused bank lines of credit in place to use in case new paper cannot be issued to generate the funds needed to pay off maturing paper.

Directly-placed paper is commercial paper that is sold to large investors without going through an agent or broker-dealer. Large issuers will deal with a select group of regular commercial paper buyers who customarily buy very large amounts.

Dealer-placed paper is sold to purchasers through a commercial-paper dealer. Most large investment firms have commercial paper desks to serve their customers' needs for short-term cash-management products.

Negotiable CDs and Bankers' Acceptances

Certificates of deposit (CDs) are issued by banks and sold to their customers. They represent a promise by the bank to repay a certain amount plus interest and, in that way, are similar to other bank deposits. In contrast to regular bank deposits, CDs are issued in specific denominations and for specified periods of time that can be of any length. In the United States, CDs are insured by the Federal Deposit Insurance Corporation (FDIC) up to a maximum value in the event the issuing bank becomes insolvent. Amounts above the maximum value are not insured and are, therefore, only as secure as the bank that issues the CD.

Typical bank CDs in the United States carry a penalty to the CD owner if the funds are withdrawn earlier than the maturity date of the CD. **Negotiable CDs**, however, permit the owner to sell the CD in the secondary market at any time. Negotiable CDs issued in the United States by U.S. banks are termed domestic CDs, whereas U.S.

dollar denominated CDs issued by foreign banks and branches of U.S. banks outside the United States are termed Eurodollar CDs. Negotiable CDs have maturities ranging from days up to five years. The interest rate paid on them is called the London Interbank Offering Rate because they are primarily issued by banks' London branches.

Bankers' acceptances are essentially guarantees by a bank that a loan will be repaid. They are created as part of commercial transactions, especially international trade. As an example, consider an importer who agrees to pay for goods shipped to him by an exporter, 45 days after the goods are shipped. The importer goes to his bank and gets a letter of credit stating that the bank will guarantee the payment, say $1 million. This letter must be sent to the bank of the exporter before the exporter will actually ship the goods. When the exporter delivers the shipping documents to her bank, she will receive the present value of the $1 million, discounted because the payment will not be made for 45 days.

The final step in the creation of a bankers' acceptance is that the exporter's bank presents the evidence of shipment to the issuing bank (the importer's bank) which then accepts the evidence of shipment. It is this accepted promise to pay $1 million in 45 days that is the bankers' acceptance. The importer will sign documents evidencing his obligation to his bank and becomes the borrower of the funds. When this final step is completed, the importer receives the documents necessary to receive the shipment of goods.

The exporter's bank can either continue to hold the acceptance or sell it to an investor, often a money market fund interested in short-term paper. The acceptance is a discount instrument and sells for the present value of the single $1 million payment to be made 45 days from the shipping date. The secondary market for bankers' acceptances is limited so their liquidity is limited and most purchasers intend to hold them until their maturity dates.

The credit risk of a bankers' acceptance is the risk that the importer (the initial borrower of the funds) and the accepting bank will both fail to make the promised payment.

LOS 54.i: Define an asset-backed security, describe the role of a special purpose vehicle in an asset-backed security's transaction, state the motivation for a corporation to issue an asset-backed security, and describe the types of external credit enhancements for asset-backed securities.

CFA® Program Curriculum, Volume 5, page 386

Credit card debt, auto loans, bank loans, and corporate receivables are often securitized in the same way as mortgages are in the MBS structure. These financial assets are the underlying collateral for bonds that are also **asset-backed securities** (ABSs). While the above types of underlying assets are the most common, innovative ABSs have also been created. In one case, singer David Bowie sold a $55 million dollar ABS issue where the underlying assets were the royalties from 25 of his albums released prior to 1990.

Role of a Special Purpose Vehicle

A **special purpose vehicle**, or *special purpose corporation*, is a separate legal entity to which a corporation transfers the financial assets for an ABS issue. The importance of this is that a legal transfer of the assets is made to the special purpose vehicle. This shields the assets from the claims of the corporation's general creditors, making it possible for the ABS issue to receive a higher credit rating than the corporation as a whole. Because the assets are sold to the special purpose vehicle, they are highly unlikely to be subject to any claims arising from the bankruptcy of the corporation, and the special purpose vehicle is termed a *bankruptcy remote* entity.

Motivation for a Corporation to Issue an Asset-Backed Security

The motivation for a corporation to issue asset-backed securities is to reduce borrowing costs. By transferring the assets into a separate entity, the entity can issue the bonds and receive a higher rating than the unsecured debt of the corporation. The higher rating reduces the required yield on the (ABS) debt.

External Credit Enhancements

Because asset-backed securities, on their own, may not receive the highest possible credit rating, the issuer may choose to enhance the credit rating by providing additional guarantees or security. Credit quality can be enhanced either externally or internally. **External credit enhancement** commonly takes the following forms:

- *Corporate guarantees*, which may be provided by the corporation creating the ABS or its parent.
- *Letters of credit*, which may be obtained from a bank for a fee.
- *Bond insurance*, which may be obtained from an insurance company or a provider specializing in underwriting such structures. This is also referred to as an *insurance wrap*.

None of these enhancements come without cost. The decision of how much enhancement to provide involves a tradeoff between the cost of enhancement and the resulting decrease in the market yield required on the bonds.

Note that the quality of a credit-enhanced security is only as good as the quality of the guarantor, and the credit rating of the security can reflect any deterioration in the guarantor's rating.

LOS 54.j: Describe collateralized debt obligations.

CFA® Program Curriculum, Volume 5, page 388

A **collateralized debt obligation** (CDO) is a debt instrument where the collateral for the promise to pay is an underlying pool of other debt obligations and even other CDOs. These underlying debt obligations can be business loans, mortgages, debt of developing countries, corporate bonds of various ratings, asset-backed securities, or even problem/non-performing loans. Tranches of the CDO are created based on the seniority of the claims to the cash flows of the underlying assets, and these are given separate credit ratings depending on the seniority of the claim, as well as the creditworthiness of the underlying pool of debt securities.

CDOs may be created by a sponsor that seeks to profit on the spread between the rate to be earned on the underlying assets and the rate promised to the CDO holder (an *arbitrage CDO*), or created by a bank or insurance company seeking to reduce its loan exposure on its balance sheet (a *balance sheet CDO*).

LOS 54.k: Describe the mechanisms available for placing bonds in the primary market and distinguish between the primary and secondary markets for bonds.

CFA® Program Curriculum, Volume 5, page 389

The **primary market** for debt (newly created debt securities) functions in a manner similar to the primary market for equities. Typically, an investment banker is involved in advising the debt issuer and in distributing (selling) the debt securities to investors. When the investment banker actually purchases the entire issue and resells it, they are said to have "underwritten" the issue. This arrangement is termed a *firm commitment* while the deal is termed a *bought deal.* In an underwritten offering of debt securities, the underwriter will typically put together a syndicate of other investment bankers to aid in distributing the securities. The underwriters can reduce their risk by preselling as much of the offering as possible to their institutional clients and hedging the interest rate risk exposure of the issue for the period they anticipate owning the securities. An alternative is for the investment banker to agree to sell all of the issue that they can and this is termed doing the offering on a *best efforts* basis.

Because the price paid for the issue and the anticipated sale price are determined between the (lead) investment bank and the issuing company, the offering is termed a *negotiated offering.* Another approach is an *auction process* where an issuer of debt securities determines the size and terms of the issue and several investment banks, or underwriting syndicates of multiple investment banks, bid on what interest rate they require to sell it. The syndicate with the lowest interest rate bid will be awarded the deal.

In the United States, securities to be offered to public investors must be registered with the SEC. When a new issue of debt securities is not registered for sale to the public, it still may be sold to a small number of investors. This is called a *private placement* or Rule 144A offering (after the rule that allows such transactions). Avoidance of the registration process is valuable to the issuer and, because a private placement involves a sale to a small number of investors/institutions, the issue can be tailored to the needs and preferences of the buyers. Because the issue cannot be sold to the public unless it is subsequently registered, the buyers will require a slightly higher interest rate to compensate them for the lack of liquidity of securities that are sold though a private placement.

The **secondary market** for debt securities includes exchanges, an over-the-counter dealer market, and electronic trading networks. Traditionally, most secondary trading in debt securities was transacted in a dealer market, with broker/dealers buying and selling bonds for and from their inventories (i.e., acting as market makers). More recently, the costs and risks of supplying the capital necessary to adequately fund bond trading operations have increased and spreads have decreased. Because of this, electronic trading has become a more important part of the secondary market for debt securities. These electronic networks can be bids and offers by a single dealer, bids and offers by multiple dealers, or simply anonymous customer bids and offers posted on an electronic trading system with a trade clearing system.

KEY CONCEPTS

LOS 54.a

Sovereign debt refers to the debt obligations of governments. U.S. Treasury securities are sovereign debt of the U.S. government and are considered free of credit risk. Sovereign debt of other countries has varying degrees of credit risk.

Sovereign debt is typically issued using one of four methods:
- Regular auction cycle with the entire issue sold at a single price.
- Regular auction cycle with bonds issued at multiple prices.
- Ad hoc auction system with no regular cycle.
- Tap system, auctioning new bonds identical to previously issued bonds.

LOS 54.b

Securities issued by the U.S. Treasury include:
- Bills—pure-discount securities maturing in four weeks, three months, or six months.
- Notes—coupon securities maturing in two, five, and ten years.
- Bonds—coupon securities maturing in 20 or 30 years.

Treasury Inflation Protected Securities (TIPS) are U.S. Treasury issues in which the coupon rate is fixed but the par value is adjusted periodically for inflation, based on changes in the CPI.

U.S. Treasuries from the most recent auction are referred to as on-the-run issues, while Treasuries from previous auctions are referred to as off-the-run issues.

LOS 54.c

Stripped Treasury securities are created by bond dealers who buy Treasury securities, separate each of their scheduled coupon and principal payments, and resell these as zero-coupon securities.

Treasury strips are traded in two forms—coupon strips and principal strips—and are taxed by the IRS on the basis of accrued interest, like other zero-coupon securities.

LOS 54.d

Agencies of the U.S. government, including federally related institutions and government-sponsored enterprises, issue bonds that are not obligations of the U.S. Treasury but are considered to be almost default risk free.

LOS 54.e

A mortgage passthrough security is backed by a pool of amortizing mortgage loans (the collateral) and has monthly cash flows that include interest payments, scheduled principal payments, and prepayments of principal.

Prepayment risk is significant for investors in passthrough securities because most mortgage loans contain a prepayment option, which allows the issuer (borrower) to make additional principal payments at any time.

Collateralized mortgage obligations (CMOs) are customized claims to the principal and/or interest payments of mortgage passthrough securities and redistribute the prepayment risk and/or maturity risk of the securities.

LOS 54.f

CMOs are created to decrease borrowing costs by redistributing prepayment risk or altering the maturity structure to better suit investor preferences.

LOS 54.g

Interest payments on state and local government securities (municipal securities, or munis) are usually exempt from U.S. federal taxes, and from state taxes in the state of issuance.

Municipal bonds include:
* Tax-backed (general obligation) bonds backed by the taxing authority of the governmental unit issuing the securities.
* Revenue bonds, backed only by the revenues from the project specifically financed by the bond issue.

LOS 54.h

Corporate debt securities include bonds, medium-term notes, and commercial paper. Bond rating agencies rate corporate bonds on capacity to repay (liquid assets and cash flow), management quality, industry prospects, corporate strategy, financial policies, credit history, overall debt levels, the collateral for the issue, and the nature of the covenants.

Corporate bonds may be secured or unsecured (called debentures). Security can be in the form of real property, financial assets, or personal property/equipment.

Medium-term notes (MTN) are issued periodically by corporations under a shelf registration, sold by agents on a best-efforts basis, and have maturities ranging from 9 months to more than 30 years.

Structured notes combine a bond with a derivative to create a security that fills a need for particular institutional investors.

Commercial paper is a short-term corporate financing vehicle and does not require registration with the SEC if its maturity is less than 270 days. CP comes in two forms:
* Directly-placed paper sold directly by the issuer.
* Dealer-placed paper sold to investors through agents/brokers.

Negotiable CDs are issued in a wide range of maturities by banks, trade in a secondary market, are backed by bank assets, and are termed Eurodollar CDs when denominated in U.S. dollars and issued outside the United States.

Bankers' acceptances are issued by banks to guarantee a future payment for goods shipped, sold at a discount to the future payment they promise, short-term, and have limited liquidity.

LOS 54.i
Asset-backed securities (ABS) are debt that is supported by the cash flows from an underlying pool of mortgages, auto loans, credit card receivables, commercial loans, or other financial assets.

A special purpose vehicle is an entity to which the assets that back an ABS are legally transferred. If the corporation transferring these assets goes bankrupt, the assets are not subject to claims from its creditors. As a result, the ABS can receive a higher credit rating than the corporation and reduce the corporation's funding costs.

External credit enhancement for an ABS can include corporate guarantees, letters of credit, or third-party bond insurance.

LOS 54.j
Collateralized debt obligations (CDOs) are backed by an underlying pool of debt securities which may be any one of a number of types: corporate bonds, loans, emerging markets debt, mortgage-backed securities, or other CDOs.

LOS 54.k
The primary market in bonds includes underwritten and best-efforts public offerings, as well as private placements.

The secondary market in bonds includes some trading on exchanges, a much larger volume of trading in a dealer market, and electronic trading networks which are an increasingly important part of the secondary market for bonds.

CONCEPT CHECKERS

1. A Treasury security is quoted at 97-17 and has a par value of $100,000. Which of the following is its quoted dollar price?
   A. $97,170.00.
   B. $97,531.25.
   C. $100,000.00.

2. An investor holds $100,000 (par value) worth of Treasury Inflation Protected Securities (TIPS) that carry a 2.5% semiannual pay coupon. If the annual inflation rate is 3%, what is the inflation-adjusted principal value of the bond after six months?
   A. $101,500.
   B. $102,500.
   C. $103,000.

3. An investor holds $100,000 (par value) worth of TIPS currently trading at par. The coupon rate of 4% is paid semiannually, and the annual inflation rate is 2.5%. What coupon payment will the investor receive at the end of the first six months?
   A. $2,000.
   B. $2,025.
   C. $2,050.

4. A Treasury note (T-note) principal strip has six months remaining to maturity. How is its price likely to compare to a 6-month Treasury bill (T-bill) that has just been issued? The T-note price should be:
   A. lower.
   B. higher.
   C. the same.

5. Which of the following statements about Treasury securities is *most accurate*?
   A. Treasury principal strips are usually created from Treasury bills.
   B. Treasury bonds may be used to create Treasury coupon strips.
   C. Treasury coupon strips make lower coupon payments than Treasury principal strips.

6. Which of the following municipal bonds typically has the *greater* risk and is issued with *higher* yields?
   A. Revenue bonds.
   B. Limited tax general obligation bonds.
   C. Unlimited tax general obligation bonds.

7. A bond issue that is serviced with the earnings from a pool of Treasury securities that have been placed in escrow is called a(n):
   A. insured bond.
   B. prefunded bond.
   C. credit-enhanced obligation.

8.   Of the following, the debt securities that are most often registered according to
     the requirements of SEC Rule 415 (shelf registration) are:
     A. corporate bonds.
     B. medium-term notes.
     C. mortgage-backed securities.

9.   A corporation issuing asset-backed securities can often improve the credit rating
     of the securities to above that of the issuing company by transferring the assets
     to a(n):
     A. asset trust.
     B. bond insurer.
     C. special purpose vehicle.

10. Which of the following is a *difference* between an on-the-run and an off-the-run
     issue? An on-the-run issue:
     A. is the most recently issued security of that type.
     B. has a shorter maturity than an off-the-run issue.
     C. is publicly traded whereas an off-the-run issue is not.

11. Compared to a public offering, a private placement of debt securities *likely* has:
     A. more liquidity and a lower yield.
     B. less liquidity and a lower yield.
     C. less liquidity and a higher yield.

12. Compared to negotiable CDs, bankers acceptances:
     A. are more liquid.
     B. have shorter maturities on average.
     C. are more likely to pay periodic interest.

13. A debt security that is collateralized by a pool of the sovereign debt of several
     developing countries is *most likely* a(n):
     A. CMO.
     B. CDO.
     C. ABS.

14. Activities in the primary market for debt securities would *least likely* include:
     A. market making.
     B. a best-efforts offering.
     C. a firm commitment.

ANSWERS – CONCEPT CHECKERS

1. **B** This value is computed as follows: dollar price =

    $97\frac{17}{32}\% \times \$100,000 = 0.9753125 \times \$100,000 = \$97,531.25.$

2. **A** The annual inflation rate is 3%, which corresponds to 1.5% semiannually. Therefore, the principal value has increased by 1.5%. So we have: new principal = $100,000 × 1.015 = $101,500.

3. **B** This coupon payment is computed as follows:

    $\text{coupon payment} = (\$100,000 \times 1.0125)\left(\frac{0.04}{2}\right) = \$2,025$

4. **C** The T-note principal strip has exactly the same cash flows (the principal) as the T-bill. Therefore, the prices of the two securities should be (about) equal. However, market imperfections, such as illiquidity, may lead to differences.

5. **B** Treasury coupon and principal strips are created by separating (stripping) the principal and coupons from Treasury notes and bonds and selling packages of these single-maturity cash flows as individual zero-coupon securities. Treasury bills cannot be used because they are already zero-coupon securities.

6. **A** Revenue bond issues are only obligated to pay principal and interest if revenue from the project that they helped fund is sufficient to service the issue. When issued, revenue bonds typically are riskier than general obligation bonds and, consequently, have higher yields.

7. **B** The cash flows generated by an escrow pool of Treasury securities are used to service prerefunded bonds. Insured bonds carry third-party guarantees. There are no securities formally known as absolute priority bonds or credit enhanced obligations (yet).

8. **B** Shelf registration is used with medium-term notes. This permits the issue to be held in inventory (on the shelf) and sold in parcels at the discretion of the issuer. Corporate bonds and MBS are usually sold all at once.

9. **C** The assets are sold to a special purpose vehicle to protect them from general claims against the issuing corporation.

10. **A** On-the-run issues are the most recently issued securities.

11. **C** Investors require a higher yield to compensate for the fact that privately placed debt is not registered for public sale and is therefore less liquid than debt registered for public sale.

12. **B** Bankers' acceptances are short-term and pay no periodic interest. Like negotiable CDs, they are as good as the credit of the issuing bank but have a very limited secondary market.

13. **B** A CDO or collateralized debt obligation is backed by an underlying pool of debt securities which may be emerging markets debt. A CMO is backed by a pool of mortgages, and an ABS is backed by financial assets.

14. **A** Market making refers to a dealer that trades in the secondary market for its own account from inventory.

The following is a review of the Analysis of Fixed Income Investments principles designed to address the learning outcome statements set forth by CFA Institute. This topic is also covered in:

UNDERSTANDING YIELD SPREADS

Study Session 15

EXAM FOCUS

Yield spreads are simply differences between the yields of any two debt securities or types of debt securities. Try to get a good grip on the spread terminology in this review and the characteristics that drive yield spreads. You should know all three theories of the term structure, not only their implications for the shape of the yield curve but also what the yield curve shape can tell us under each of the three theories. Learn the relationships between taxable and after-tax yields and between tax-free and taxable equivalent yields well.

LOS 55.a: Identify the interest rate policy tools available to a central bank.

CFA® Program Curriculum, Volume 5, page 408

While interest rates are determined by a variety of economic conditions, in the United States the Federal Reserve (Fed) attempts to manage short-term rates through its *monetary policy tools*. The **four interest rate tools of the Fed** are as follows:

1. **The discount rate** is the rate at which banks can borrow reserves from the Fed. A lower rate tends to increase bank reserves, encourage lending, and decrease interest rates. A higher discount rate has the opposite effect, raising rates.

2. **Open market operations** refers to the buying or selling of Treasury securities by the Fed in the open market. When the Fed buys securities, cash replaces securities in investor accounts, more funds are available for lending, and interest rates decrease. Sales of securities by the Fed have the opposite effect, reducing cash balances and funds available for lending as well as increasing rates.

3. **Bank reserve requirements** are the percentage of deposits that banks must retain (not loan out). By increasing the percentage of deposits banks are required to retain as *reserves,* the Fed effectively decreases the funds that are available for lending. This decrease in amounts available for lending will tend to increase interest rates. A decrease in the percentage reserve requirement will increase the funds available for loans and tends to decrease interest rates.

4. **Persuading banks to tighten or loosen their credit policies**. By asking banks to alter their lending policies, the Fed attempts to affect their willingness to lend. Encouraging lending will tend to decrease rates and vice versa.

The most commonly used policy tool is *open market operations*.

LOS 55.b: Describe a yield curve and the various shapes of the yield curve.

CFA® Program Curriculum, Volume 5, page 410

We have mentioned yield curves previously as just a plot of yields by years to maturity. For a view of a current Treasury yield curve and related information, you can look at www.bloomberg.com/markets/rates/index.html. The Treasury yield curve shows the yields for U.S. Treasury securities (bills, notes, and bonds) with maturities from three months to 30 years.

We use four general shapes to describe yield curves:

1. Normal or upward sloping.

2. Inverted or downward sloping.

3. Flat.

4. Humped.

These four shapes are illustrated in Figure 1.

Figure 1: Yield Curve Shapes

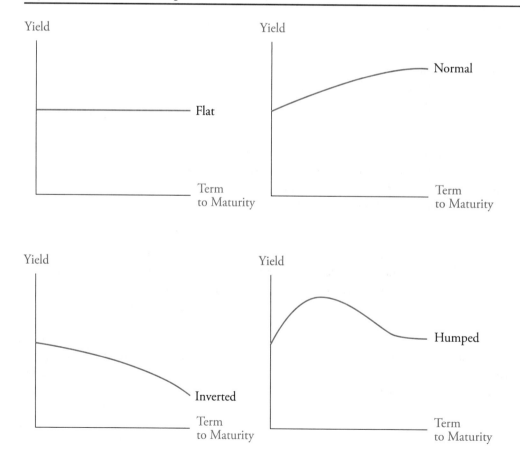

Yield curves can take on just about any shape, so don't think these examples are the only ones observed. These four are representative of general types, and you need to be familiar with what is meant by an "upward sloping" or "normal" yield curve and by an "inverted" or "downward sloping" yield curve. Humped and flat yield curves usually go by just those descriptive names and shouldn't present any problem. Just remember that a flat yield curve means that yields are all equal at every maturity.

LOS 55.c: Explain the basic theories of the term structure of interest rates and describe the implications of each theory for the shape of the yield curve.

CFA® Program Curriculum, Volume 5, page 413

The **pure expectations theory** states that the yield for a particular maturity is an average (not a simple average) of the short-term rates that are expected in the future. If short-term rates are expected to rise in the future, interest rate yields on longer maturities will be higher than those on shorter maturities, and the yield curve will be upward sloping. If short-term rates are expected to fall over time, longer maturity bonds will be offered at lower yields.

Proponents of the **liquidity preference theory** believe that, in addition to expectations about future short-term rates, investors require a risk premium for holding longer term bonds. This is consistent with the fact that interest rate risk is greater for longer maturity bonds.

Under this theory, the size of the liquidity premium will depend on how much additional compensation investors require to induce them to take on the greater risk of longer maturity bonds or, alternatively, how strong their preference for the greater liquidity of shorter term debt is. An illustration of the effect of a liquidity premium on a yield curve, where expected future short-term rates are constant, is presented in Figure 2.

Figure 2: Liquidity Premium

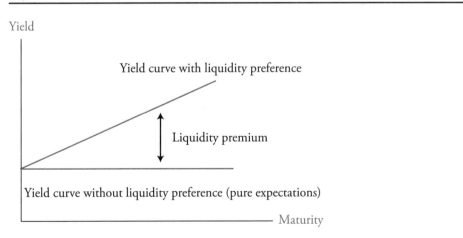

The **market segmentation theory** is based on the idea that investors and borrowers have preferences for different *maturity ranges*. Under this theory, the supply of bonds (desire to borrow) and the demand for bonds (desire to lend) determine equilibrium yields for the various maturity ranges. Institutional investors may have strong preferences for maturity ranges that closely match their liabilities. Life insurers and pension funds may prefer long maturities due to the long-term nature of the liabilities they must fund. A commercial bank that has liabilities of a relatively short maturity may prefer to invest in shorter-term debt securities. Another argument for the market segmentation theory is that there are legal or institutional policy restrictions that prevent investors from purchasing securities with maturities outside a particular maturity range. The determination of yields for various maturity ranges of the yield curve is illustrated in Figure 3.

Figure 3: Market Segmentation Theory and the Yield Curve

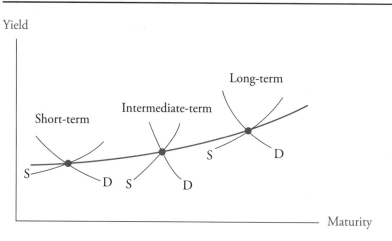

A somewhat weaker version of the market segmentation theory is the *preferred habitat theory*. Under this theory, yields also depend on supply and demand for various maturity ranges, but investors can be induced to move from their preferred maturity ranges when yields are sufficiently higher in other (non-preferred) maturity ranges.

Term Structure Theories and the Shape of the Yield Curve

The **pure expectations theory** by itself has no implications for the shape of the yield curve. The various expectations and the shapes that are consistent with them are:

> Short-term rates expected to rise in the future → upward sloping yield curve
> Short-term rates are expected fall in the future → downward sloping yield curve
> Short-term rates expected to rise then fall → humped yield curve
> Short-term rates expected to remain constant → flat yield curve

The shape of the yield curve, under the pure expectations theory, provides us with information about investor expectations about future short-term rates.

Under the **liquidity preference theory**, the yield curve may take on any of the shapes we have identified. If rates are expected to fall a great deal in the future, even adding a liquidity premium to the resulting negatively sloped yield curve can result in a downward sloping yield curve. A humped yield curve could still be humped even with a liquidity premium added to all the yields. Also note that, under the liquidity preference theory, an upward sloping yield curve can be consistent with expectations of declining short-term rates in the future. This case is illustrated in Figure 4.

Figure 4: Liquidity Premium Added to Decreasing Expected Rates

The **market segmentation theory** of the term structure is consistent with any yield curve shape. Under this theory, it is supply and demand for debt securities at each maturity range that determines the yield for that maturity range. There is no specific linkage among the yields at different maturities, although, under the *preferred habitat theory*, higher rates at an adjacent maturity range can induce investors to purchase bonds with maturities outside their preferred range of maturities.

LOS 55.d: Define a spot rate.

CFA® Program Curriculum, Volume 5, page 415

Yield to maturity is the single discount rate that makes the present value of a bond's promised cash flows equal to its market price. Actually, the appropriate discount rates for cash flows that come at different points in time are typically not all the same. The discount rate for a payment that comes one year from now is not necessarily the same discount rate that should be applied to a payment that comes five or ten years from now. That is, the spot-rate yield curve is not *flat* (horizontal).

The appropriate discount rates for individual future payments are called **spot rates**. The spot rates for different time periods that correctly value (produce a value equal to market price) the cash flows from a Treasury bond are called **arbitrage-free** Treasury spot rates, or the *theoretical Treasury spot-rate curve*. We will examine the methodology for estimating these rates and why they are called "arbitrage-free" spot rates a bit later. Here we just introduce the idea of spot rates to differentiate them from coupon bond yields (YTMs). Conceptually, spot rates are the discount rates for (yields on) zero-coupon bonds, securities that have only a single cash flow at a future date. A simple example (with annual rather than semiannual payments) will illustrate this concept as applied to coupon bonds.

Consider an annual-pay bond with a 10% coupon rate and three years to maturity. This bond will make three payments. For a $1,000 bond, these payments will be $100 in one year, $100 at the end of two years, and $1,100 three years from now. Suppose we are given the following spot rates:

1 year = 8%

2 year = 9%

3 year = 10%

Discounting each promised payment by its corresponding spot rate, we can value the bond as:

$$\frac{100}{1.08} + \frac{100}{1.09^2} + \frac{1,100}{1.10^3} = 1,003.21$$

LOS 55.e: Calculate and compare yield spread measures.

CFA® Program Curriculum, Volume 5, page 416

A yield spread is simply the difference between the yields on two bonds or two types of bonds. Three different yield spread measures are as follows:

1. The **absolute yield spread** is simply the difference between yields on two bonds. This simple measure is sometimes called the *nominal spread*. Absolute yield spreads are usually expressed in basis points (100ths of 1%).

   absolute yield spread = yield on the higher-yield bond − yield on the lower-yield bond

2. The **relative yield spread** is the absolute yield spread expressed as a percentage of the yield on the benchmark bond.

   $$\text{relative yield spread} = \frac{\text{absolute yield spread}}{\text{yield on the benchmark bond}}$$

3. The **yield ratio** is the ratio of the yield on the subject bond to the yield on the benchmark bond.

   $$\text{yield ratio} = \frac{\text{subject bond yield}}{\text{benchmark bond yield}}$$

Note that the yield ratio is simply one plus the relative yield spread. The calculation of these yield spread measures is illustrated in the following example.

Example: Computing yield spreads

Consider two bonds, X and Y. Their respective yields are 6.50% and 6.75%. Using bond X as the benchmark bond, compute the absolute yield spread, the relative yield spread, and the yield ratio for these bonds.

Answer:

absolute yield spread = 6.75% – 6.50% = 0.25% or 25 basis points
relative yield spread = 0.25% / 6.50% = 0.038 = 3.8%
yield ratio = 6.75% / 6.50% = 1.038

The most commonly used yield spread is the *absolute* yield spread, even though it is the most simplistic. A shortcoming of the absolute yield spread is that it may remain constant, even though overall rates rise or fall. In this case, the effect of rising or falling rates on spreads is captured by the relative yield spread or the yield ratio.

For example, consider two yields that rise from 6.5% and 7.0% to 7.0% and 7.5%, respectively. The absolute yield spread remains constant at 50 basis points, while the relative spread falls from 7.69% to 7.14% and the yield ratio decreases from 1.077 to 1.071.

LOS 55.f: Describe credit spreads and relationships between credit spreads and economic conditions.

CFA® Program Curriculum, Volume 5, page 418

A **credit (or quality) spread** is the difference in yields between two issues that are similar in all respects except for credit rating. An example of a credit spread is the difference in yields between long AA rated general obligation (GO) municipal bonds and long A rated GO munis (an intramarket spread as well). Obviously, these spreads show the effect of credit quality on yields and reveal the risk-return tradeoff the investor can expect (i.e., how much added return an investor can earn by investing in issues with higher perceived credit risk).

Credit spreads are related to the state of the economy. During an expanding economy, credit spreads decline as corporations are expected to have stronger cash flows. On the other hand, during economic contractions, cash flows are pressured, leading to a greater probability of default and higher yields on lower-quality issues. When investors anticipate an economic downturn, they often sell low-quality issues and buy high-quality issues, including Treasuries. This *flight to quality* puts downward pressure on the prices of low-quality issues, raising their yields.

LOS 55.g: Describe how embedded options affect yield spreads.

CFA® Program Curriculum, Volume 5, page 420

A call option on a bond is an option the bond issuer holds and will only be exercised if it is advantageous to the issuer to do so. From the bondholder's perspective, a noncallable bond is preferred to a bond that is otherwise identical but callable. Investors will require a higher yield on a callable bond, compared to the same bond without the call feature. Therefore, yield spreads to a benchmark bond, such as a similar maturity Treasury issue, are higher for the callable bond. By the same reasoning, yield spreads must be greater to compensate bondholders for the prepayment option embedded in mortgage passthrough securities.

The inclusion of a put provision or a conversion option with a bond will have the opposite effect; the choice of whether to exercise either of these options is the bondholder's. Compared to an identical option-free bond, a putable bond will have a lower yield spread to Treasuries due to the value of the put feature included with the bond.

The fact that option provisions affect yield spreads is important because this tells us that spreads for bonds with embedded options are not purely premiums for credit risk, liquidity differences, and maturity (duration) risk.

LOS 55.h: Explain how liquidity and issue-size affects the yield spread of a bond relative to other similar securities.

CFA® Program Curriculum, Volume 5, page 422

Bonds that have *less liquidity have higher spreads* to Treasuries. Investors prefer more liquidity to less and will pay a premium for greater liquidity. A higher price for a bond that is identical to another in all aspects except that it is more actively traded—and therefore more liquid—translates into a lower yield compared to the less liquid bond.

Liquidity is affected by the size of an issue. *Larger issues normally have greater liquidity* because they are more actively traded in the secondary market. Empirical evidence suggests that issues with *greater size have lower yield spreads*. When compared with identical but smaller issues, larger-size issues have lower yields due to their greater liquidity.

LOS 55.i: Calculate the after-tax yield of a taxable security and the tax-equivalent yield of a tax-exempt security.

CFA® Program Curriculum, Volume 5, page 423

The **after-tax yield** on a taxable security can be calculated as:

after-tax yield = taxable yield $\times$ (1 − marginal tax rate)

> **Example: Computing after-tax yield**
>
> What is the after-tax yield on a corporate bond with a yield of 10% for an investor with a 40% marginal tax rate?
>
> **Answer:**
>
> Investors are concerned with after-tax returns. The marginal tax rate is the percentage that must be paid in taxes on one additional dollar of income, in this case interest income.
>
> For an investor with a marginal tax rate of 40%, 40 cents of every additional dollar of taxable interest income must be paid in taxes. For a taxable bond that yields 10%, the after-tax yield to an investor with a 40% marginal tax rate will be:
>
> 10%(1 − 0.4) = 6.0% after tax

Tax-exempt securities can offer lower yields compared to taxable securities because the yields they offer are after-tax yields. The higher an investor's marginal tax rate, the greater the attractiveness of a tax exempt issue compared to a taxable issue. The **taxable-equivalent yield** is the yield a particular investor must earn on a taxable bond to have the same after-tax return they would receive from a particular tax-exempt issue. The calculation is just a rearrangement of the after-tax yield formula listed previously.

$$\text{taxable-equivalent yield} = \frac{\text{tax-free yield}}{(1 - \text{marginal tax rate})}$$

Example: Taxable-equivalent yield

Consider a municipal bond that offers a yield of 4.5%. If an investor is considering buying a fully taxable Treasury security offering a 6.75% yield, should she buy the Treasury security or the municipal bond, given that her marginal tax rate is 35%?

Answer:

We can approach this problem from two perspectives. First, the taxable equivalent yield on the municipal bond is $\dfrac{4.5\%}{(1-0.35)} = 6.92\%$, which is higher than the taxable yield, so the municipal bond is preferred.

Alternatively, the after-tax return on the taxable bond is $0.0675 \times (1-0.35) = 4.39\%$.

Thus, the after-tax return on the municipal bond (4.5%) is greater than the after-tax yield on the taxable bond (4.39%), and the municipal bond is preferred.

Either approach gives the same answer; she should buy the municipal bond.

Professor's Note: Because investors have different marginal tax rates, investors will have different tax-equivalent yields. Thus, the Treasury yield curve is not the appropriate benchmark to use for municipal bond yield spreads. The AAA rated municipal general obligation yield curve is the benchmark for municipal yield spreads.

LOS 55.j: Define LIBOR and explain its importance to funded investors who borrow short term.

CFA® Program Curriculum, Volume 5, page 427

We previously mentioned the **London Interbank Offered Rate** (LIBOR) in reference to the rates paid on negotiable CDs by banks and bank branches located in London. LIBOR has become the most important benchmark or reference rate for floating-rate debt securities and short-term lending. LIBOR is determined each day and published by the British Bankers' Association for several currencies, including the U.S., Canadian, and Australian dollars, the Euro, Japanese yen, British pounds, and Swiss francs, among others. While the maturity of the CDs that banks invest in can range from overnight to five years, LIBOR is most important for short-term rates of one year or less.

A **funded investor** is one who borrows to finance an investment position. The importance of LIBOR in this context is as a measure of the funding costs because the loans to finance the investment are most often floating-rate loans or short-term loans where the reference rate is published LIBOR. Recall that floating-rate loans are based on a reference rate plus a margin. A funded investor with a borrowing rate of 2-month (60-day) LIBOR + 40 basis points would have a borrowing cost (annualized) of 2.6% when 2-month LIBOR is quoted at 2.2%. The profits of such a funded investor would depend on his or her ability to earn greater than a 2.6% annual rate on the investments funded in such a manner.

KEY CONCEPTS

LOS 55.a
The Federal Reserve Board's tools for affecting short-term interest rates are the discount rate, open-market operations, the reserve requirement, and persuasion to influence banks' lending policies.

LOS 55.b
Yield curves represent the plot of yield against maturity.

The general yield curve shapes are upward or downward sloping, flat, or humped.

LOS 55.c
Theories of the yield curve and their implications for the shape of the yield curve are:
- The *pure expectations theory* argues that rates at longer maturities depend only on expectations of future short-term rates and is consistent with any yield curve shape.
- The *liquidity preference theory* of the term structure states that longer-term rates reflect investors' expectations about future short-term rates and an increasing liquidity premium to compensate investors for exposure to greater amounts of interest rate risk at longer maturities. The liquidity preference theory can be consistent with a downward sloping curve if an expected decrease in short-term rates outweighs the liquidity premium.
- The *market segmentation theory* argues that lenders and borrowers have preferred maturity ranges and that the shape of the yield curve is determined by the supply and demand for securities within each maturity range, independent of the yield in other maturity ranges. It is consistent with any yield curve shape and in a somewhat weaker form is known as the preferred habitat theory.

LOS 55.d
Treasury spot rates are the appropriate discount rates for single cash flows (coupon or principal payments) from a U.S. Treasury security, given the time until the payment is to be received.

LOS 55.e
Types of yield spreads:
- The *absolute yield spread* is the difference between the yield on a particular security or sector and the yield of a reference (benchmark) security or sector, which is often on-the-run Treasury securities of like maturity.
- The *relative yield spread* is the absolute yield spread expressed as a percentage of the benchmark yield. This is arguably a superior measure to the absolute spread, since it will reflect changes in the level of interest rates even when the absolute spread remains constant.
- The *yield ratio* is the ratio of the yield on a security or sector to the yield on a benchmark security or sector; it is simply one plus the relative yield spread.

LOS 55.f

A credit spread is the yield difference between two bond issues due to differences in their credit ratings.

Credit spreads narrow when the economy is healthy and expanding, while they increase during contractions/recessions reflecting a flight to (higher) quality by investors.

LOS 55.g

Call options and prepayment options increase yields and yield spreads compared to option-free bonds.

Put options and conversion options decrease yields and yield spreads compared to comparable option-free bonds.

LOS 55.h

Bonds with less liquidity are less desirable and must offer a higher yield. Larger bond issues are more liquid and, other things equal, will have lower yield spreads.

LOS 55.i

To compare a tax-exempt bond with a taxable issue, use either of the following:
- After-tax yield = taxable yield × (1 − marginal tax rate), and compare it to tax-exempt yield.
- Taxable-equivalent yield $= \dfrac{\text{tax-free yield}}{(1 - \text{marginal tax rate})}$, and compare it to a taxable yield.

LOS 55.j

LIBOR for various currencies is determined from rates at which large London banks loan money to each other and is the most important reference rate globally for floating-rate debt and short-term loans of various maturities.

CONCEPT CHECKERS

1. Under the pure expectations theory, an inverted yield curve is interpreted as evidence that:
   A. demand for long-term bonds is falling.
   B. short-term rates are expected to fall in the future.
   C. investors have very little demand for liquidity.

2. According to the liquidity preference theory, which of the following statements is *least accurate*?
   A. All else equal, investors prefer short-term securities over long-term securities.
   B. Investors perceive little risk differential between short-term and long-term securities.
   C. Borrowers will pay a premium for long-term funds to avoid having to roll over short-term debt.

3. With respect to the term structure of interest rates, the market segmentation theory holds that:
   A. an increase in demand for long-term borrowings could lead to an inverted yield curve.
   B. expectations about the future of short-term interest rates are the major determinants of the shape of the yield curve.
   C. the yield curve reflects the maturity demands of financial institutions and investors.

4. The most commonly used tool of the Fed to control interest rates is:
   A. the discount rate.
   B. the bank reserve requirement.
   C. open market operations.

5. For two bonds that are alike in all respects except maturity, the relative yield spread is 7.14%. The yield ratio is *closest* to:
   A. 0.714.
   B. 1.0714.
   C. 107.14.

6. Assume the following yields for different bonds issued by a corporation:
   - 1-year bond: 5.50%.
   - 2-year bond: 6.00%.
   - 3-year bond: 7.00%.

   If a 3-year U.S. Treasury is yielding 5%, then what is the *absolute* yield spread on the 3-year corporate issue?
   A. 0.40.
   B. 100 bp.
   C. 200 bp.

7. Assume the following corporate yield curve:
    *   1-year bond: 5.00%.
    *   2-year bond: 6.00%.
    *   3-year bond: 7.00%.

    If a 3-year U.S. Treasury yielding 6% is the benchmark bond, the *relative* yield spread on the 3-year corporate is:
    A. 16.67%.
    B. 1.167.
    C. 14.28%.

8. If a U.S. investor is forecasting that the yield spread between U.S. Treasury bonds and U.S. corporate bonds is going to widen, which of the following beliefs would he be also *most likely* to hold?
    A. The economy is going to expand.
    B. The economy is going to contract.
    C. There will be no change in the economy.

9. For a Treasury bond and a corporate bond that are alike in all respects except credit risk, the yield ratio is 1.0833. If the yield on the corporate bond is 6.5%, the Treasury (benchmark) bond yield is *closest* to:
    A. 5.50%.
    B. 6.00%.
    C. 8.33%.

10. Given two bonds that are equivalent in all respects except tax status, the marginal tax rate that will make an investor indifferent between an 8.2% taxable bond and a 6.2% tax-exempt bond is *closest* to:
    A. 24.39%.
    B. 37.04%.
    C. 43.47%.

11. Which of the following statements *most accurately* describes the relationship between the economic health of a nation and credit spreads?
    A. Credit spreads and economic well-being are not correlated.
    B. Credit spreads decrease during an expanding economy because corporate cash flows are expected to rise.
    C. Credit spreads increase during an expanding economy because corporations invest in more speculative projects.

12. Which of the following *most accurately* describes the relationship between liquidity and yield spreads relative to Treasury issues? All else being equal, bonds with:
    A. less liquidity have lower yield spreads to Treasuries.
    B. greater liquidity have higher yield spreads to Treasuries.
    C. less liquidity have higher yield spreads to Treasuries.

13. A narrowing of credit spreads would have the *least* impact on the value of which of the following investments?
    A. AAA corporate bond.
    B. 30-year Treasury bond.
    C. BB+ rated corporate bond.

14. Assume an investor is in the 31% marginal tax bracket. She is considering the purchase of either a 7.5% corporate bond that is selling at par or a 5.25% tax-exempt municipal bond that is also selling at par. Given that the two bonds are comparable in all respects except their tax status, the investor should buy the:
    A. corporate bond, because it has the higher yield of 7.50%.
    B. municipal bond, because its taxable-equivalent yield is 7.61%.
    C. corporate bond, because its after-tax yield is higher.

ANSWERS – CONCEPT CHECKERS

1. **B**   An inverted or downward-sloping yield curve, under the pure expectations theory, indicates that short-term rates are expected to decline in the future.

2. **B**   Rational investors feel that long-term bonds have more risk exposure than short-term securities (i.e., long-term securities are less liquid and subject to more price volatility). The other statements are correct.

3. **C**   The market segmentation theory holds that certain types of financial institutions and investors prefer to confine (most of) their investment activity to certain maturity ranges of the fixed-income market and that supply and demand forces within each segment ultimately determine the shape of the yield curve.

4. **C**   Open market operations are carried on frequently. The Fed's selling of Treasuries in the open market takes money out of the economy, reducing the amount of loanable funds and increasing interest rates. The opposite occurs when the Fed buys Treasuries in the open market.

5. **B**   The yield ratio is 1 + relative yield spread, or 1 + 0.0714 = 1.0714.

6. **C**   Absolute yield spread = yield on the 3-year corporate issue – yield on the on-the-run 3-year Treasury issue = 7.00% – 5.00% = 2.00% or 200 bp.

7. **A**   The yield on the corporate is 7%, so the relative yield spread is $\dfrac{7\% - 6\%}{6\%}$, which is 1/6 or 16.67% of the 3-year Treasury yield.

8. **B.** A contracting economy means lower corporate earnings which increases the probability of default on debt and increases yield spreads between corporate issues and Treasuries at a particular maturity.

9. **B** $\text{yield ratio} = \dfrac{\text{corporate bond yield}}{\text{Treasury bond yield}} = 1.0833$. Given that the corporate bond yield is 6.5%, the Treasury bond yield can be calculated as: $\dfrac{6.5\%}{1.0833} = 6.0\%$.

10. **A**   The tax rate that makes investors indifferent between two otherwise equivalent bonds is determined by solving for the tax rate in the equation: tax-exempt yield = (1 – tax rate) × taxable yield. Rearranging this relationship, we have:

$$\text{marginal tax rate} = 1 - \dfrac{\text{tax-exempt rate}}{\text{taxable rate}} = 1 - \dfrac{6.2}{8.2} = 24.39\%.$$

11. **B**   As an economy expands, credit spreads decline as expected corporate earnings rise. This is because, with stronger earnings, corporations are less likely to default on their debt.

12. **C**   The less liquidity a bond has, the higher its yield spread relative to Treasuries. This is because investors require a higher yield to compensate them for giving up liquidity, which results in a greater spread over Treasury issues, which are very liquid.

13. **B**   Because we usually speak of credit spreads as yield spreads to Treasuries, a change in the yield spread does not imply any change in the values of Treasuries.

14. **B** The taxable-equivalent yield on this municipal bond is $\dfrac{5.25}{(1-0.31)} = \dfrac{5.25}{0.69} = 7.61\%$.

Because this is higher than the yield on the (taxable) corporate bond, the municipal bond is preferred. Alternatively, the after-tax yield on the corporate is 7.5% (1 – 0.31) = 5.175%, which is less than the tax-exempt yield, leading to the same decision.

INTRODUCTION TO THE VALUATION OF DEBT SECURITIES

Study Session 16

EXAM FOCUS

Bond valuation is all about calculating the present value of the promised cash flows. If your time-value-of-money (TVM) skills are not up to speed, take the time now to revisit the Study Session 2 review of TVM concepts. The material in this topic review is very important. Calculating the value of a bond by discounting expected cash flows should become an easy exercise. The final material, on discounting a bond's expected cash flows using spot rates and the idea of "arbitrage-free" bond valuation, is quite important as well. A good understanding here will just make what follows easier to understand.

LOS 56.a: Explain steps in the bond valuation process.

CFA® Program Curriculum, Volume 5, page 447

The general procedure for valuing fixed-income securities (or any security) is to take the present values of all the expected cash flows and add them up to get the value of the security.

There are three steps in the bond valuation process:

Step 1: **Estimate the cash flows** over the life of the security. For a bond, there are two types of cash flows: (1) the coupon payments and (2) the return of principal.

Step 2: **Determine the appropriate discount rate** based on the risk of (uncertainty about) the receipt of the estimated cash flows.

Step 3: **Calculate the present value of the estimated cash flows** by multiplying the bond's expected cash flows by the appropriate discount factors.

LOS 56.b: Describe types of bonds for which estimating the expected cash flows is difficult.

CFA® Program Curriculum, Volume 5, page 448

Certainly, one problem in estimating future cash flows for bonds is predicting defaults and any potential credit problems that make the receipt of future cash flows uncertain. Aside from credit risk, however, we can identify three situations where estimating future cash flows poses additional difficulties.

1. **The principal repayment stream is not known with certainty.** This category includes bonds with embedded options (puts, calls, prepayment options, and accelerated sinking fund provisions). For these bonds, the future stream of principal payments is

uncertain and will depend to a large extent on the future path of interest rates. For example, lower rates will increase prepayments of mortgage passthrough securities, and principal will be repaid earlier.

2. **The coupon payments are not known with certainty.** With floating-rate securities, future coupon payments depend on the path of interest rates. With some floating-rate securities, the coupon payments may depend on the price of a commodity or the rate of inflation over some future period.

3. **The bond is convertible or exchangeable into another security.** Without information about future stock prices and interest rates, we don't know when the cash flows will come or how large they will be.

LOS 56.c: Calculate the value of a bond (coupon and zero-coupon).

CFA® Program Curriculum, Volume 5, page 449

For a Treasury bond, the appropriate rate used to value the promised cash flows is the risk-free rate. This may be a single rate, used to discount all of the cash flows, or a series of discount rates that correspond to the times until each cash flow arrives.

For non-Treasury securities, we must add a risk premium to the risk-free (Treasury) rate to determine the appropriate discount rate. This risk premium is one of the yield spread measures covered in the previous review and is the added yield to compensate for greater risk (credit risk, liquidity risk, call risk, prepayment risk, and so on). When using a single discount rate to value bonds, the risk premium is added to the risk-free rate to get the appropriate discount rate for all of the expected cash flows.

yield on a risky bond = yield on a default-free bond + risk premium

Other things being equal, the riskier the security, the higher the yield differential (or risk premium) we need to add to the on-the-run Treasury yields.

Calculating the Value of a Coupon Bond

Valuation with a single yield (discount rate). Recall that we valued an annuity using the time value of money keys on the calculator. For an option-free coupon bond, the coupon payments can be valued as an annuity. In order to take into account the payment of the par value at maturity, we will enter this final payment as the future value. This is the basic difference between valuing a coupon bond and valuing an annuity.

For simplicity, consider a security that will pay $100 per year for ten years and make a single $1,000 payment at maturity (in ten years). If the appropriate discount rate is 8% for all the cash flows, the value is:

$$\frac{100}{1.08} + \frac{100}{1.08^2} + \frac{100}{1.08^3} + \frac{100}{1.08^4} + ... + \frac{100}{1.08^{10}} + \frac{1,000}{1.08^{10}}$$

$= \$1,134.20 = $ present value of expected cash flows

This is simply the sum of the present values of the future cash flows, $100 per year for ten years and $1,000 (the principal repayment) to be received at the end of the tenth year, at the same time as the final coupon payment.

The calculator solution is:

N = 10; PMT = 100; FV = 1,000; I/Y = 8; CPT → PV = –$1,134.20

where:
N   = number of years
PMT = the *annual* coupon payment
I/Y   = the *annual* discount rate
FV   = the par value or selling price at the end of an assumed holding period

> *Professor's Note: Take note of a couple of points here. The discount rate is entered as a whole number in percent, 8, not 0.08. The ten coupon payments of $100 each are taken care of in the N = 10 entry, the principal repayment is in the FV = 1,000 entry. Lastly, note that the PV is negative; it will be the opposite sign to the sign of PMT and FV. The calculator is just "thinking" that if you receive the payments and future value (you own the bond), you must pay the present value of the bond today (you must buy the bond). That's why the PV amount is negative; it is a cash outflow to a bond buyer. Just make sure that you give the payments and future value the same sign, and then you can ignore the sign on the answer (PV).*

Valuation with a single yield and semiannual cash flows. Let's calculate the value of the same bond with semiannual payments.

Rather than $100 per year, the security will pay $50 every six months. Adjust the discount rate of 8% per year to 4% per six months. The par value remains $1,000.

The calculator solution is:

N = 20; PMT = 50; FV = 1,000; I/Y = 4; CPT PV = –1,135.90

where:
N   = number of semiannual periods
PMT = the semiannual coupon payment
I/Y   = the semiannual discount rate
FV   = the par value

Calculating the Value of a Zero-Coupon Bond

Because a zero-coupon bond has only a single payment at maturity, the value of a zero is simply the present value of the par or face value. Given the yield to maturity, the calculation on a semiannual basis is:

$$\text{bond value} = \frac{\text{maturity value}}{(1+i)^{\text{number of years} \times 2}}$$

Study Session 16
Cross-Reference to CFA Institute Assigned Reading #56 – Introduction to the Valuation of Debt Securities

Study Session 16

Note that this valuation model requires just three pieces of information:

1. The bond's maturity value, assumed to be $1,000.
2. The semiannual discount rate, i.
3. The life of the bond, N years.

Alternatively, using the TVM keys, we can enter:

PMT = 0; FV = par; N = # years × 2; I/Y = YTM/2 = semiannual discount rate; CPT → PV

Although zero-coupon bonds do not pay coupons, it is customary to value zero-coupon bonds using semiannual discount rates. Note that N is now two times the number of years to maturity and that the semiannual discount rate is one-half the yield to maturity expressed as a BEY.

Example: Valuing a zero-coupon bond

Compute the value of a 10-year, $1,000 face value zero-coupon bond with a yield to maturity of 8%.

Answer:

To find the value of this bond given its yield to maturity of 8% (a 4% semiannual rate), we can calculate:

$$\text{bond value} = \frac{1,000}{\left(1 + \frac{0.08}{2}\right)^{10\times2}} = \frac{1,000}{\left(1.04\right)^{20}} = \$456.39$$

Or, use the following inputs:

$$N = 10 \times 2 = 20; \ FV = 1,000; \ I/Y = \frac{8}{2} = 4; \ PMT = 0; \ CPT \rightarrow PV = -\$456.39$$

The difference between the current price of the bond ($456.39) and its par value ($1,000) is the amount of compound interest that will be earned over the 10-year life of the issue.

Professor's Note: Exam questions will likely specify whether annual or semiannual discounting should be used. Just be prepared to value a zero-coupon bond either way.

LOS 56.d: Explain how the price of a bond changes if the discount rate changes and as the bond approaches its maturity date.

CFA® Program Curriculum, Volume 5, page 450

Prior to maturity, a bond can be selling at a significant discount or premium to par value. However, regardless of its required yield, the price will converge to par value as maturity approaches. Consider a bond with $1,000 par value and a 3-year life paying 6% semiannual coupons. The bond values corresponding to required yields of 3%, 6%, and 12% as the bond approaches maturity are presented in Figure 1.

Figure 1: Bond Values and the Passage of Time

Time to Maturity	YTM = 3%	YTM = 6%	YTM = 12%
3.0 years	$1,085.46	$1,000.00	$852.48
2.5	1,071.74	1,000.00	873.63
2.0	1,057.82	1,000.00	896.05
1.5	1,043.68	1,000.00	919.81
1.0	1,029.34	1,000.00	945.00
0.5	1,014.78	1,000.00	971.69
0.0	1,000.00	1,000.00	1,000.00

To compute the change in bond value due to the passage of time, just revalue the bond with the number of periods (remaining until maturity) reduced. The value of a 6% bond with three years until maturity and a yield to maturity of 3% is FV = 1,000; PMT = 30; N = 6; I/Y = 1.5; CPT → PV = $1,085.46. To see the effect of the passage of time (with the yield to maturity held constant) just enter N = 5 CPT → PV to get the value one period (six months) from now of $1,071.74, or N = 4 CPT → PV to get the value two periods (one year) from now of $1,057.82.

The change in value associated with the passage of time for the three bonds represented in Figure 1 is presented graphically in Figure 2.

Figure 2: Premium, Par, and Discount Bonds

LOS 56.e: Calculate the change in value of a bond given a change in its discount rate.

CFA® Program Curriculum, Volume 5, page 450

Bond values and bond yields are inversely related. An *increase* in the discount rate will *decrease* the present value of a bond's expected cash flows; a decrease in the discount rate will increase the present value of a bond's expected cash flows. The change in bond value in response to a change in the discount rate can be calculated as the difference between the present values of the cash flows at the two different discount rates.

Example: Changes in required yield

A bond has a par value of $1,000, a 6% semiannual coupon, and three years to maturity. Compute the bond values when the yield to maturity is 3%, 6%, and 12%.

Answer:

$$\text{At I}/\text{Y} = \frac{3}{2}; \text{N} = 3 \times 2; \text{FV} = 1{,}000; \text{PMT} = \frac{60}{2}; \text{CPT} \to \text{PV} = -1{,}085.458$$

$$\text{At I}/\text{Y} = \frac{6}{2}; \text{N} = 3 \times 2; \text{FV} = 1{,}000; \text{PMT} = \frac{60}{2}; \text{CPT} \to \text{PV} = -1{,}000.000$$

$$\text{At I}/\text{Y} = \frac{12}{2}; \text{N} = 3 \times 2; \text{FV} = 1{,}000; \text{PMT} = \frac{60}{2}; \text{CPT} \to \text{PV} = -852.480$$

We have illustrated here a point covered earlier; if the yield to maturity equals the coupon rate, the bond value is equal to par. If the yield to maturity is higher (lower) than the coupon rate, the bond is trading at a discount (premium) to par.

We can now calculate the percentage change in price for changes in yield. If the required yield decreases from 6% to 3%, the value of the bond increases by:

$$\frac{1{,}085.46}{1{,}000.00} - 1 = 8.546\%.$$

If the yield increases from 6% to 12%, the bond value decreases by:

$$\frac{852.48}{1{,}000.00} - 1 = -14.752\%.$$

 Professor's Note: Notice that in these calculations, you only need to change the interest rate (I/Y) and then compute PV once the values of N, PMT, and FV have been entered. The TVM keys remember the values for these inputs even after the calculator has been turned off!

Price-yield profile. If you plot a bond's yield to its corresponding value, you'll get a graph like the one shown in Figure 3. Here we see that higher prices are associated with lower yields. This graph is called the *price-yield curve*. Note that it is not a straight line but is curved. For option-free bonds, the price-yield curve is convex toward the origin, meaning it looks like half of a smile.

Study Session 16
Cross-Reference to CFA Institute Assigned Reading #56 – Introduction to the Valuation of Debt Securities

Study Session 16

Figure 3: The Price-Yield Profile

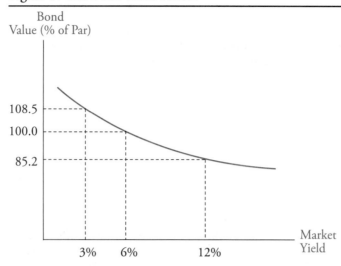

LOS 56.f: Explain and demonstrate the use of the arbitrage-free valuation approach and describe how a dealer can generate an arbitrage profit if a bond is mispriced.

CFA® Program Curriculum, Volume 5, page 462

Yield to maturity is a summary measure and is essentially an internal rate of return based on a bond's cash flows and its market price. In the traditional valuation approach, we get the yield to maturity of bonds with maturity and risk characteristics similar to those of the bond we wish to value. Then we use this rate to discount the cash flows of the bond to be valued.

With the **arbitrage-free valuation approach**, we *discount each cash flow using a discount rate that is specific to the maturity of each cash flow*. Again, these discount rates are called **spot rates** and can be thought of as the required rates of return on zero-coupon bonds maturing at various times in the future.

The arbitrage-free valuation approach simply says that the value of a Treasury bond based on (Treasury) spot rates must be equal to the value of the parts (i.e., the sum of the present values of all of the expected cash flows). If this is not the case, there must be an arbitrage opportunity. If a bond is selling for less than the sum of the present values of its expected cash flows, an arbitrageur will buy the bond and sell the pieces. If the bond is selling for more than the sum of the values of the pieces (individual cash flows), one could buy the pieces, package them to make a bond, and then sell the bond package to earn an arbitrage profit.

The first step in checking for arbitrage-free valuation is to value a coupon bond using the appropriate spot rates. The second step is to compare this value to the market price of the bond. If the computed value is not equal to the market price, there is an arbitrage profit to be earned by buying the lower-priced alternative (either the bond or the individual cash flows) and selling the higher-priced alternative. Of course, this assumes that there are zero-coupon bonds available that correspond to the coupon bond's cash flows.

Example: Arbitrage-free valuation

Consider a 6% Treasury note with 1.5 years to maturity. Spot rates (expressed as yields to maturity) are: 6 months = 5%, 1 year = 6%, and 1.5 years = 7%. If the note is selling for $992, compute the arbitrage profit, and explain how a dealer would perform the arbitrage.

Answer:

To value the note, note that the cash flows (per $1,000 par value) will be $30, $30, and $1,030 and that the semiannual discount rates are half the stated yield to maturity.

Using the semiannual spot rates, the present value of the expected cash flows is:

$$\text{present value using spot rates} = \frac{30}{1.025} + \frac{30}{1.03^2} + \frac{1,030}{1.035^3} = \$986.55$$

This value is less than the market price of the note, so we will buy the individual cash flows (zero-coupon bonds), combine them into a 1.5-year note package, and sell the package for the market price of the note. This will result in an immediate and riskless profit of 992.00 – 986.55 = $5.45 per bond.

Determining whether a bond is over- or undervalued is a two-step process. First, compute the value of the bond using either the spot rates or yield to maturity, remembering that both are often given as two times the semiannual discount rate(s). Second, compare this value to the market price given in the problem to see which is higher.

How a Dealer Can Generate an Arbitrage Profit

Recall that the Treasury STRIPS program allows dealers to divide Treasury bonds into their coupon payments (by date) and their maturity payments in order to create zero-coupon securities. The program also allows reconstitution of Treasury bonds/notes by putting the individual cash flows back together to create Treasury securities. Ignoring any costs of performing these transformations, the ability to separate and reconstitute Treasury securities will insure that the arbitrage-free valuation condition is met.

The STRIPS program allows for just the arbitrage we outlined previously. If the price of the bond is greater than its arbitrage-free value, a dealer could buy the individual cash flows and sell the package for the market price of the bond. If the price of the bond is less than its arbitrage-free value, an arbitrageur can make an immediate and riskless profit by purchasing the bond and selling the parts for more than the cost of the bond.

Such arbitrage opportunities and the related buying of bonds priced too low and sales of bonds priced too high will force the bond prices toward equality with their arbitrage-free values, eliminating further arbitrage opportunities.

KEY CONCEPTS

LOS 56.a

To value a bond, one must:
- Estimate the amount and timing of the bond's future payments of interest and principal.
- Determine the appropriate discount rate(s).
- Calculate the sum of the present values of the bond's cash flows.

LOS 56.b

Certain bond features, including embedded options, convertibility, or floating rates, can make the estimation of future cash flows uncertain, which adds complexity to the estimation of bond values.

LOS 56.c

To compute the value of an option-free coupon bond, value the coupon payments as an annuity and add the present value of the principal repayment at maturity.

The value of a zero-coupon bond calculated using a semiannual discount rate, i (one-half its annual yield to maturity), is:

$$\text{bond value} = \frac{\text{maturity value}}{(1 + i)^{\text{number of years} \times 2}}$$

LOS 56.d

When interest rates (yields) do not change, a bond's price will move toward its par value as time passes and the maturity date approaches.

To compute the change in value that is attributable to the passage of time, revalue the bond with a smaller number of periods to maturity.

LOS 56.e

The change in value that is attributable to a change in the discount rate can be calculated as the change in the bond's present value based on the new discount rate (yield).

LOS 56.f

A Treasury spot yield curve is considered "arbitrage-free" if the present values of Treasury securities calculated using these rates are equal to equilibrium market prices.

If bond prices are not equal to their arbitrage-free values, dealers can generate arbitrage profits by buying the lower-priced alternative (either the bond or the individual cash flows) and selling the higher-priced alternative (either the individual cash flows or a package of the individual cash flows equivalent to the bond).

CONCEPT CHECKERS

1. An analyst observes a 5-year, 10% coupon bond with semiannual payments. The face value is £1,000. How much is each coupon payment?
    A. £25.
    B. £50.
    C. £100.

2. A 20-year, 10% annual-pay bond has a par value of $1,000. What would this bond be trading for if it were being priced to yield 15% as an annual rate?
    A. $685.14.
    B. $687.03.
    C. $828.39.

3. An analyst observes a 5-year, 10% semiannual-pay bond. The face amount is £1,000. The analyst believes that the yield to maturity for this bond should be 15%. Based on this yield estimate, the price of this bond would be:
    A. £828.40.
    B. £1,189.53.
    C. £1,193.04.

4. Two bonds have par values of $1,000. Bond A is a 5% annual-pay, 15-year bond priced to yield 8% as an annual rate; the other (Bond B) is a 7.5% annual-pay, 20-year bond priced to yield 6% as an annual rate. The values of these two bonds would be:

	Bond A	Bond B
A.	$740.61	$847.08
B.	$740.61	$1,172.04
C.	$743.22	$1,172.04

5. Bond A is a 15-year, 10.5% semiannual-pay bond priced with a yield to maturity of 8%, while Bond B is a 15-year, 7% semiannual-pay bond priced with the same yield to maturity. Given that both bonds have par values of $1,000, the prices of these two bonds would be:

	Bond A	Bond B
A.	$1,216.15	$913.54
B.	$1,216.15	$944.41
C.	$746.61	$913.54

Use the following data to answer Questions 6 through 8.

An analyst observes a 20-year, 8% option-free bond with semiannual coupons. The required semiannual-pay yield to maturity on this bond was 8%, but suddenly it drops to 7.25%.

6. As a result of the drop, the price of this bond:
    A. will increase.
    B. will decrease.
    C. will stay the same.

7. Prior to the change in the required yield, what was the price of the bond?
    A. 92.64.
    B. 100.00.
    C. 107.85.

8. The percentage change in the price of this bond when the rate decreased is *closest* to:
    A. 7.86%.
    B. 7.79%.
    C. 8.00%.

9. Treasury spot rates (expressed as semiannual-pay yields to maturity) are as follows: 6 months = 4%, 1 year = 5%, 1.5 years = 6%. A 1.5-year, 4% Treasury note is trading at $965. The arbitrage trade and arbitrage profit are:
    A. buy the bond, sell the pieces, earn $7.09 per bond.
    B. sell the bond, buy the pieces, earn $7.09 per bond.
    C. sell the bond, buy the pieces, earn $7.91 per bond.

10. A $1,000, 5%, 20-year annual-pay bond has a yield of 6.5%. If the yield remains unchanged, how much will the bond value increase over the next three years?
    A. $13.62.
    B. $13.78.
    C. $13.96.

11. The value of a 17-year, zero-coupon bond with a maturity value of $100,000 and a semiannual-pay yield of 8.22% is *closest* to:
    A. $24,618.
    B. $25,425.
    C. $26,108.

ANSWERS – CONCEPT CHECKERS

1. **B** $CPN = 1,000 \times \dfrac{0.10}{2} = £50$

2. **B**   bond value = $\sum\limits_{t=1}^{20} \dfrac{100}{(1+0.15)^t} + \dfrac{1,000}{(1+0.15)^{20}} = \$687.03$

   N = 20; I/Y = 15; FV = 1,000; PMT = 100; CPT → PV = –$687.03

3. **A**   N = 10; I/Y = 7.5; FV = 1,000; PMT = 50; CPT → PV = –$828.40

4. **C**   Bond A: N = 15; I/Y = 8; FV = 1,000; PMT = 50; CPT → PV = –$743.22

   Bond B: N = 20; I/Y = 6; FV = 1,000; PMT = 75; CPT → PV = –$1,172.04

   Because the coupon on Bond A is less than its required yield, the bond will sell at a discount; conversely, because the coupon on Bond B is greater than its required yield, the bond will sell at a premium.

5. **A**   Bond A: N = 15 × 2 = 30; I/Y = $\dfrac{8}{2}$ = 4; FV = 1,000; PMT = $\dfrac{105}{2}$ = 52.50;

   CPT → PV = –$1,216.15

   Bond B: N = 15 × 2 = 30; I/Y = $\dfrac{8}{2}$ = 4; FV = 1,000; PMT = $\dfrac{70}{2}$ = 35;

   CPT → PV = –$913.54

6. **A**   The price-yield relationship is inverse. If the required yield falls, the bond's price will rise, and vice versa.

7. **B**   If YTM = stated coupon rate ⇒ bond price = 100 or par value.

8. **A**   The new value is 40 = N, $\dfrac{7.25}{2}$ = I/Y, 40 = PMT, 1,000 = FV

   CPT → PV = –1,078.55, an increase of 7.855%

9. **A**   arbitrage-free value = $\dfrac{20}{1.02} + \dfrac{20}{1.025^2} + \dfrac{1020}{1.03^3} = \$972.09$

   Since the bond price ($965) is less, buy the bond and sell the pieces for an arbitrage profit of $7.09 per bond.

10. **A**   With 20 years to maturity, the value of the bond with an annual-pay yield of 6.5% is 20 = N, 50 = PMT, 1,000 = FV, 6.5 = I/Y, CPT – PV = –834.72. With 17 = N, CPT → PV = –848.34, so the value will increase $13.62.

11. **B** $\quad \text{PMT} = 0, \text{N} = 2 \times 17 = 34, \text{ I}/\text{Y} = \dfrac{8.22}{2} = 4.11, \text{FV} = 100,000$

$\text{CPT} \rightarrow \text{PV} = -25,424.75, \text{ or}$

$\dfrac{100,000}{(1.0411)^{34}} = \$25,424.76$

YIELD MEASURES, SPOT RATES, AND FORWARD RATES

EXAM FOCUS

This topic review gets a little more specific about yield measures and introduces current yield, yield to maturity, and yield to call. Please pay particular attention to the concept of a bond equivalent yield and how to convert various yields to a bond equivalent basis. The other important thing about the yield measures here is to understand what they are telling you so that you understand their limitations.

The final section of this review introduces forward rates. The relationship between forward rates and spot rates is an important one. At a minimum, you should be prepared to solve for spot rates given forward rates and to solve for an unknown forward rate given two spot rates. You should also get a firm grip on the concept of an option-adjusted spread, when it is used and how to interpret it, as well as how and when it differs from a zero-volatility spread.

LOS 57.a: Describe the sources of return from investing in a bond.

CFA® Program Curriculum, Volume 5, page 492

Debt securities that make explicit interest payments have **three sources of return**:

1. The periodic *coupon interest payments* made by the issuer.

2. The *recovery of principal, along with any capital gain or loss* that occurs when the bond matures, is called, or is sold.

3. *Reinvestment income*, or the income earned from reinvesting the periodic coupon payments (i.e., the compound interest on reinvested coupon payments).

The interest earned on reinvested income is an important source of return to bond investors. The uncertainty about how much reinvestment income a bondholder will realize is what we have previously addressed as *reinvestment risk*.

LOS 57.b: Calculate and interpret traditional yield measures for fixed-rate bonds and explain their limitations and assumptions.

CFA® Program Curriculum, Volume 5, page 493

Current yield is the simplest of all return measures, but it offers limited information. This measure looks at just one source of return: *a bond's annual interest income—it does* not consider capital gains/losses or reinvestment income. The formula for the current yield is:

$$\text{current yield} = \frac{\text{annual cash coupon payment}}{\text{bond price}}$$

Example: Computing current yield

Consider a 20-year, $1,000 par value, 6% *semiannual-pay* bond that is currently trading at $802.07. Calculate the current yield.

Answer:

The *annual* cash coupon payments total:

annual cash coupon payment = par value × stated coupon rate = $1,000 × 0.06 = $60

Because the bond is trading at $802.07, the current yield is:

$$\text{current yield} = \frac{60}{802.07} = 0.0748, \text{ or } 7.48\%.$$

Note that current yield is based on *annual* coupon interest so that it is the same for a semiannual-pay and annual-pay bond with the same coupon rate and price.

Yield to maturity (YTM) is an annualized internal rate of return, based on a bond's price and its promised cash flows. For a bond with semiannual coupon payments, the yield to maturity is stated as two times the semiannual internal rate of return implied by the bond's price. The formula that relates the bond price (including accrued interest) to YTM for a semiannual coupon bond is:

$$\text{bond price} = \frac{CPN_1}{\left(1 + \frac{YTM}{2}\right)} + \frac{CPN_2}{\left(1 + \frac{YTM}{2}\right)^2} + \cdots + \frac{CPN_{2N} + Par}{\left(1 + \frac{YTM}{2}\right)^{2N}}$$

where:
bond price = full price including accrued interest
CPN_t = the (semiannual) coupon payment received after t semiannual periods
N = number of years to maturity
YTM = yield to maturity

YTM and price contain the same information. That is, given the YTM, you can calculate the price and given the price, you can calculate the YTM.

We cannot easily solve for YTM from the bond price. Given a bond price and the coupon payment amount, we could solve it by trial and error, trying different values of YTM until the present value of the expected cash flows is equal to price. Fortunately, your calculator will do exactly the same thing, only faster. It uses a trial and error algorithm to find the discount rate that makes the two sides of the pricing formula equal.

> **Example: Computing YTM**
>
> Consider a 20-year, $1,000 par value bond, with a 6% coupon rate (semiannual payments) with a full price of $802.07. Calculate the YTM.
>
> **Answer:**
>
> Using a financial calculator, you'd find the YTM on this bond as follows:
>
> PV = –802.07; N = 20 × 2 = 40; FV = 1,000; PMT = 60/2 = 30; CPT → I/Y = 4.00
>
> 4% is the semiannual discount rate, $\dfrac{YTM}{2}$ in the formula, so the YTM = 2 × 4% = 8%.
>
> Note that the signs of PMT and FV are positive, and the sign of PV is negative; you must do this to avoid the dreaded "Error 5" message on the TI calculator. If you get the "Error 5" message, you can assume you have not assigned a negative value to the price (PV) of the bond and a positive sign to the cash flows to be received from the bond.

There are certain relationships that exist between different yield measures, depending on whether a bond is trading at par, at a discount, or at a premium. These relationships are shown in Figure 1.

Figure 1: Par, Discount, and Premium Bond

Bond Selling at:	Relationship
Par	coupon rate = current yield = yield to maturity
Discount	coupon rate < current yield < yield to maturity
Premium	coupon rate > current yield > yield to maturity

These conditions will hold in all cases; every discount bond will have a nominal yield (coupon rate) that is less than its current yield and a current yield that is less than its YTM.

The yield to maturity calculated in the previous example (2 × the semiannual discount rate) is referred to as a **bond equivalent yield** (BEY), and we will also refer to it as a semiannual YTM or semiannual-pay YTM. If you are given yields that are identified as BEY, you will know that you must divide by two to get the semiannual discount rate. With bonds that make annual coupon payments, we can calculate an **annual-pay yield to maturity**, which is simply the internal rate of return for the expected annual cash flows.

Example: Calculating YTM for annual coupon bonds

Consider an annual-pay 20-year, $1,000 par value, with a 6% coupon rate and a full price of $802.07. Calculate the *annual-pay YTM*.

Answer:

The relation between the price and the annual-pay YTM on this bond is:

$$802.07 = \sum_{t=1}^{20} \frac{60}{(1+\text{YTM})^t} + \frac{1,000}{(1+\text{YTM})^{20}} \Rightarrow \text{YTM} = 8.019\%.$$

Here we have separated the coupon cash flows and the principal repayment.

The calculator solution is:

PV = −802.07; N = 20; FV = 1,000; PMT = 60; CPT → I/Y = 8.019; 8.019% is the annual-pay YTM.

Use a discount rate of 8.019%, and you'll find the present value of the bond's future cash flows (annual coupon payments and the recovery of principal) will equal the current market price of the bond. *The discount rate is the bond's YTM.*

For zero-coupon Treasury bonds, the convention is to quote the yields as BEYs (semiannual-pay YTMs).

Example: Calculating YTM for zero-coupon bonds

A 5-year Treasury STRIP is priced at $768. Calculate the semiannual-pay YTM and annual-pay YTM.

Answer:

The direct calculation method, based on the geometric mean covered in Quantitative Methods, is:

$$\text{the semiannual-pay YTM or BEY} = \left[\left(\frac{1,000}{768} \right)^{\frac{1}{10}} - 1 \right] \times 2 = 5.35\%.$$

$$\text{the annual-pay YTM} = \left(\frac{1,000}{768} \right)^{\frac{1}{5}} - 1 = 5.42\%.$$

Using the TVM calculator functions:

PV = −768; FV = 1,000; PMT = 0; N = 10; CPT → I/Y = 2.675% × 2 = 5.35% for the semiannual-pay YTM, and PV = −768; FV = 1,000; PMT = 0; N = 5; CPT → I/Y = 5.42% for the annual-pay YTM.

The annual-pay YTM of 5.42% means that $768 earning compound interest of 5.42% per year would grow to $1,000 in five years.

The **yield to call** is used to calculate the yield on callable bonds that are selling at a premium to par. For bonds trading at a premium to par, the *yield to call* may be less than the yield to maturity. This can be the case when the call price is below the current market price.

The calculation of the yield to call is the same as the calculation of yield to maturity, except that the *call price is substituted* for the par value in FV and the *number of semiannual periods until the call date is substituted* for periods to maturity, *N*. When a bond has a period of call protection, we calculate the **yield to first call** over the period until the bond may first be called, and use the first call price in the calculation as FV. In a similar manner, we can calculate the yield to any subsequent call date using the appropriate call price.

If the bond contains a provision for a call at *par* at some time in the future, we can calculate the *yield to first par call* using the number of years until the par call date and par for the maturity payment. If you have a good understanding of the yield to maturity measure, the YTC is not a difficult calculation; just be very careful about the number of years to the call and the call price for that date. An example will illustrate the calculation of these yield measures.

Example: Computing the YTM, YTC, and yield to first par call

Consider a 20-year, 10% semiannual-pay bond with a full price of 112 that can be called in five years at 102 and called at par in seven years. Calculate the YTM, YTC, and yield to first par call.

 Professor's Note: Bond prices are often expressed as a percent of par (e.g., 100 = par).

Answer:

The **YTM** can be calculated as: N = 40; PV = –112; PMT = 5; FV = 100; CPT → I/Y = 4.361% × 2 = 8.72% = YTM.

To compute the **yield to first call** (YTFC), we substitute the number of semiannual periods until the first call date (10) for N, and the first call price (102) for FV, as follows:

N = 10; PV = –112; PMT = 5; **FV = 102**;

CPT → I/Y = 3.71% and 2 × 3.71 = 7.42% = YTFC

To calculate the **yield to first par call** (YTFPC), we will substitute the number of semiannual periods until the first par call date (14) for N and par (100) for FV as follows:

N = 14; PV = –112; PMT = 5; **FV = 100**;

CPT → I/Y = 3.873% × 2 = 7.746% = YTFPC

Note that the yield to call, 7.42%, is significantly lower than the yield to maturity, 8.72%. If the bond were trading at a discount to par value, there would be no reason to calculate the yield to call. For a discount bond, the YTC will be higher than the YTM since the bond will appreciate more rapidly with the call to at least par and, perhaps, an even greater call price. Bond yields are quoted on a yield to call basis when the YTC is less than the YTM, which can only be the case for bonds trading at a premium to the call price.

The **yield to worst** is the worst yield outcome of any that are possible given the call provisions of the bond. In the above example, the yield to first call is less than the YTM and less than the yield to first par call. So, the worst possible outcome is a yield of 7.42%; the yield to first call is the *yield to worst*.

The **yield to refunding** refers to a specific situation where a bond is currently callable and current rates make calling the issue attractive to the issuer, but where the bond covenants contain provisions giving protection from refunding until some future date. The calculation of the yield to refunding is just like that of YTM or YTC. The difference here is that the yield to refunding would use the call price, but the date (and therefore the number of periods used in the calculation) is the date when refunding protection ends. Recall that bonds that are callable, but not currently refundable, can be called using funds from sources other than the issuance of a lower coupon bond.

The **yield to put** (YTP) is used if a bond has a put feature and is selling at a discount. The yield to put will likely be higher than the yield to maturity. The yield to put calculation is just like the yield to maturity with the number of semiannual periods until the put date as N, and the put price as FV.

Example: Computing YTM and YTP

Consider a 3-year, 6%, $1,000 *semiannual-pay* bond. The bond is selling for a full price of $925.40. The first put opportunity is at par in two years. Calculate the YTM and the YTP.

Answer:

Yield to maturity is calculated as:

N = 6; FV = 1,000; PMT = 30; PV = –925.40; CPT → I/Y = 4.44 × 2 = 8.88% = YTM

Yield to put is calculated as:

N = 4; FV = 1,000; PMT = 30; PV = –925.40; CPT → I/Y = 5.11 × 2 = 10.22% = YTP

In this example, the yield to put is higher than the YTM and, therefore, would be the appropriate yield to look at for this bond.

The **cash flow yield** (CFY) is used for mortgage-backed securities and other amortizing asset-backed securities that have monthly cash flows. In many cases, the amount of the principal repayment can be greater than the amount required to amortize the loan over its original life. Cash flow yield (CFY) incorporates an assumed schedule of monthly cash flows based on assumptions as to how prepayments are likely to occur. Once we have projected the monthly cash flows, we can calculate CFY as a *monthly* internal rate of return based on the market price of the security.

 Professor's Note: I believe you are more likely to be required to interpret a CFY than to calculate one. If you need to calculate a CFY, just use the cash flow keys, put the price of the security as a negative value as CF_0, enter the monthly cash flows sequentially as CFn's, and solve for IRR, which will be a monthly rate.

The following formula is used to convert a (monthly) CFY into bond equivalent form:

$$\text{bond equivalent yield} = \left[\left(1 + \text{monthly CFY}\right)^6 - 1\right] \times 2$$

Here, we have converted the monthly yield into a semiannual yield and then doubled it to make it equivalent to a semiannual-pay YTM or bond equivalent yield.

A limitation of the CFY measure is that actual prepayment rates may differ from those assumed in the calculation of CFY.

The Assumptions and Limitations of Traditional Yield Measures

The primary *limitation of the yield to maturity measure* is that it does not tell us the compound rate of return that we will realize on a fixed-income investment over its life. This is because we do not know the rate of interest we will realize on the reinvested coupon payments (the reinvestment rate). Reinvestment income can be a significant part of the overall return on a bond. As noted earlier, the uncertainty about the return on reinvested cash flows is referred to as *reinvestment risk*. It is higher for bonds with higher coupon rates, other things equal, and potentially higher for callable bonds as well.

The realized yield on a bond is the actual compound return that was earned on the initial investment. It is usually computed at the end of the investment horizon. For a bond to have a *realized yield* equal to its YTM, all cash flows prior to maturity must be reinvested at the YTM, and the bond must be held until maturity. If the average reinvestment rate is below the YTM, the realized yield will be below the YTM. For this reason, it is often stated that: *The yield to maturity assumes cash flows will be reinvested at the YTM and assumes that the bond will be held until maturity.*

The other internal rate of return measures, YTC and YTP, suffer from the same shortcomings since they are calculated like YTMs and do not account for reinvestment income. The CFY measure is also an internal rate of return measure and can differ greatly from the realized yield if reinvestment rates are low, since scheduled principal payments and prepayments must be reinvested along with the interest payments.

LOS 57.c: Explain the reinvestment assumption implicit in calculating yield to maturity and describe the factors that affect reinvestment risk.

CFA® Program Curriculum, Volume 5, page 495

Reinvestment income is important because if the reinvestment rate is less than the YTM, the realized yield on the bond will be less than the YTM. The realized yield will always be between the YTM and the assumed reinvestment rate.

If a bondholder holds a bond until maturity and reinvests all coupon interest payments, the total amount generated by the bond over its life has three components:

1. Bond principal.

2. Coupon interest.

3. Interest on reinvested coupons.

Once we calculate the total amount needed for a particular level of compound return over a bond's life, we can subtract the principal and coupon payments to determine the amount of reinvestment income necessary to achieve the target yield. An example will illustrate this calculation.

Example: Required reinvestment income for a bond

If you purchase a 6%, 10-year Treasury bond at par, how much reinvestment income must be generated over its life to provide the investor with a compound return of 6% on a semiannual basis?

Answer:

Assuming the bond has a par value of $100, we first calculate the total value that must be generated ten years (20 semiannual periods) from now as:

$$100(1.03)^{20} = \$180.61$$

There are 20 bond coupons of $3 each, totaling $60, and a payment of $100 of principal at maturity.

Therefore, the required reinvestment income over the life of the bond is:

$$180.61 - 100 - 60 = \$20.61$$

Professor's Note: If we had purchased the bond at a premium or discount, we would still use the purchase price (which would not equal 100) and the required compound return to calculate the total future dollars required, and then subtract the maturity value and the total coupon payments to get the required reinvestment income.

Factors That Affect Reinvestment Risk

Other things being equal, a coupon bond's **reinvestment risk** will *increase* with:

- *Higher coupons*—because there's more cash flow to reinvest.
- *Longer maturities*—because more of the total value of the investment is in the coupon cash flows (and interest on coupon cash flows).

In both cases, the amount of reinvested income will play a bigger role in determining the bond's total return and, therefore, introduce more reinvestment risk. A noncallable zero-coupon bond has no reinvestment risk over its life because there are no cash flows to reinvest prior to maturity.

LOS 57.d: Calculate and interpret the bond equivalent yield of an annual-pay bond and the annual-pay yield of a semiannual-pay bond.

CFA® Program Curriculum, Volume 5, page 494

This LOS requires that you be able to turn a semiannual return into an annual return, and an annual return into a semiannual return.

> **Example: Comparing bonds with different coupon frequencies**
>
> Suppose that a corporation has a semiannual coupon bond trading in the United States with a YTM of 6.25%, and an annual coupon bond trading in Europe with a YTM of 6.30%. Which bond has the greater yield?
>
> **Answer:**
>
> To determine the answer, we can convert the yield on *the annual-pay bond* to a (semiannual-pay) bond equivalent yield. That is:
>
> $$\text{BEY of an annual-pay bond} = [(1 + \text{annual YTM})^{\frac{1}{2}} - 1] \times 2$$
>
> Thus, the BEY of the 6.30% annual-pay bond is:
>
> $$[(1 + 0.0630)^{0.5} - 1] \times 2 = [1.031 - 1] \times 2 = 0.031 \times 2 = 0.062 = 6.2\%$$
>
> The 6.25% semiannual-pay bond provides the better (bond equivalent) yield.
>
> Alternatively, we could convert the YTM of the semiannual-pay bond (which is a bond equivalent yield) to an equivalent annual-pay basis. The equivalent annual yield (EAY—*sometimes known as the effective annual yield*) to the 6.25% semiannual-pay YTM is:
>
> $$\text{equivalent annual yield} = \left(1 + \frac{0.0625}{2}\right)^2 - 1 = 0.0635 \rightarrow 6.35\%$$

The EAY of the semiannual-pay bond is 6.35%, which is greater than the 6.3% for the annual-pay bond. Therefore, the semiannual-pay bond has a greater yield as long as we put the yields on an equivalent basis, calculating both as annual yields or calculating both as bond equivalent yields (semiannual yields × 2).

LOS 57.e: Describe the calculation of the theoretical Treasury spot rate curve and calculate the value of a bond using spot rates.

CFA® Program Curriculum, Volume 5, page 508

The par yield curve gives the YTMs of bonds currently trading near their par values (YTM ≈ coupon rate) for various maturities. Here, we need to use these yields to get the theoretical Treasury spot rate curve by a process called **bootstrapping**.

The method of bootstrapping can be a little confusing, so let's first get the main idea and then go through a more realistic and detailed example. The general idea is that we will solve for spot rates by knowing the prices of coupon bonds. We always know one spot rate to begin with and then calculate the spot rate for the next longer period. When we know two spot rates, we can get the third based on the market price of a bond with three cash flows by using the spot rates to get the present values of the first two cash flows.

As an example of this method, consider that we know the prices and yields of three annual-pay bonds as shown in Figure 2. All three bonds are trading at par or $1,000.

Figure 2: Prices and Yield for Three Annual-Pay Bonds

Maturity	Coupon	Yield	Price
1 year	3%	3%	$1,000
2 years	4%	4%	$1,000
3 years	5%	5%	$1,000

Because the 1-year bond makes only one payment (it's an annual-pay bond) of $1,030 at maturity, the 1-year spot rate is 3%, the yield on this single payment. The 2-year bond makes two payments, a $40 coupon in one year and a $1,040 payment at maturity in two years. Because the spot rate to discount the 2-year bond's first cash flow is 3%, and because we know that the sum of the present values of the bond's cash flows must equal its (no-arbitrage) price of $1,000, we can write:

$$\frac{40}{1.03} + \frac{1,040}{(1 + \text{2-year spot rate})^2} = \$1,000$$

Based on this, we can solve for the 2-year spot rate as follows:

1. $\dfrac{1,040}{(1 + \text{2-year spot})^2} = 1,000 - \dfrac{40}{1.03} = 1,000 - 38.83 = 961.17$

2. $\dfrac{1,040}{961.17} = (1 + \text{2-year spot})^2 = 1.082$

3. $\text{2-year spot} = (1.082)^{\frac{1}{2}} - 1 = 0.04019 = 4.019\%$

Now that we have both the 1-year and 2-year spot rates, we can use the cash flows and price of the 3-year bond to write:

$$\frac{50}{1.03} + \frac{50}{(1.04019)^2} + \frac{1,050}{(1 + \text{3-year spot})^3} = 1,000$$

And solve for the 3-year spot rate:

$$1,000 - \frac{50}{1.03} - \frac{50}{(1.04019)^2} = \frac{1,050}{(1 + \text{3-year spot})^3}$$

$$1,000 - 48.54 - 46.21 = \frac{1,050}{(1 + \text{3-year spot})^3}$$

$$905.25 = \frac{1,050}{(1 + \text{3-year spot})^3}$$

$$\left(\frac{1,050}{905.25}\right)^{\frac{1}{3}} - 1 = \text{3-year spot} = 0.05069 = 5.069\%$$

So, we can state that:

$$\frac{50}{1.03} + \frac{50}{(1.04019)^2} + \frac{1,050}{(1.05069)^3} = \$1,000$$

We have just solved for the 2-year and 3-year spot rates by the method of bootstrapping.

In practice, Treasury bonds pay semiannually, and their YTMs are semiannual-pay YTMs. The next example illustrates the method of bootstrapping when coupons are paid semiannually.

Consider the yields on coupon Treasury bonds trading at par given in Figure 3. YTM for the bonds is expressed as a bond equivalent yield (semiannual-pay YTM).

Figure 3: Par Yields for Three Semiannual-Pay Bonds

Maturity	YTM	Coupon	Price
6 months	5%	5%	100
1 year	6%	6%	100
18 months	7%	7%	100

The bond with six months left to maturity has a semiannual discount rate of $0.05 / 2 = 0.025 = 2.5\%$ or 5% on an annual BEY basis. Because this bond will only make one payment of 102.5 in six months, the YTM is the spot rate for cash flows to be received six months from now.

The bootstrapping process proceeds from this point using the fact that the 6-month annualized spot rate is 5% together with the price/YTM information on the 1-year bond. We will use the formula for valuing a bond using spot rates that we covered earlier.

Noting that the 1-year bond will make two payments, one in six months of 3.0 and one in one year of 103.0, and that the appropriate spot rate to discount the coupon payment (which comes six months from now), we can write:

$$\frac{3}{1.025} + \frac{103}{\left(1 + \frac{S_{1.0}}{2}\right)^2} = 100, \text{ where } S_{1.0} \text{ is the annualized 1-year spot rate,}$$

and solve for $\frac{S_{1.0}}{2}$ as: $\dfrac{103}{\left(1 + \frac{S_{1.0}}{2}\right)^2} = 100 - \dfrac{3}{1.025} = 100 - 2.927 = 97.073$

$$\frac{103}{97.073} = \left(1 + \frac{S_{1.0}}{2}\right)^2, \text{ so } \sqrt{\frac{103}{97.073}} - 1 = \frac{S_{1.0}}{2}$$

$$= 0.030076 \text{ and } S_{1.0} = 2 \times 0.030076 = 0.060152 = 6.0152\%$$

Now that we have the 6-month and 1-year spot rates, we can use this information and the price of the 18-month bond to set the bond price equal to the value of the bond's cash flows as:

$$\frac{3.5}{1.025} + \frac{3.5}{(1.030076)^2} + \frac{103.5}{\left(1 + \frac{S_{1.5}}{2}\right)^3} = 100,$$

where $S_{1.5}$ is the annualized 1.5-year spot rate, and solve for $\frac{S_{1.5}}{2}$

$$\frac{103.5}{\left(1 + \frac{S_{1.5}}{2}\right)^3} = 100 - \frac{3.5}{1.025} - \frac{3.5}{(1.030076)^2} = 100 - 3.415 - 3.30 = 93.285$$

$$\frac{103.5}{93.285} = \left(1 + \frac{S_{1.5}}{2}\right)^3, \text{ so } \left(\frac{103.5}{93.285}\right)^{\frac{1}{3}} - 1 = \frac{S_{1.5}}{2}$$

$$\frac{S_{1.5}}{2} = 0.0352$$

$$S_{1.5} = 0.0705 = 7.05\%$$

To summarize the method of bootstrapping spot rates from the par yield curve:

1. Begin with the 6-month spot rate.

2. Set the value of the 1-year bond equal to the present value of the cash flows with the 1-year spot rate divided by two as the only unknown.

3. Solve for the 1-year spot rate.

4. Use the 6-month and 1-year spot rates and equate the present value of the cash flows of the 1.5-year bond equal to its price, with the 1.5-year spot rate as the only unknown.

5. Solve for the 1.5-year spot rate.

 Professor's Note: You are responsible for "describing" this calculation, not for computing theoretical spot rates.

Example: Valuing a bond using spot rates

Given the following spot rates (in BEY form):

> 0.5 years = 4%
> 1.0 years = 5%
> 1.5 years = 6%

Calculate the value of a 1.5-year, 8% Treasury bond.

Answer:

Simply lay out the cash flows and discount by the spot rates, which are one-half the quoted rates since they are quoted in BEY form.

$$\frac{4}{\left(1+\dfrac{0.04}{2}\right)^1} + \frac{4}{\left(1+\dfrac{0.05}{2}\right)^2} + \frac{104}{\left(1+\dfrac{0.06}{2}\right)^3} = 102.9$$

or, with the TVM function:

> N = 1; PMT = 0; I/Y = 2; FV = 4; CPT → PV = −3.92
> N = 2; PMT = 0; I/Y = 2.5; FV = 4; CPT → PV = −3.81
> N = 3; PMT = 0; I/Y = 3; FV = 104; CPT → PV = −95.17

Add these values together to get 102.9.

LOS 57.f: Explain nominal, zero-volatility, and option-adjusted spreads and the relations among these spreads and option cost.

CFA® Program Curriculum, Volume 5, page 513

The **nominal spread** is the simplest of the spread measures to use and to understand. It is simply an issue's YTM minus the YTM of a Treasury security of similar maturity. Therefore, the use of the nominal spread suffers from the same limitations as the YTM. YTM uses a single discount rate to value the cash flows, so it *ignores the shape of the spot yield curve.* In fact, YTM for a coupon bond is theoretically correct only to the extent that the spot rate curve is flat.

The Zero-Volatility Spread

One way to get a bond's nominal spread to Treasuries is to add different amounts to the yield of a comparable Treasury bond, and value the bond with those YTMs. The amount added to the Treasury yield that produces a bond value equal to the market price of the bond must be the nominal yield spread.

This may seem like an odd way to get the spread, but it makes sense when you see how the **zero-volatility spread**, or static spread, is calculated. The zero-volatility spread (*Z*-spread) is the equal amount that we must add to each rate on the Treasury spot yield curve in order to make the present value of the risky bond's cash flows equal to its market price. Instead of measuring the spread to YTM, the zero-volatility spread measures the spread to Treasury spot rates necessary to produce a spot rate curve that correctly prices a risky bond (i.e., produces its market price).

For a risky bond, the value obtained from discounting the expected cash flows at Treasury spot rates will be too high because the Treasury spot rates are lower than those appropriate for a risky bond. In order to value it correctly, we have to increase each of the Treasury spot rates by some equal amount so that the present value of the risky bond's cash flows discounted at the (increased) spot rates equals the market value of the bond. The following example will illustrate the process for calculating the *Z*-spread.

Example: Zero-volatility spread

1-, 2-, and 3-year spot rates on Treasuries are 4%, 8.167%, and 12.377%, respectively. Consider a 3-year, 9% annual coupon corporate bond trading at 89.464. The YTM is 13.50%, and the YTM of a 3-year Treasury is 12%. Compute the nominal spread and the zero-volatility spread of the corporate bond.

Answer:

The *nominal spread* is:

$$\text{nominal spread} = \text{YTM}_{\text{Bond}} - \text{YTM}_{\text{Treasury}} = 13.50 - 12.00 = 1.50\%.$$

To compute the *Z*-spread, set the present value of the bond's cash flows equal to today's market price. Discount each cash flow at the appropriate zero-coupon bond spot rate *plus* a fixed spread equals ZS. Solve for ZS in the following equation and you have the *Z*-spread:

$$89.464 = \frac{9}{\left(1.04 + \text{ZS}\right)^1} + \frac{9}{\left(1.08167 + \text{ZS}\right)^2} + \frac{109}{\left(1.12377 + \text{ZS}\right)^3} \Rightarrow$$

$$\text{ZS} = 1.67\% \text{ or } 167 \text{ basis points}$$

Note that this spread is found by trial-and-error. In other words, pick a number "ZS," plug it into the right-hand side of the equation, and see if the result equals 89.464. If the right-hand side equals the left, then you have found the *Z*-spread. If not, pick another "ZS" and start over.

 Professor's Note: This is not a calculation you are expected to make; this example is to help you understand how a Z-spread differs from a nominal spread.

There are two primary factors that influence the difference between the nominal spread and the *Z*-spread for a security.

- The steeper the benchmark spot rate curve, the greater the difference between the two spread measures. There is no difference between the nominal and *Z*-spread when the spot yield curve is flat. If the spot yield curve is upward sloping, the *Z*-spread is larger than the nominal spread. The *Z*-spread is less than the nominal spread when the spot yield curve is negatively sloped.
- The earlier the bond principal is paid, the greater the difference between the two spread measures. For a given positively sloped yield curve, an amortizing security, such as an MBS, will have a greater difference between its *Z*-spread and nominal spread than a coupon bond will.

The Option-Adjusted Spread

The **option-adjusted spread** (OAS) measure is used when a bond has embedded options. A callable bond, for example, must have a greater yield than an identical option-free bond, and a greater nominal spread or *Z*-spread. Without accounting for the value of the options, these spread measures will suggest the bond is a great value when, in fact, the additional yield is compensation for call risk. Loosely speaking, the *option-adjusted spread* takes the option yield component out of the *Z*-spread measure; the option-adjusted spread is the spread to the Treasury spot rate curve that the bond would have if it were option-free. The OAS is the spread for non-option characteristics like credit risk, liquidity risk, and interest rate risk.

 Professor's Note: The actual method of calculation is reserved for Level II; for our purposes, however, an understanding of what the OAS is will be sufficient.

Embedded Option Cost

If we calculate an option-adjusted spread for a callable bond, it will be less than the bond's *Z*-spread. The difference is the extra yield required to compensate for the call option. Calling that extra yield the option cost, we can write:

Z-spread – OAS = option cost in percent

Example: Cost of an embedded option

Suppose you learn that a bond is callable and has an OAS of 135bp. You also know that similar bonds have a *Z*-spread of 167 basis points. Compute the cost of the embedded option.

Answer:

The option cost = *Z*-spread – OAS = 167 – 135 = 32 basis points.

For embedded short calls (e.g., callable bonds): option cost > 0 (you receive compensation for writing the option to the issuer) → OAS < *Z*-spread. In other words, you *require more yield on the callable bond* than for an option-free bond.

For embedded puts (e.g., putable bonds), option cost < 0 (i.e., you must pay for the option) → OAS > *Z*-spread. In other words, you *require less yield on the putable bond* than for an option-free bond.

LOS 57.g: Explain a forward rate and calculate spot rates from forward rates, forward rates from spot rates, and the value of a bond using forward rates.

CFA® Program Curriculum, Volume 5, page 520

A **forward rate** is a borrowing/lending rate for a loan to be made at some future date. The notation used must identify both the length of the lending/borrowing period and when in the future the money will be loaned/borrowed. Thus, $_1f_1$ is the rate for a 1-year loan one year from now and $_1f_2$ is the rate for a 1-year loan to be made two years from now, and so on. Rather than introduce a separate notation, we can represent the current 1-year rate as $_1f_0$. To get the present values of a bond's expected cash flows, we need to discount each cash flow by the forward rates for each of the periods until it is received. (The present value of $1 to be received in period n, discounted by the forward rates for periods 1 to n, is called the **forward discount factor** for period n.)

The Relationship Between Short-Term Forward Rates and Spot Rates

The idea here is that *borrowing for three years at the 3-year rate or borrowing for 1-year periods, three years in succession, should have the same cost.*

This relation is illustrated as $(1 + S_3)^3 = (1 + _1f_0)(1 + _1f_1)(1 + _1f_2)$ and the reverse as $S_3 = [(1 + _1f_0)(1 + _1f_1)(1 + _1f_2)]^{1/3} - 1$, which is the geometric mean we covered in Quantitative Methods.

Example: Computing spot rates from forward rates

If the current 1-year rate is 2%, the 1-year forward rate ($_1f_1$) is 3% and the 2-year forward rate ($_1f_2$) is 4%, what is the 3-year spot rate?

Answer:

$$S_3 = [(1.02)(1.03)(1.04)]^{1/3} - 1 = 2.997\%$$

This can be interpreted to mean that a dollar compounded at 2.997% for three years would produce the same ending value as a dollar that earns compound interest of 2% the first year, 3% the next year, and 4% for the third year.

 Professor's Note: You can get a very good approximation of the 3-year spot rate with the simple average of the forward rates. In the previous example, we calculated 2.997% and the simple average of the three annual rates is $\frac{2+3+4}{3} = 3\%$.

Forward Rates Given Spot Rates

We can use the same relationship we used to calculate spot rates from forward rates to calculate forward rates from spot rates.

Our basic relation between forward rates and spot rates (for two periods) is:

$$(1 + S_2)^2 = (1 + {_1}f_0)(1 + {_1}f_1)$$

Which, again, tells us that an investment has the same expected yield (borrowing has the same expected cost) whether we invest (borrow) for two periods at the 2-period spot rate, S_2, or for one period at the current rate, S_1, and for the next period at the expected forward rate, ${_1}f_1$. Clearly, given two of these rates, we can solve for the other.

Example: Computing a forward rate from spot rates

The 2-period spot rate, S_2, is 8% and the current 1-period (spot) rate is 4% (this is both S_1 and ${_1}f_0$). Calculate the forward rate for one period, one period from now, ${_1}f_1$.

Answer:

The following figure illustrates the problem.

Finding a Forward Rate

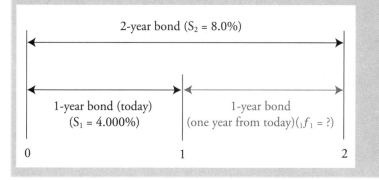

From our original equality, $(1 + S_2)^2 = (1 + S_1)(1 + {_1}f_1)$, we can get $\dfrac{(1+S_2)^2}{(1+S_1)} - 1 = {_1}f_1$

or, because we know that both choices have the same payoff in two years:

$$(1.08)^2 = (1.04)(1 + {_1}f_1)$$

$$(1 + {_1}f_1) = \frac{(1.08)^2}{(1.04)}$$

$${_1}f_1 = \frac{(1.08)^2}{(1.04)} - 1 = \frac{1.1664}{1.04} - 1 = 12.154\%$$

In other words, investors are willing to accept 4.0% on the 1-year bond today (when they could get 8.0% on the 2-year bond today) only because they can get 12.154% on a 1-year bond one year from today. This future rate that can be locked in today is a *forward rate*.

Similarly, we can back other forward rates out of the spot rates. We know that:

$$(1 + S_3)^3 = (1 + S_1)(1 + {_1}f_1)(1 + {_1}f_2)$$

And that:

$$(1 + S_2)^2 = (1 + S_1)(1 + {_1}f_1), \text{ so we can write } (1 + S_3)^3 = (1 + S_2)^2(1 + {_1}f_2)$$

This last equation says that investing for three years at the 3-year spot rate should produce the same ending value as investing for two years at the 2-year spot rate and then for a third year at ${_1}f_2$, the 1-year forward rate, two years from now.

Solving for the forward rate, ${_1}f_2$, we get:

$$\frac{(1+S_3)^3}{(1+S_2)^2} - 1 = {_1}f_2$$

Example: Forward rates from spot rates

Let's extend the previous example to three periods. The current 1-year spot rate is 4.0%, the current 2-year spot rate is 8.0%, and the current 3-year spot rate is 12.0%. Calculate the 1-year forward rates one and two years from now.

Answer:

We know the following relation must hold:

$$(1 + S_2)^2 = (1 + S_1)(1 + {}_1f_1)$$

We can use it to solve for the 1-year forward rate one year from now:

$$(1.08)^2 = (1.04)(1 + {}_1f_1), \text{ so } {}_1f_1 = \frac{(1.08)^2}{(1.04)} - 1 = 12.154\%$$

We also know that the relations:

$$(1 + S_3)^3 = (1 + S_1)(1 + {}_1f_1)(1 + {}_1f_2)$$

and, equivalently $(1 + S_3)^3 = (1 + S_2)^2(1 + {}_1f_2)$ must hold.

Substituting values for S_3 and S_2, we have:

$$(1.12)^3 = (1.08)^2 \times (1 + {}_1f_2)$$

so that the 1-year forward rate two years from now is:

$$_1f_2 = \frac{(1.12)^3}{(1.08)^2} - 1 = 20.45\%$$

To verify these results, we can check our relations by calculating:

$$S_3 = [1(1.04)(1.12154)(1.2045)]^{1/3} - 1 = 12.00\%$$

This may all seem a bit complicated, but the basic relation, that borrowing for successive periods at 1-period rates should have the same cost as borrowing at multiperiod spot rates, can be summed up as:

$$(1 + S_2)^2 = (1 + S_1)(1 + {}_1f_1) \text{ for two periods, and } (1 + S_3)^3 = (1 + S_2)^2(1 + {}_1f_2) \text{ for three periods.}$$

Study Session 16

Professor's Note: Simple averages also give decent approximations for calculating forward rates from spot rates. In the above example, we had spot rates of 4% for one year and 8% for two years. Two years at 8% is 16%, so if the first-year rate is 4%, the second-year rate is close to 16 – 4 = 12% (actual is 12.154). Given a 2-year spot rate of 8% and a 3-year spot rate of 12%, we could approximate the 1-year forward rate from time two to time three as (3 × 12) – (2 × 8) = 20. That may be close enough (actual is 20.45) to answer a multiple-choice question and, in any case, serves as a good check to make sure the exact rate you calculate is reasonable.

We can also calculate implied forward rates for loans for more than one period. Given spot rates of: 1-year = 5%, 2-year = 6%, 3-year = 7%, and 4-year = 8%, we can calculate $_2f_2$.

The implied forward rate on a 2-year loan two years from now is:

$$\left[\frac{(1+S_4)^4}{(1+S_2)^2}\right]^{\frac{1}{2}} - 1 = \left(\frac{1.08^4}{1.06^2}\right)^{\frac{1}{2}} - 1 = 10.04\%.$$

Professor's Note: The approximation works for multi-period forward rates as well. Here, we have $\frac{(4 \times 8 - 6 \times 2)}{2} = 10$. The difference between two years at 6% and four years at 8% is approximately 20%. Since that is for two years, we divide by two to get an annual rate of approximately 10%.

Valuing a Bond Using Forward Rates

Example: Computing a bond value using forward rates

The current 1-year rate ($_1f_0$) is 4%, the 1-year forward rate for lending from time = 1 to time = 2 is $_1f_1$ = 5%, and the 1-year forward rate for lending from time = 2 to time = 3 is $_1f_2$ = 6%. Value a 3-year annual-pay bond with a 5% coupon and a par value of $1,000.

Answer:

$$\text{bond value} = \frac{50}{1 + {}_1f_0} + \frac{50}{(1 + {}_1f_0)(1 + {}_1f_1)} + \frac{1,050}{(1 + {}_1f_0)(1 + {}_1f_1)(1 + {}_1f_2)} =$$

$$\frac{50}{1.04} + \frac{50}{(1.04)(1.05)} + \frac{1,050}{(1.04)(1.05)(1.06)} = \$1,000.98$$

Professor's Note: If you think this looks a little like valuing a bond using spot rates, as we did for arbitrage-free valuation, you are right. The discount factors are equivalent to spot rate discount factors.

KEY CONCEPTS

LOS 57.a
Three sources of return to a coupon bond:
- Coupon interest payments.
- Reinvestment income on the coupon cash flows.
- Capital gain or loss on the principal value.

LOS 57.b
Yield to maturity (YTM) for a semiannual-pay coupon bond is calculated as two times the semiannual discount rate that makes the present value of the bond's promised cash flows equal to its market price plus accrued interest. For an annual-pay coupon bond, the YTM is simply the annual discount rate that makes the present value of the bond's promised cash flows equal to its market price plus accrued interest.

The current yield for a bond is its annual interest payment divided by its market price.

Yield to call (put) is calculated as a YTM but with the number of periods until the call (put) and the call (put) price substituted for the number of periods to maturity and the maturity value.

The cash flow yield is a monthly internal rate of return based on a presumed prepayment rate and the current market price of a mortgage-backed or asset-backed security.

These yield measures are limited by their common assumptions that: (1) all cash flows can be discounted at the same rate; (2) the bond will be held to maturity, with all coupons reinvested to maturity at a rate of return that equals the bond's YTM; and (3) all coupon payments will be made as scheduled.

LOS 57.c
YTM is not the realized yield on an investment unless the reinvestment rate is equal to the YTM.

The amount of reinvestment income required to generate the YTM over a bond's life is the difference between the purchase price of the bond, compounded at the YTM until maturity, and the sum of the bond's interest and principal cash flows.

Reinvestment risk is higher when the coupon rate is greater (maturity held constant) and when the bond has longer maturity (coupon rate held constant).

LOS 57.d
The bond-equivalent yield of an annual-pay bond is:

$$BEY = \left[\sqrt{(1 + \text{annual-pay YTM})} - 1 \right] \times 2$$

The annual-pay yield can be calculated from the YTM of a semiannual-pay bond as:

$$EAY = \left(1 + \frac{\text{semiannual-pay YTM}}{2}\right)^2 - 1$$

LOS 57.e
The theoretical Treasury spot rate curve is derived by calculating the spot rate for each successive period N based on the spot rate for period $N - 1$ and the market price of a bond with N coupon payments.

To compute the value of a bond using spot rates, discount each separate cash flow using the spot rate corresponding to the number of periods until the cash flow is to be received.

LOS 57.f
Three commonly used yield spread measures:
- *Nominal spread*: bond YTM – Treasury YTM.
- *Zero-volatility spread* (*Z*-spread or static spread): the equal amount of additional yield that must be added to each Treasury spot rate to get spot rates that will produce a present value for a bond equal to its market price.
- *Option-adjusted spread* (OAS): spread to the spot yield curve after adjusting for the effects of embedded options. OAS reflects the spread for credit risk and liquidity risk primarily.

There is no difference between the nominal and *Z*-spread when the yield curve is flat. The steeper the spot yield curve and the earlier bond principal is paid (amortizing securities), the greater the difference in the two spread measures.

The option cost for a bond with an embedded option is *Z*-spread – OAS.

For callable bonds, *Z*-spread > OAS and option cost > 0.

For putable bonds, *Z*-spread < OAS and option cost < 0.

LOS 57.g
Forward rates are current lending/borrowing rates for short-term loans to be made in future periods.

A spot rate for a maturity of N periods is the geometric mean of forward rates over the N periods. The same relation can be used to solve for a forward rate given spot rates for two different periods.

To value a bond using forward rates, discount the cash flows at times 1 through N by the product of one plus each forward rate for periods 1 to N, and sum them.

CONCEPT CHECKERS

Use the following data to answer Questions 1 through 4.

An analyst observes a Widget & Co. 7.125%, 4-year, semiannual-pay bond trading at 102.347% of par (where par = $1,000). The bond is callable at 101 in two years and putable at 100 in two years.

1. What is the bond's current yield?
   A. 6.962%.
   B. 7.328%.
   C. 7.426%.

2. What is the bond's yield to maturity?
   A. 3.225%.
   B. 5.864%.
   C. 6.450%.

3. What is the bond's yield to call?
   A. 3.167%.
   B. 5.664%.
   C. 6.334%.

4. What is the bond's yield to put?
   A. 4.225%.
   B. 5.864%.
   C. 6.450%.

5. Based on semiannual compounding, what would the YTM be on a 15-year, zero-coupon, $1,000 par value bond that's currently trading at $331.40?
   A. 3.750%.
   B. 5.151%.
   C. 7.500%.

6. An analyst observes a bond with an *annual* coupon that's being priced to yield 6.350%. What is this issue's bond equivalent yield?
   A. 3.175%.
   B. 3.126%.
   C. 6.252%.

7. An analyst determines that the cash flow yield of GNMA Pool 3856 is 0.382% *per month*. What is the bond equivalent yield?
   A. 4.628%.
   B. 9.363%.
   C. 9.582%.

8. If the YTM equals the actual compound return an investor realizes on an investment in a coupon bond purchased at a premium to par, it is *least likely* that:
   A. cash flows will be paid as promised.
   B. the bond will not be sold at a capital loss.
   C. cash flows will be reinvested at the YTM rate.

9. The 4-year spot rate is 9.45%, and the 3-year spot rate is 9.85%. What is the 1-year forward rate three years from today?
   A. 8.258%.
   B. 9.850%.
   C. 11.059%.

10. An investor purchases a bond that is putable at the option of the holder. The option has value. He has calculated the *Z*-spread as 223 basis points. The option-adjusted spread will be:
   A. equal to 223 basis points.
   B. less than 223 basis points.
   C. greater than 223 basis points.

Use the following data to answer Questions 11 and 12.

Given:
- Current 1-year rate = 5.5%.
- One-year forward rate one year from today = 7.63%.
- One-year forward rate two years from today = 12.18%.
- One-year forward rate three years from today = 15.5%.

11. The value of a 4-year, 10% annual-pay, $1,000 par value bond would be *closest* to:
   A. $995.89.
   B. $1,009.16.
   C. $1,085.62.

12. Using annual compounding, the value of a 3-year, zero-coupon, $1,000 par value bond would be:
   A. $785.
   B. $852.
   C. $948.

13. A bond's nominal spread, zero-volatility spread, and option-adjusted spread will all be equal for a coupon bond if:
   A. the yield curve is flat.
   B. the bond is option free.
   C. the yield curve is flat and the bond has no embedded options.

14. The zero-volatility spread will be zero:
    A. if the yield curve is flat.
    B. for a zero-coupon bond.
    C. for an on-the-run Treasury bond.

15. Assume the Treasury spot-rate yield curve is upward sloping. Compared to the nominal yield spread between a Treasury bond and an option-free corporate bond of similar maturity, the *Z*-spread will be:
    A. greater than the nominal spread.
    B. less than the nominal spread.
    C. equal to the nominal spread.

CHALLENGE PROBLEMS

1. An investor buys a 10-year, 7% coupon, semiannual-pay bond for 92.80. He sells it three years later, just after receiving the sixth coupon payment, when its yield to maturity is 6.9%. Coupon interest has been placed in an account that yields 5% (BEY). State the sources of return on this bond and calculate the dollar return from each source based on a $100,000 bond.

2. What is the yield on a bond equivalent basis of an annual-pay 7% coupon bond priced at par?

3. What is the annual-pay yield to maturity of a 7% coupon semi-annual pay bond?

4. The yield to maturity on a bond equivalent basis on 6-month and 1-year T-bills are 2.8% and 3.2%, respectively. A 1.5-year, 4% Treasury note is selling at par.
   A. What is the 18-month Treasury spot rate?
   B. If a 1.5-year semiannual-pay corporate bond with a 7% coupon is selling for 102.395, what is the nominal spread for this bond? Is the zero-volatility spread (in basis points) 127, 130, or 133?

5. Assume the following spot rates (as BEYs).

Years to Maturity	Spot Rates
0.5	4.0%
1.0	4.4%
1.5	5.0%
2.0	5.4%

   A. What is the 6-month forward rate one year from now?
   B. What is the 1-year forward rate one year from now?
   C. What is the value of a 2-year, 4.5% coupon Treasury note?

Study Session 16
Cross-Reference to CFA Institute Assigned Reading #57 – Yield Measures, Spot Rates, and Forward Rates

Study Session 16

6. Assume the current 6-month rate is 3.5% and the 6-month forward rates (all as BEYs) are those in the following table.

Periods From Now	Forward Rates
1	3.8%
2	4.0%
3	4.4%
4	4.8%

A. Calculate the corresponding spot rates.

B. What is the value of a 1.5-year, 4% Treasury note?

7. Consider the following three bonds that all have par values of $100,000.
    I.   A 10-year zero coupon bond priced at 48.20.
    II. A 5-year 8% semiannual-pay bond priced with a YTM of 8%.
    III. A 5-year 9% semiannual-pay bond priced with a YTM of 8%.

Rank the three bonds in terms of how important reinvestment income is to an investor who wishes to realize the stated YTM of the bond at purchase by holding it to maturity.

ANSWERS – CONCEPT CHECKERS

1. **A**   current yield $= \dfrac{71.25}{1,023.47} = 0.06962$, or 6.962%

2. **C** $1,023.47 = \sum_{t=1}^{8} \dfrac{35.625}{(1+\text{YTM}/2)^t} + \dfrac{1,000}{(1+\text{YTM}/2)^8} \Rightarrow \text{YTM} = 6.450\%$

    N = 8; FV = 1,000; PMT = 35.625; PV = −1,023.47 → CPT I/Y = 3.225 × 2 = 6.45%

3. **C** $1,023.47 = \sum_{t=1}^{4} \dfrac{35.625}{(1+\text{YTC}/2)^t} + \dfrac{1,010}{(1+\text{YTC}/2)^4} \Rightarrow \text{YTC} = 6.334\%$

    N = 4; FV = 1,010; PMT = 35.625; PV = −1,023.47; CPT → I/Y = 3.167 × 2 = 6.334%

4. **B** $1,023.47 = \sum_{t=1}^{4} \dfrac{35.625}{(1+\text{YTP}/2)^t} + \dfrac{1,000}{(1+\text{YTP}/2)^4} \Rightarrow \text{YTP} = 5.864\%$

    N = 4; FV = 1,000; PMT = 35.625; PV = −1,023.47; CPT → I/Y = 2.932 × 2 = 5.864%

5. **C** $\left[\left(\dfrac{1,000}{331.40} \right)^{\frac{1}{30}} - 1 \right] \times 2 = 7.5\%$ or,

    Solving with a financial calculator:

    N = 30; FV = 1,000; PMT = 0; PV = −331.40; CPT → I/Y = 3.750 × 2 = 7.500%

6. **C**   bond equivalent yield $= [(1 + \text{EAY})^{1/2} - 1] \times 2 = [(1.0635)^{1/2} - 1] \times 2 = 6.252\%$

7. **A**   bond equivalent yield $= [(1 + \text{CFY})^6 - 1] \times = [(1.00382)^6 - 1] \times 2 = 4.628\%$

8. **B**   For a bond purchased at a premium to par value, a decrease in the premium over time (a capital loss) is already factored into the calculation of YTM.

9. **A** $(1.0945)^4 = (1.0985)^3 \times (1 + {}_1f_3)$

    $\dfrac{(1.0945)^4}{(1.0985)^3} - 1 = {}_1f_3 = 8.258\%$

10. **C**   For embedded puts (e.g., putable bonds): option cost < 0, $\Rightarrow$ OAS > Z-spread.

11. **B**   Spot rates: $S_1 = 5.5\%$.

$S_2 = [(1.055)(1.0763)]^{1/2} - 1 = 6.56\%$

$S_3 = [(1.055)(1.0763)(1.1218)]^{1/3} - 1 = 8.39\%$

$S_4 = [(1.055)(1.0763)(1.1218)(1.155)]^{1/4} - 1 = 10.13\%$

Bond value:
N = 1; FV = 100; I/Y = 5.5; CPT → PV=   −94.79
N = 2; FV = 100; I/Y = 6.56; CPT → PV=   −88.07
N = 3; FV = 100; I/Y = 8.39; CPT → PV=   −78.53
N = 4; FV = 1,100; I/Y = 10.13; CPT → PV=   −747.77
Total: $1,009.16

12. **A**   Find the spot rate for 3-year lending:

$S_3 = [(1.055)(1.0763)(1.1218)]^{1/3} - 1 = 8.39\%$

Value of the bond: N = 3; FV = 1,000; I/Y = 8.39; CPT→PV = −785.29

or $\dfrac{\$1,000}{(1.055)(1.0763)(1.1218)} = \$785.05$

13. **C**   If the yield curve is flat, the nominal spread and the Z-spread are equal. If the bond is option-free, the Z-spread and OAS are equal.

14. **C**   A Treasury bond is the best answer. The Treasury spot yield curve will correctly price an on-the-run Treasury bond at its arbitrage-free price, so the Z-spread is zero.

15. **A**   The Z-spread will be greater than the nominal spread when the spot yield curve is upward sloping.

ANSWERS – CHALLENGE PROBLEMS

1.   The three sources of return are coupon interest payments, recovery of principal/capital gain or loss, and reinvestment income.

Coupon interest payments: 0.07 / 2 × $100,000 × 6 = $21,000

Recovery of principal/capital gain or loss: Calculate the sale price of the bond:
N = (10 − 3) × 2 = 14; I/Y = 6.9 / 2 = 3.45; PMT = 0.07 / 2 × 100,000 = 3,500; FV = 100,000; CPT → PV = −100,548

Capital gain = 100,548 − 92,800 = $7,748

Reinvestment income: We can solve this by treating the coupon payments as a 6-period annuity, calculating the future value based on the semiannual interest rate, and subtracting the coupon payments. The difference must be the interest earned by reinvesting the coupon payments.

N = 3 × 2 = 6; I/Y = 5 / 2 = 2.5; PV = 0; PMT = −3,500; CPT → FV = $22,357

Reinvestment income = 22,357 − (6 × 3,500) = $1,357

2. BEY = 2 × semiannual discount rate

    semiannual discount rate = $(1.07)^{1/2} - 1 = 0.344 = 3.44\%$

    BEY = 2 × 3.44% = 6.88%

3. annual-pay YTM = $\left(1 + \dfrac{0.07}{2}\right)^2 - 1 = 0.0712 = 7.12\%$

4. A. Because the T-bills are zero-coupon instruments, their YTMs are the 6-month and 1-year spot rates. To solve for the 1.5-year spot rate, we set the bond's market price equal to the present value of its (discounted) cash flows:

    $$100 = \frac{2}{1 + \dfrac{0.028}{2}} + \frac{2}{\left(1 + \dfrac{0.032}{2}\right)^2} + \frac{102}{\left(1 + \dfrac{S_{1.5}}{2}\right)^3}$$

    $$100 = 1.9724 + 1.9375 + \frac{102}{\left(1 + \dfrac{S_{1.5}}{2}\right)^3}$$

    $$\left(1 + \frac{S_{1.5}}{2}\right)^3 = \frac{102}{100 - 1.9724 - 1.9375} = 1.0615$$

    $$1 + \frac{S_{1.5}}{2} = 1.0615^{1/3} = 1.0201$$

    $$S_{1.5} = 0.0201 \times 2 = 0.0402 = 4.02\%$$

    B. Compute the YTM on the corporate bond:

    N = 1.5 × 2 = 3; PV = −102.395; PMT = 7 / 2 = 3.5; FV = 100; CPT → I/Y = 2.6588 × 2 = 5.32%

    nominal spread = $YTM_{Bond} - YTM_{Treasury}$ = 5.32% − 4.0% = 1.32%, or 132 bp

    Solve for the zero-volatility spread by setting the present value of the bond's cash flows equal to the bond's price, discounting each cash flow by the Treasury spot rate plus a fixed Z-spread.

    $$102.4 = \frac{3.5}{1 + \dfrac{0.028 + ZS}{2}} + \frac{3.5}{\left(1 + \dfrac{0.032 + ZS}{2}\right)^2} + \frac{103.5}{\left(1 + \dfrac{0.0402 + ZS}{2}\right)^3}$$

    Substituting each of the choices into this equation gives the following bond values:

Z-spread	Bond value
127 bp	102.4821
130 bp	102.4387
133 bp	102.3953

Since the price of the bond is 102.395, a *Z*-spread of 133 bp is the correct one.

Note that, assuming one of the three zero-volatility spreads given is correct, you could calculate the bond value using the middle spread (130) basis points, get a bond value (102.4387) that is too high, and know that the higher zero-volatility spread is the only one that could generate a present value equal to the bond's market price.

Also note that according to the LOS, you are not responsible for this calculation. Working through this example, however, should ensure that you understand the concept of a zero-volatility spread well.

5. A. $$\left(1+\frac{S_{1.5}}{2}\right)^3 = \left(1+\frac{S_{1.0}}{2}\right)^2 \left(1+\frac{0.5f_{1.0}}{2}\right)$$

$$\left(1+\frac{0.5f_{1.0}}{2}\right) = \frac{\left(1+\frac{S_{1.5}}{2}\right)^3}{\left(1+\frac{S_{1.0}}{2}\right)^2} = \frac{1.025^3}{1.022^2} = 1.03103$$

$$_{0.5}f_{1.0} = 0.03103 \times 2 = 0.0621 = 6.21\%$$

B. $_1f_1$ here refers to the 1-year rate, one year from today, expressed as a BEY.

$$\left(1+\frac{S_2}{2}\right)^4 = \left(1+\frac{S_1}{2}\right)^2 \left(1+\frac{_1f_1}{2}\right)^2$$

$$\left(1+\frac{_1f_1}{2}\right)^2 = \frac{\left(1+\frac{S_2}{2}\right)^4}{\left(1+\frac{S_1}{2}\right)^2}$$

$$\frac{_1f_1}{2} = \sqrt{\frac{\left(1+\frac{S_2}{2}\right)^4}{\left(1+\frac{S_1}{2}\right)^2}} - 1$$

$$\frac{_1f_1}{2} = \sqrt{\frac{\left(1+\frac{0.054}{2}\right)^4}{\left(1+\frac{0.044}{2}\right)^2}} - 1 = 0.0320$$

$$_1f_1 = 2 \times 0.0320 = 6.40\%$$

Note that the approximation 2 × 5.4 – 4.4 = 6.4 works very well here and is quite a bit less work.

C. Discount each of the bond's cash flows (as a percent of par) by the appropriate spot rate:

$$\text{bond value} = \frac{2.25}{1+\dfrac{0.040}{2}} + \frac{2.25}{\left(1+\dfrac{0.044}{2}\right)^2} + \frac{2.25}{\left(1+\dfrac{0.050}{2}\right)^3} + \frac{102.25}{\left(1+\dfrac{0.054}{2}\right)^4}$$

$$= \frac{2.25}{1.02} + \frac{2.25}{1.0445} + \frac{2.25}{1.0769} + \frac{102.25}{1.1125} = 98.36$$

6. A. $\left(1+\dfrac{S_{1.0}}{2}\right)^2 = \left(1+\dfrac{S_{0.5}}{2}\right)\left(1+\dfrac{{}_{0.5}f_{0.5}}{2}\right) = \left(1+\dfrac{0.035}{2}\right)\left(1+\dfrac{0.038}{2}\right) = 1.0368$

$\dfrac{S_{1.0}}{2} = 1.0368^{1/2} - 1 = 0.0182$

$S_{1.0} = 0.0182 \times 2 = 0.0364 = 3.64\%$

$\left(1+\dfrac{S_{1.5}}{2}\right)^3 = \left(1+\dfrac{S_{0.5}}{2}\right)\left(1+\dfrac{{}_{0.5}f_{0.5}}{2}\right)\left(1+\dfrac{{}_{0.5}f_{1.0}}{2}\right)$

$$= \left(1+\dfrac{0.035}{2}\right)\left(1+\dfrac{0.038}{2}\right)\left(1+\dfrac{0.040}{2}\right) = 1.0576$$

$\dfrac{S_{1.5}}{2} = 1.0576^{1/3} - 1 = 0.0188$

$S_{1.5} = 0.0188 \times 2 = 0.0376 = 3.76\%$

$\left(1+\dfrac{S_{2.0}}{2}\right)^4 = \left(1+\dfrac{S_{0.5}}{2}\right)\left(1+\dfrac{{}_{0.5}f_{0.5}}{2}\right)\left(1+\dfrac{{}_{0.5}f_{1.0}}{2}\right)\left(1+\dfrac{{}_{0.5}f_{1.5}}{2}\right)$

$$= \left(1+\dfrac{0.035}{2}\right)\left(1+\dfrac{0.038}{2}\right)\left(1+\dfrac{0.040}{2}\right)\left(1+\dfrac{0.044}{2}\right) = 1.0809$$

$\dfrac{S_{2.0}}{2} = 1.0809^{1/4} - 1 = 0.0196$

$S_{2.0} = 0.0196 \times 2 = 0.0392 = 3.92\%$

B. $\dfrac{2}{1+\dfrac{0.035}{2}} + \dfrac{2}{\left(1+\dfrac{0.0364}{2}\right)^2} + \dfrac{102}{\left(1+\dfrac{0.0376}{2}\right)^3} = 100.35$

7. Reinvestment income is most important to the investor with the 9% coupon bond, followed by the 8% coupon bond and the zero-coupon bond. In general, reinvestment risk increases with the coupon rate on a bond.

The following is a review of the Analysis of Fixed Income Investments principles designed to address the learning outcome statements set forth by CFA Institute. This topic is also covered in:

INTRODUCTION TO THE MEASUREMENT OF INTEREST RATE RISK

Study Session 16

EXAM FOCUS

This topic review is about the relation of yield changes and bond price changes, primarily based on the concepts of duration and convexity. There is really nothing in this study session that can be safely ignored; the calculation of duration, the use of duration, and the limitations of duration as a measure of bond price risk are all important. You should work to understand what convexity is and its relation to the interest rate risk of fixed-income securities. There are two important formulas: the formula for effective duration and the formula for estimating the price effect of a yield change based on both duration and convexity. Finally, you should get comfortable with how and why the convexity of a bond is affected by the presence of embedded options.

LOS 58.a: Distinguish between the full valuation approach (the scenario analysis approach) and the duration/convexity approach for measuring interest rate risk, and explain the advantage of using the full valuation approach.

CFA® Program Curriculum, Volume 5, page 556

The full valuation or **scenario analysis approach** to measuring interest rate risk is based on applying the valuation techniques we have learned for a given change in the yield curve (i.e., for a given *interest rate scenario*). For a single option-free bond, this could be simply, "if the YTM increases by 50 bp or 100 bp, what is the impact on the value of the bond?" More complicated scenarios can be used as well, such as the effect on the bond value of a steepening of the yield curve (long-term rates increase more than short-term rates). If our valuation model is good, the exercise is straightforward: plug in the rates described in the interest rate scenario(s), and see what happens to the values of the bonds. For more complex bonds, such as callable bonds, a pricing model that incorporates yield volatility as well as specific yield curve change scenarios is required to use the full valuation approach. If the valuation models used are sufficiently good, this is the theoretically preferred approach. Applied to a portfolio of bonds, one bond at a time, we can get a very good idea of how different interest rate change scenarios will affect the value of the portfolio. Using this approach with extreme changes in interest rates is called **stress testing** a bond portfolio.

The **duration/convexity approach** provides an approximation of the actual interest rate sensitivity of a bond or bond portfolio. Its main advantage is its simplicity compared to the full valuation approach. The full valuation approach can get quite complex and time consuming for a portfolio of more than a few bonds, especially if some of the bonds have more complex structures, such as call provisions. As we will see shortly, limiting our scenarios to parallel yield curve shifts and settling for an estimate of interest rate risk allows us to use the summary measures, duration, and convexity. This greatly simplifies the process of estimating the value impact of overall changes in yield.

Compared to the duration/convexity approach, the full valuation approach is more precise and can be used to evaluate the price effects of more complex interest rate scenarios. Strictly speaking, the duration-convexity approach is appropriate only for estimating the effects of parallel yield curve shifts.

Example: The full valuation approach

Consider two option-free bonds. Bond X is an 8% annual-pay bond with five years to maturity, priced at 108.4247 to yield 6% (N = 5; PMT = 8.00; FV = 100; I/Y = 6.00%; CPT → PV = −108.4247).

Bond Y is a 5% annual-pay bond with 15 years to maturity, priced at 81.7842 to yield 7%.

Assume a $10 million face-value position in each bond and two scenarios. The first scenario is a parallel shift in the yield curve of +50 basis points, and the second scenario is a parallel shift of +100 basis points. Note that the bond price of 108.4247 is the price per $100 of par value. With $10 million of par value bonds, the market value will be $10.84247 million.

Answer:

The full valuation approach for the two simple scenarios is illustrated in the following figure.

The Full Valuation Approach

		Market Value of:			
Scenario	Yield Δ	Bond X (in millions)	Bond Y (in millions)	Portfolio	Portfolio Value Δ%
Current	+0 bp	$10.84247	$8.17842	$19.02089	
1	+50 bp	$10.62335	$7.79322	$18.41657	−3.18%
2	+100 bp	$10.41002	$7.43216	$17.84218	−6.20%

N = 5; PMT = 8; FV = 100; I/Y = 6% + 0.5%; CPT → PV = −106.2335

N = 5; PMT = 8; FV = 100; I/Y = 6% + 1%; CPT → PV = −104.1002

N = 15; PMT = 5; FV = 100; I/Y = 7% + 0.5%; CPT → PV = −77.9322

N = 15; PMT = 5; FV = 100; I/Y = 7% + 1%; CPT → PV = −74.3216

Portfolio value change 50 bp: (18.41657 − 19.02089) / 19.02089 = −0.03177 = −3.18%

Portfolio value change 100 bp: (17.84218 – 19.02089) / 19.02089 = –0.06197 = –6.20%

It's worth noting that, on an individual bond basis, the effect of an increase in yield on the bonds' values is less for Bond X than for Bond Y (i.e., with a 50 bp increase in yields, the value of Bond X falls by 2.02%, while the value of Bond Y falls by 4.71%; and with a 100 bp increase, X falls by 3.99%, while Y drops by 9.12%). This, of course, is totally predictable since Bond Y is a longer-term bond and has a lower coupon—both of which mean more interest rate risk.

Professor's Note: Let's review the effects of bond characteristics on duration (price sensitivity). Holding other characteristics the same, we can state the following:

- *Higher (lower) coupon means lower (higher) duration.*
- *Longer (shorter) maturity means higher (lower) duration.*
- *Higher (lower) market yield means lower (higher) duration.*

Finance professors love to test these relations.

LOS 58.b: Describe the price volatility characteristics for option-free, callable, prepayable, and putable bonds when interest rates change.

LOS 58.c: Describe positive convexity and negative convexity, and their relation to bond price and yield.

CFA® Program Curriculum, Volume 5, page 560

We established earlier that the relation between price and yield for a straight coupon bond is negative. An increase in yield (discount rate) leads to a decrease in the value of a bond. The precise nature of this relationship for an option-free, 8%, 20-year bond is illustrated in Figure 1.

Figure 1: Price-Yield Curve for an Option-Free, 8%, 20-Year Bond

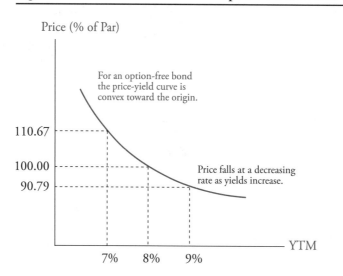

First, note that the price-yield relationship is negatively sloped, so the price falls as the yield rises. Second, note that the relation follows a curve, not a straight line. Because the curve is convex (toward the origin), we say that an option-free bond has **positive convexity**. Because of its positive convexity, the price of an option-free bond *increases more when yields fall than it decreases when yields rise*. In Figure 1, we have illustrated that, for an 8%, 20-year option-free bond, a 1% decrease in the YTM will increase the price to 110.67, a *10.67% increase* in price. A 1% increase in YTM will cause the bond value to decrease to 90.79, a *9.22% decrease* in value.

If the price-yield relation were a straight line, there would be no difference between the price increase and the price decline in response to equal decreases and increases in yields. Convexity is a good thing for a bond owner; for a given volatility of yields, price increases are larger than price decreases. The convexity property is often expressed by saying, "a bond's price falls at a decreasing rate as yields rise." For the price-yield relationship to be convex, the slope (rate of decrease) of the curve must be decreasing as we move from left to right (i.e., towards higher yields).

Note that the duration (interest rate sensitivity) of a bond at any yield is (absolute value of) the slope of the price-yield function at that yield. The convexity of the price-yield relation for an option-free bond can help you remember a result presented earlier, that the duration of a bond is less at higher market yields.

Callable Bonds, Prepayable Securities, and Negative Convexity

With a **callable** or **prepayable debt**, the upside price appreciation in response to decreasing yields is limited (sometimes called price compression). Consider the case of a bond that is currently callable at 102. The fact that the issuer can call the bond at any time for $1,020 per $1,000 of face value puts an effective upper limit on the value of the bond. As Figure 2 illustrates, as yields fall and the price approaches $1,020, the price-yield curve rises more slowly than that of an identical but noncallable bond. When the price begins to *rise at a decreasing rate* in response to further decreases in yield, the price-yield curve bends over to the left and exhibits **negative convexity**.

Thus, in Figure 2, so long as yields remain *below level y'*, callable bonds will exhibit *negative convexity*; however, at yields *above level y'*, those same callable bonds will exhibit *positive convexity*. In other words, at higher yields the value of the call options becomes very small so that a callable bond will act very much like a noncallable bond. It is only at lower yields that the callable bond will exhibit negative convexity.

Figure 2: Price-Yield Function of a Callable vs. an Option-Free Bond

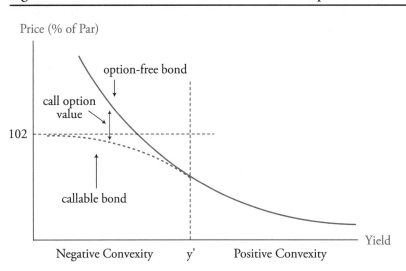

In terms of price sensitivity to interest rate changes, the slope of the price-yield curve at any particular yield tells the story. Note that as yields fall, the slope of the price-yield curve for the callable bond decreases, becoming almost zero (flat) at very low yields. This tells us how a call feature affects price sensitivity to changes in yield. At higher yields, the interest rate risk of a callable bond is very close or identical to that of a similar option-free bond. At lower yields, the price volatility of the callable bond will be much lower than that of an identical but noncallable bond.

The effect of a prepayment option is quite similar to that of a call; at low yields it will lead to negative convexity and reduce the price volatility (interest rate risk) of the security. Note that when yields are low and callable and prepayable securities exhibit less interest rate risk, reinvestment risk rises. At lower yields, the probability of a call and the prepayment rate both rise, increasing the risk of having to reinvest principal repayments at the lower rates.

The Price Volatility Characteristics of Putable Bonds

The value of a put increases at higher yields and decreases at lower yields opposite to the value of a call option. Compared to an option-free bond, a **putable bond** will have *less* price volatility at higher yields. This comparison is illustrated in Figure 3.

Figure 3: Comparing the Price-Yield Curves for Option-Free and Putable Bonds

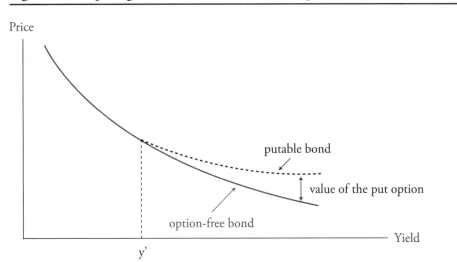

In Figure 3, the price of the putable bond falls more slowly in response to increases in yield above y' because the value of the embedded put rises at higher yields. The slope of the price-yield relation is flatter, indicating less price sensitivity to yield changes (lower duration) for the putable bond at higher yields. At yields below y', the value of the put is quite small, and a putable bond's price acts like that of an option-free bond in response to yield changes.

LOS 58.d: Calculate and interpret the effective duration of a bond, given information about how the bond's price will increase and decrease for given changes in interest rates.

CFA® Program Curriculum, Volume 5, page 569

In our introduction to the concept of duration, we described it as the ratio of the percentage change in price to change in yield. Now that we understand convexity, we know that the price change in response to rising rates is smaller than the price change in response to falling rates for option-free bonds. The formula we will use for calculating the **effective duration** of a bond uses the average of the price changes in response to equal increases and decreases in yield to account for this fact. If we have a callable bond that is trading in the area of negative convexity, the price increase is smaller than the price decrease, but using the average still makes sense.

The formula for calculating the effective duration of a bond is:

$$\text{effective duration} = \frac{\left(\text{bond price when yields fall} - \text{bond price when yields rise}\right)}{2 \times \left(\text{initial price}\right) \times \left(\text{change in yield in decimal form}\right)}$$

which we will sometimes write as $\text{duration} = \dfrac{V_- - V_+}{2V_0(\Delta y)}$

where:
V_- = bond value if the yield decreases by Δy
V_+ = bond value if the yield increases by Δy
V_0 = initial bond price
Δy = change in yield used to get V_- and V_+, *expressed in decimal form*

Consider the following example of this calculation.

Example: Calculating effective duration

Consider a 20-year, semiannual-pay bond with an 8% coupon that is currently priced at $908.00 to yield 9%. If the yield declines by 50 basis points (to 8.5%), the price will increase to $952.30, and if the yield increases by 50 basis points (to 9.5%), the price will decline to $866.80. Based on these price and yield changes, calculate the effective duration of this bond.

Answer:

Let's approach this intuitively to gain a better understanding of the formula. We begin by computing the average of the percentage change in the bond's price for the yield increase and the percentage change in price for a yield decrease. We can calculate this as:

$$\text{average } \textit{percentage } \text{price change} = \frac{\left(\$952.30 - \$866.80\right)}{2 \times \$908.00} = 0.0471\%, \text{ or } 4.71\%$$

The 2 in the denominator is to obtain the average price change, and the $908 in the denominator is to obtain this average change as a percentage of the current price.

To get the duration (to scale our result for a 1% change in yield), the final step is to divide this average percentage price change by the change in interest rates that caused it. In the example, the yield change was 0.5%, which we need to write in decimal form as 0.005. Our estimate of the duration is:

$$\frac{0.0471}{0.005} = \frac{4.71\%}{0.50\%} = 9.42 = \text{duration}$$

Using the formula previously given, we have:

$$\text{effective duration} = \frac{\left(\$952.3 - \$866.8\right)}{2 \times \$908 \times 0.005} = 9.416$$

The interpretation of this result, as you should be convinced by now, is that a 1% change in yield produces an approximate change in the price of this bond of 9.42%. Note, however, that this estimate of duration was based on a change in yield of 0.5% and will perform best for yield changes close to this magnitude. Had we used a yield change of 0.25% or 1%, we would have obtained a slightly different estimate of effective duration.

This is an important concept, and you are required to learn the formula for the calculation. To further help you understand this formula and remember it, consider the following.

The price increase in response to a 0.5% decrease in rates was $\dfrac{\$44.30}{\$908} = 4.879\%$.

The price decrease in response to a 0.5% increase in rates was $\dfrac{\$41.20}{\$908} = 4.537\%$.

The average of the percentage price increase and the percentage price decrease is 4.71%. Because we used a 0.5% change in yield to get the price changes, we need to double this and get a 9.42% change in price for a 1% change in yield. The duration is 9.42.

For bonds with no embedded options, modified duration and effective duration will be equal or very nearly equal. In order to calculate effective duration for a bond with an embedded option, we need a pricing model that takes account of how the cash flows change when interest rates change.

LOS 58.e: Calculate the approximate percentage price change for a bond, given the bond's effective duration and a specified change in yield.

CFA® Program Curriculum, Volume 5, page 570

Multiply effective duration by the change in yield to get the magnitude of the price change and then change the sign to get the direction of the price change right (yield up, price down).

percentage change in bond price = –effective duration × change in yield in percent

Example: Using effective duration

What is the expected percentage price change for a bond with an effective duration of nine in response to an increase in yield of 30 basis points?

Answer:

$$-9 \times 0.3\% = -2.7\%$$

We expect the bond's price to decrease by 2.7% in response to the yield change. If the bond were priced at $980, the new price is $980 \times (1 - 0.027) = \$953.54$.

LOS 58.f: Distinguish among the alternative definitions of duration and explain why effective duration is the most appropriate measure of interest rate risk for bonds with embedded options.

CFA® Program Curriculum, Volume 5, page 576

The formula we used to calculate duration based on price changes in response to equal increases and decreases in YTM, $\text{duration} = \dfrac{V_- - V_+}{2V_0(\Delta y)}$, is the formula for effective (option-adjusted) duration. This is the preferred measure because it gives a good approximation of interest rate sensitivity for both option-free bonds and *bonds with embedded options*.

Macaulay duration is an estimate of a bond's interest rate sensitivity based on the time, in years, until promised cash flows will arrive. Since a 5-year zero-coupon bond has only one cash flow five years from today, its Macaulay duration is five. The change in value in response to a 1% change in yield for a 5-year zero-coupon bond is approximately 5%. A 5-year coupon bond has some cash flows that arrive earlier than five years from today (the coupons), so its Macaulay duration is less than five. This is consistent with what we learned earlier: the higher the coupon, the less the price sensitivity (duration) of a bond.

Macaulay duration is the earliest measure of duration, and because it was based on the time, duration is often stated as years. Because Macaulay duration is based on the expected cash flows for an option-free bond, it is not an appropriate estimate of the price sensitivity of bonds with embedded options.

Modified duration is derived from Macaulay duration and offers a slight improvement over Macaulay duration in that it takes the current YTM into account. Like Macaulay duration, and for the same reasons, modified duration is not an appropriate measure of interest rate sensitivity for bonds with embedded options. For option-free bonds, however, effective duration (based on small changes in YTM) and modified duration will be very similar.

Professor's Note: The LOS here do not require that you calculate either Macaulay duration or modified duration, only effective duration. For your own understanding, however, note that the relation is

$$\text{modified duration} = \frac{\text{Macaulay duration}}{1 + \text{periodic market yield}}$$. *This accounts for the fact we*

learned earlier that duration decreases as YTM increases. Graphically, the slope of the price-yield curve is less steep at higher yields.

Effective Duration for Bonds With Embedded Options

As noted earlier, in comparing the various duration measures, both Macaulay and modified duration are calculated directly from the promised cash flows for a bond with no adjustment for the effect of any embedded options on cash flows. Effective duration is calculated from expected price changes in response to changes in yield that explicitly take into account a bond's option provisions (i.e., they are in the price-yield function used).

Interpreting Duration

We can interpret duration in three different ways.

First, duration is the slope of the price-yield curve at the bond's current YTM. Mathematically, the slope of the price-yield curve is the first derivative of the price-yield curve with respect to yield.

A second interpretation of duration, as originally developed by Macaulay, is a weighted average of the time (in years) until each cash flow will be received. The weights are the proportions of the total bond value that each cash flow represents. The answer, again, comes in years.

A third interpretation of duration is the approximate percentage change in price for a 1% change in yield. This interpretation, price sensitivity in response to a change in yield, is the preferred, and most intuitive, interpretation of duration.

Professor's Note: The fact that duration was originally calculated and expressed in years has been a source of confusion for many candidates and finance students. Practitioners regularly speak of "longer duration securities." This confusion is the reason for this part of the LOS. The most straightforward interpretation of duration is the one that we have used up to this point: "It is the approximate percentage change in a bond's price for a 1% change in YTM." If you see duration expressed in years, just ignore the years and use the number. Questions might ask whether duration becomes longer or shorter in response to a change; longer means higher or more interest rate sensitivity. A duration of 6.82 years means that for a 1% change in YTM, a bond's value will change approximately 6.82%. This is the best way to interpret duration.

LOS 58.g: Calculate the duration of a portfolio, given the duration of the bonds comprising the portfolio, and explain the limitations of portfolio duration.

CFA® Program Curriculum, Volume 5, page 580

The concept of duration can also be applied to portfolios. In fact, one of the benefits of duration as a measure of interest rate risk is that the **duration of a portfolio** is simply the weighted average of the durations of the individual securities in the portfolio. Mathematically, the duration of a portfolio is:

$$\text{portfolio duration} = w_1 D_1 + w_2 D_2 + \ldots + w_N D_N$$

where:

w_i = market value of bond i divided by the market value of the portfolio
D_i = the duration of bond i
N = the number of bonds in the portfolio

Example: Calculating portfolio duration

Suppose you have a two-security portfolio containing Bonds A and B. The market value of Bond A is $6,000, and the market value of Bond B is $4,000. The duration of Bond A is 8.5, and the duration of Bond B is 4.0. Calculate the duration of the portfolio.

Answer:

First, find the weights of each bond. Because the market value of the portfolio is $10,000 = $6,000 + $4,000, the weight of each security is as follows:

$$\text{weight in Bond A} = \frac{\$6,000}{\$10,000} = 60\%$$

$$\text{weight in Bond B} = \frac{\$4,000}{\$10,000} = 40\%$$

Using the formula for the duration of a portfolio, we get:

$$\text{portfolio duration} = (0.6 \times 8.5) + (0.4 \times 4.0) = 6.7$$

Limitations of Portfolio Duration

The limitations of portfolio duration as a measure of interest rate sensitivity stem from the fact that yields may not change equally on all the bonds in the portfolio. With a portfolio that includes bonds with different maturities, credit risks, and embedded options, there is no reason to suspect that the yields on individual bonds will change by equal amounts when the yield curve changes. As an example, a steepening of the yield curve can increase yields on long-term bonds and leave the yield on short-term bonds unchanged. It is for this reason that we say that duration is a good measure of the sensitivity of portfolio value to *parallel* changes in the yield curve.

LOS 58.h: Describe the convexity measure of a bond and estimate a bond's percentage price change, given the bond's duration and convexity and a specified change in interest rates.

CFA® Program Curriculum, Volume 5, page 581

Convexity is a measure of the curvature of the price-yield curve. The more curved the price-yield relation is, the greater the convexity. A straight line has a convexity of zero. If the price-yield curve were, in fact, a straight line, the convexity would be zero. The reason we care about convexity is that the more curved the price-yield relation is, the worse our duration-based estimates of bond price changes in response to changes in yield are.

As an example, consider again an 8%, 20-year Treasury bond priced at $908 so that it has a yield to maturity of 9%. We previously calculated the effective duration of this bond as 9.42. Figure 4 illustrates the differences between actual bond price changes and duration-based estimates of price changes at different yield levels.

Figure 4: Duration-Based Price Estimates vs. Actual Bond Prices

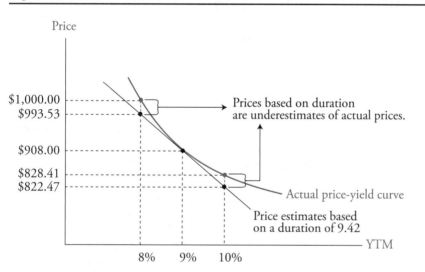

Based on a value of 9.42 for duration, we would estimate the new prices after 1% changes in yield (to 8% and to 10%) as 1.0942 × 908 = $993.53 and (1 − 0.0942) × 908 = $822.47, respectively. These price estimates are shown in Figure 4 along the straight line tangent to the actual price-yield curve.

The actual price of the 8% bond at a YTM of 8% is, of course, par value ($1,000). Based on a YTM of 10%, the actual price of the bond is $828.41, about $6 higher than our duration based estimate of $822.47. Note that price estimates based on duration are less than the actual prices for both a 1% increase and a 1% decrease in yield.

Figure 4 illustrates why convexity is important and why estimates of price changes based solely on duration are inaccurate. If the price-yield relation were a straight line

Study Session 16

(i.e., if convexity were zero), duration alone would provide good estimates of bond price changes for changes in yield of any magnitude. The greater the convexity, the greater the error in price estimates based solely on duration.

A Bond's Approximate Percentage Price Change Based on Duration and Convexity

By combining duration and convexity, we can obtain a more accurate estimate of the percentage change in price of a bond, especially for relatively large changes in yield. The formula for estimating a bond's percentage price change based on its convexity and duration is:

percentage change in price = duration effect + convexity effect

$$= \left\{ \left[-\text{duration} \times (\Delta y) \right] + \left[\text{convexity} \times (\Delta y)^2 \right] \right\} \times 100$$

With Δy entered as a decimal, the "× 100" is necessary to get an answer in percent.

> **Example: Estimating price changes with duration and convexity**
>
> Consider an 8% Treasury bond with a current price of $908 and a YTM of 9%. Calculate the percentage change in price of both a 1% increase and a 1% decrease in YTM based on a duration of 9.42 and a convexity of 68.33.
>
> **Answer:**
>
> The duration effect, as we calculated earlier, is 9.42 × 0.01 = 0.0942 = 9.42%. The convexity effect is 68.33 × 0.01² × 100 = 0.00683 × 100 = 0.683%. The total effect for a *decrease in yield of 1%* (from 9% to 8%) is 9.42% + 0.683% = +10.103%, and the estimate of the new price of the bond is 1.10103 × 908 = 999.74. This is much closer to the actual price of $1,000 than our estimate using only duration.
>
> The total effect for an *increase in yield of 1%* (from 9% to 10%) is –9.42% + 0.683% = –8.737%, and the estimate of the bond price is (1 – 0.08737)(908) = $828.67. Again, this is much closer to the actual price ($828.40) than the estimate based solely on duration.

There are a few points worth noting here. First, the convexity adjustment is always positive when convexity is positive because $(\Delta y)^2$ is always positive. This goes along with the illustration in Figure 4, which shows that the duration-only based estimate of a bond's price change suffered from being an underestimate of the percentage increase in the bond price when yields fell, and an overestimate of the percentage decrease in the bond price when yields rose. Recall, that for a callable bond, convexity can be negative at low yields. When convexity is negative, the convexity adjustment to the duration-only based estimate of the percentage price change will be negative for both yield increases and yield decreases.

 Professor's Note: Different dealers may calculate the convexity measure differently. Often the measure is calculated in a way that requires an analyst to divide the measure by two to get the correct convexity adjustment.

LOS 58.i: Distinguish between modified convexity and effective convexity.

CFA® Program Curriculum, Volume 5, page 584

Effective convexity takes into account changes in cash flows due to embedded options, while modified convexity does not. The difference between modified convexity and effective convexity mirrors the difference between modified duration and effective duration. Recall that modified duration is calculated without any adjustment to a bond's cash flows for embedded options. Also recall that effective duration was appropriate for bonds with embedded options because the inputs (prices) were calculated under the assumption that the cash flows could vary at different yields because of the embedded options in the securities. Clearly, effective convexity is the appropriate measure to use for bonds with embedded options, since it is based on bond values that incorporate the effect of embedded options on the bond's cash flows.

LOS 58.j: Calculate the price value of a basis point (PVBP), and explain its relationship to duration.

CFA® Program Curriculum, Volume 5, page 584

The **price value of a basis point** (PVBP) is the dollar change in the price/value of a bond or a portfolio when the yield changes by one basis point, or 0.01%. We can calculate the PVBP directly for a bond by changing the YTM by one basis point and computing the change in value. As a practical matter, we can use duration to calculate the price value of a basis point as:

price value of a basis point = duration × 0.0001 × bond value

The following example demonstrates this calculation.

Example: Calculating the price value of a basis point

A bond has a market value of $100,000 and a duration of 9.42. What is the price value of a basis point?

Answer:

Using the duration formula, the percentage change in the bond's price for a change in yield of 0.01% is 0.01% × 9.42 = 0.0942%. We can calculate 0.0942% of the original $100,000 portfolio value as 0.000942 × 100,000 = $94.20. If the bond's yield increases (decreases) by one basis point, the portfolio value will fall (rise) by $94.20. $94.20 is the (duration-based) price value of a basis point for this bond.

We could also directly calculate the price value of a basis point for this bond by increasing the YTM by 0.01% (0.0001) and calculating the change in bond value. This would give us the PVBP for an increase in yield. This would be very close to our duration-based estimate because duration is a very good estimate of interest rate risk for small changes in yield. We can ignore the convexity adjustment here because it is of very small magnitude: $(\Delta y)^2 = (0.0001)^2 = 0.00000001$, which is very small indeed!

LOS 58.k: Describe the impact of yield volatility on the interest rate risk of a bond.

CFA® Program Curriculum, Volume 5, page 585

Earlier in this topic review, we introduced duration as a measure of interest rate risk. A bond with a lower duration is less affected by a given change in yield than a bond with greater duration. Here we combine a bond's duration with its yield volatility in assessing its interest rate risk.

Consider a Treasury bond with a duration of 7 and a similar single-B rated corporate bond with a duration of 5. Based on duration alone, we would say that the Treasury bond has more interest rate risk. If, however, the volatility of the market yield on the corporate bond is sufficiently greater than the volatility of the market yield on the Treasury bond, the corporate bond can have greater price volatility due to yield (interest rate) changes than the Treasury bond. Investors must consider both the effects of yield changes on bond values and how volatile yields are when estimating interest rate risk. One measure of price risk that considers both these components is value-at-risk (VaR).

KEY CONCEPTS

LOS 58.a
The full valuation approach to measuring interest rate risk involves using a pricing model to value individual bonds and can be used to find the price impact of any scenario of interest rate/yield curve changes. Its advantages are its flexibility and precision.

The duration/convexity approach is based on summary measures of interest rate risk and, while simpler to use for a portfolio of bonds than the full valuation approach, is theoretically correct only for parallel shifts in the yield curve.

LOS 58.b
Callable bonds and prepayable securities will have less price volatility (lower duration) at low yields, compared to option-free bonds.

Putable bonds will have less price volatility at high yields, compared to option-free bonds.

LOS 58.c
Option-free bonds have a price-yield relationship that is curved (convex toward the origin) and are said to exhibit positive convexity. In this case, bond prices fall less in response to an increase in yield than they rise in response to an equal-sized decrease in yield.

Callable bonds exhibit negative convexity at low yield levels. In this case, bond prices rise less in response to a decrease in yield than they fall in response to an equal-sized increase in yield.

LOS 58.d
Effective duration is calculated as the ratio of the average percentage price change for an equal-sized increase and decrease in yield, to the change in yield.

$$\text{effective duration} = \frac{V_- - V_+}{2V_0(\Delta y)}$$

LOS 58.e
Approximate percentage change in bond price = –duration × change in yield in percent.

LOS 58.f
The most intuitive interpretation of duration is as the percentage change in a bond's price for a 1% change in yield to maturity.

Macaulay duration and modified duration are based on a bond's promised cash flows.

Effective duration is appropriate for estimating price changes in bonds with embedded options because it takes into account the effect of embedded options on a bond's cash flows.

LOS 58.g
The duration of a bond portfolio is equal to a weighted average of the individual bond durations, where the weights are the proportions of total portfolio value in each bond position.

Portfolio duration is limited because it gives the sensitivity of portfolio value only to yield changes that are equal for all bonds in the portfolio, an unlikely scenario for most portfolios.

LOS 58.h
Because of convexity, the duration measure is a poor approximation of price sensitivity for yield changes that are not absolutely small. The convexity adjustment accounts for the curvature of the price-yield relationship.

Incorporating both duration and convexity, we can estimate the percentage change in price in response to a change in yield of (Δy) as:

$$\left\{ \left[(-\text{duration})(\Delta y) \right] + \left[(\text{convexity})(\Delta y)^2 \right] \right\} \times 100$$

LOS 58.i
Effective convexity considers expected changes in cash flows that may occur for bonds with embedded options, while modified convexity does not.

LOS 58.j
Price value of a basis point (PVBP) is an estimate of the change in a bond's or a bond portfolio's value for a one basis point change in yield.

$$\text{PVBP} = \text{duration} \times 0.0001 \times \text{bond (or portfolio) value}$$

LOS 58.k
Yield volatility is the standard deviation of the changes in the yield of a bond. Uncertainty about a bond's future price due to changes in yield results from both a bond's price sensitivity to yield changes (its duration) and also from the volatility of its yield in the market.

CONCEPT CHECKERS

1. Why is the price/yield profile of a callable bond less convex than that of an otherwise identical option-free bond? The price:
    A. increase is capped from above, at or near the call price as the required yield decreases.
    B. increase is capped from above, at or near the call price as the required yield increases.
    C. decrease is limited from below, at or near the call price as the required yield increases.

2. The 4.65% semiannual-pay Portage Health Authority bonds have exactly 17 years to maturity and are currently priced to yield 4.39%. Using the full valuation approach, the interest rate exposure (in percent of value) for these bonds, given a 75 basis point increase in required yield, is *closest* to:
    A. –9.104%.
    B. –9.031%.
    C. –8.344%.

3. A 14% semiannual-pay coupon bond has six years to maturity. The bond is currently trading at par. Using a 25 basis point change in yield, the effective duration of the bond is *closest* to:
    A. 0.389.
    B. 3.889.
    C. 3.970.

4. Suppose that the bond in Question 3 is callable at par today. Using a 25 basis point change in yield, the bond's effective duration assuming that its price cannot exceed 100 is *closest* to:
    A. 1.972.
    B. 1.998.
    C. 19.72.

5. The modified duration of a bond is 7.87. The percentage change in price using duration for a yield decrease of 110 basis points is *closest* to:
    A. –8.657%.
    B. +7.155%.
    C. +8.657%.

6. A bond has a convexity of 57.3. The convexity effect if the yield decreases by 110 basis points is *closest* to:
    A. –1.673%.
    B. +0.693%.
    C. +1.673%.

7. Assume a bond has an effective duration of 10.5 and a convexity of 97.3. Using both of these measures, the estimated percentage change in price for this bond, in response to a decline in yield of 200 basis points, is *closest* to:
    A. 19.05%.
    B. 22.95%.
    C. 24.89%.

8.   An analyst has determined that if market yields rise by 100 basis points, a certain high-grade corporate bond will have a convexity effect of 1.75%. Further, she's found that the total estimated percentage change in price for this bond should be –13.35%. Given this information, it follows that the bond's percentage change in price due to duration is:
A.   –15.10%.
B.   –11.60%.
C.   +16.85%.

9.   The total price volatility of a typical noncallable bond can be found by:
A.   adding the bond's convexity effect to its effective duration.
B.   adding the bond's negative convexity to its modified duration.
C.   subtracting the bond's negative convexity from its positive convexity.

10.   The current price of a $1,000, 7-year, 5.5% semiannual coupon bond is $1,029.23. The bond's PVBP is *closest* to:
A. $0.05.
B. $0.60.
C. $5.74.

11.   The effect on a bond portfolio's value of a decrease in yield would be *most accurately* estimated by using:
A.   the full valuation approach.
B.   the price value of a basis point.
C.   both the portfolio's duration and convexity.

12.   An analyst has noticed lately that the price of a particular bond has risen less when the yield falls by 0.1% than the price falls when rates increase by 0.1%. She could conclude that the bond:
A.   is an option-free bond.
B.   has an embedded put option.
C.   has negative convexity.

13.   Which of the following measures is *lowest* for a currently callable bond?
A.   Macaulay duration.
B.   Effective duration.
C.   Modified duration.

Study Session 16
Cross-Reference to CFA Institute Assigned Reading #58 – Introduction to the Measurement of Interest Rate Risk

Page 153

CHALLENGE PROBLEMS

Use the following information to answer Questions 1 through 6.

A bond dealer provides the following selected information on a portfolio of fixed-income securities.

Par Value	Market Price	Coupon	Modified Duration	Effective Duration	Effective Convexity
$2 million	100	6.5%	8	8	154
$3 million	93	5.5%	6	1	50
$1 million	95	7%	8.5	8.5	130
$4 million	103	8%	9	5	−70

1. What is the effective duration for the portfolio?

2. Calculate the price value of a basis point for this portfolio.

3. Which bond(s) likely has (have) no embedded options? (identify bonds by coupon)

4. Which bond(s) is (are) likely callable?

5. Which bond(s) is (are) likely putable?

6. What is the approximate price change for the 7% bond if its yield to maturity increases by 25 basis points?

7. Why might two bond dealers differ in their estimates of a portfolio's effective duration?

8. Why might portfolio effective duration be an inadequate measure of interest rate risk for a bond portfolio even if we assume the bond effective durations are correct?

ANSWERS – CONCEPT CHECKERS

1. **A**   As the required yield decreases on a callable bond, the rate of increase in the price of the bond begins to slow down and eventually level off as it approaches the call price, a characteristic known as "negative convexity."

2. **C**   We need to compare the value of the bond today to the value if the YTM increases by 0.75%.

    Price today = 103.092

    $N = 34$; $PMT = \dfrac{4.65}{2} = 2.325$; $FV = 100$;

    $I/Y = \dfrac{4.39}{2} = 2.195\%$; $CPT \to PV = -103.092$

    Price after a 75 basis point increase in the YTM is 94.490

    $N = 34$; $PMT = \dfrac{4.65}{2} = 2.325$; $FV = 100$;

    $I/Y = \dfrac{5.14}{2} = 2.57\%$; $CPT \to PV = -94.490$

    Interest rate exposure $= \dfrac{94.490 - 103.092}{103.092} = -8.344\%$

3. **C** $V_{-} = 100.999$

    $N = 12$; $PMT = \dfrac{14.00}{2} = 7.00$; $FV = 100$;

    $I/Y = \dfrac{13.75}{2} = 6.875\%$; $CPT \to PV = -100.999$

    $V_{+} = 99.014$

    $N = 12$; $PMT = \dfrac{14.00}{2} = 7.00$; $FV = 100$;

    $I/Y = \dfrac{14.25}{2} = 7.125\%$; $CPT \to PV = -99.014$

    $V_{0} = 100.000$

    $\Delta y = 0.0025$

    $\text{duration} = \dfrac{V_{-} - V_{+}}{2V_{0}(\Delta y)} = \dfrac{100.999 - 99.014}{2(100)0.0025} = 3.970$

4. **A** $V_- = 100$

   $V_+ = 99.014$

   $V_0 = 100$

   $\Delta y = 0.0025$

   $$\text{duration} = \frac{V_- - V_+}{2V_0(\Delta y)} = \frac{100 - 99.014}{2(100)0.0025} = 1.972$$

5. **C** $\text{Est.}[\Delta V\_\%] = -7.87 \times (-1.10\%) = 8.657\%$

6. **B** $\text{convexity effect} = \text{convexity} \times (\Delta y)^2 = \left[57.3(0.011)^2\right] \times 100 = 0.693\%$

7. **C** Total estimated price change = (duration effect + convexity effect)

   $$\left\{\left[-10.5 \times (-0.02)\right] + \left[97.3 \times (-0.02)^2\right]\right\} \times 100 = 21.0\% + 3.89\% = 24.89\%$$

8. **A** Total percentage change in price = duration effect + convexity effect. Thus:

   $-13.35 = \text{duration effect} + 1.75 \Rightarrow \text{duration effect} = -15.10\%\cdot$

   (Note: the duration effect must be negative because yields are rising.)

9. **A** Total percentage change in price = duration effect + convexity effect. Thus:

   Total percentage change in price = effective duration + convexity effect.

   (Note: since this is a noncallable bond, you can use either effective or modified duration in the above equation.)

10. **B** PVBP = initial price – price if yield is changed by 1 basis point. First, we need to calculate the yield so that we can calculate the price of the bond with a 1 basis point change in yield. Using a financial calculator: PV = –1,029.23; FV = 1,000; PMT = 27.5 = (0.055 × 1,000) / 2; N = 14 = 2 × 7 years; CPT → I/Y = 2.49998, multiplied by 2 = 4.99995, or 5.00%. Next, compute the price of the bond at a yield of 5.00% + 0.01%, or 5.01%. Using the calculator: FV = 1,000; PMT = 27.5; N = 14; I/Y = 2.505 (5.01 / 2); CPT → PV = $1,028.63. Finally, PVBP = $1,029.23 – $1,028.63 = $0.60.

11. **A** The full valuation approach is the most complex method, but also the most accurate.

12. **C** A bond with negative convexity will rise less in price in response to a decrease in yield than it will fall in response to an equal-sized increase in rates.

13. **B** The interest rate sensitivity of a bond with an embedded call option will be less than that of an option-free bond. Effective duration takes the effect of the call option into account and will, therefore, be less than Macaulay or modified duration.

ANSWERS – CHALLENGE PROBLEMS

1. Portfolio effective duration is the weighted average of the effective durations of the portfolio bonds.

    Numerators in weights are market values (par value × price as percent of par). Denominator is total market value of the portfolio.

    $$\frac{2}{9.86}(8) + \frac{2.79}{9.86}(1) + \frac{0.95}{9.86}(8.5) + \frac{4.12}{9.86}(5) = 4.81 \text{ (weights are in millions)}$$

2. Price value of a basis point can be calculated using effective duration for the portfolio and the portfolio's market value, together with a yield change of 0.01%. Convexity can be ignored for such a small change in yield.

    4.81 × 0.0001 × 9,860,000 = $4,742.66

3. The 6.5% and 7% coupon bonds likely have no embedded options. For both of these bonds, modified duration and effective duration are identical, which would be the case if they had no embedded options. (It is possible that these bonds have options that are so far out of the money that the bond prices act as if there is no embedded option. One example might be a conversion option to common stock at $40 per share when the market value of the shares is $2.)

4. The 8% bond is likely callable. It is trading at a premium, its effective duration is less than modified duration, and it exhibits negative convexity. Remember, call price can be above par.

5. The 5.5% bond is likely putable. It is trading at a significant discount, its effective duration is much lower than its modified duration (close to zero in fact), and its convexity is positive but low. Note that a putable bond may trade below par when the put price is below par (also if there is risk that the issuer cannot honor the put). If it were callable, we would expect its modified and effective durations to be closer in value because the market price is significantly below likely call prices.

6. Based on the effective duration and effective convexity of the 7% bond, the approximate price change is:

    [−8.5 × 0.0025] + [130 × 0.0025^2] × 950,000 = −$19,415.63

7. In order to estimate effective duration, the dealers must use a pricing model for the bonds and choose a specific yield change. Differences in models or the yield change used can lead to differences in their estimates of effective duration.

8. Effective duration is based on small changes in yield and is appropriate for parallel changes in the yield curve (or equal changes in the yields to maturity for all portfolio bonds). Other types of yield changes will make portfolio duration an inadequate measure of portfolio interest rate risk.

FUNDAMENTALS OF CREDIT ANALYSIS

Study Session 16

EXAM FOCUS

This topic review introduces credit analysis, primarily for corporate bonds, but considerations for credit analysis of high yield, sovereign, and municipal bonds are also covered. Focus on credit ratings, credit spreads, and the impact on return when ratings and spreads change.

LOS 59.a: Describe credit risk and credit-related risks affecting corporate bonds.

CFA® Program Curriculum, Volume 5, page 606

Credit risk is the risk associated with losses stemming from the failure of a borrower to make timely and full payments of interest or principal. Credit risk has two components: *default risk* and *loss severity*.

- **Default risk** is the probability that a borrower (bond issuer) fails to pay interest or repay principal when due.
- **Loss severity**, or *loss given default*, refers to the value a bond investor will lose if the issuer defaults. Loss severity can be stated as a monetary amount or as a percentage of a bond's value (principal and unpaid interest).

The **expected loss** is equal to the default risk multiplied by the loss severity. Expected loss can likewise be stated as a monetary value or as a percentage of a bond's value.

The **recovery rate** is the percentage of a bond's value an investor will receive if the issuer defaults. Loss severity as a percentage is equal to one minus the recovery rate.

Bonds with credit risk trade at higher yields than bonds thought to be free of credit risk. The difference in yield between a credit-risky bond and a credit-risk-free bond of similar maturity is called its **yield spread**. For example, if a 5-year corporate bond is trading at a spread of +250 basis points to Treasuries and the yield on 5-year Treasury notes is 4.0%, the yield on the corporate bond is 4.0% + 2.5% = 6.5%.

Bond prices are inversely related to spreads; a wider spread implies a lower bond price and a narrower spread implies a higher price. The size of the spread reflects the creditworthiness of the issuer and the liquidity of the market for its bonds. **Spread risk** is the possibility that a bond's spread will widen due to one or both of these factors.

- **Credit migration risk** or **downgrade risk** is the possibility that spreads will increase because the issuer has become less creditworthy. As we will see later in this topic review, credit rating agencies assign ratings to bonds and issuers, and may upgrade or downgrade these ratings over time.
- **Market liquidity risk** is the risk of receiving less than market value when selling a bond and is reflected in the size of the bid-ask spreads. Market liquidity risk is greater for the bonds of less creditworthy issuers and for the bonds of smaller issuers with relatively little publicly traded debt.

LOS 59.b: Describe seniority rankings of corporate debt and explain the potential violation of the priority of claims in a bankruptcy proceeding.

CFA® Program Curriculum, Volume 5, page 609

Each category of debt from the same issuer is ranked according to a **priority of claims** in the event of a default. A bond's priority of claims to the issuer's assets and cash flows is referred to as its **seniority ranking**.

Debt can be either **secured debt** or **unsecured debt**. Secured debt is backed by collateral, while unsecured debt or *debentures* represent a general claim to the issuer's assets and cash flows. Secured debt has higher priority of claims than unsecured debt.

Secured debt can be further distinguished as *first lien* or *first mortgage* (where a specific asset is pledged), *senior secured*, or *junior secured* debt. Unsecured debt is further divided into *senior*, *junior*, and *subordinated* gradations. The highest rank of unsecured debt is senior unsecured. Subordinated debt ranks below other unsecured debt.

The general seniority rankings for debt repayment priority are the following:

- First lien or first mortgage.
- Senior secured debt.
- Junior secured debt.
- Senior unsecured debt.
- Senior subordinated debt.
- Subordinated debt.
- Junior subordinated debt.

All debt within the same category is said to rank **pari passu**, or have same priority of claims. All senior secured debt holders, for example, are treated alike in a corporate bankruptcy.

Recovery rates are highest for debt with the highest priority of claims and decrease with each lower rank of seniority. The lower the seniority ranking of a bond, the higher its credit risk. Investors require a higher yield to accept a lower seniority ranking.

In the event of a default or reorganization, senior lenders have claims on the assets before junior lenders and equity holders. A strict priority of claims, however, is not always applied in practice. Although in theory the priority of claims is absolute, in many cases lower-priority debt holders (and even equity investors) may get paid even if senior debt holders are not paid in full.

Bankruptcies can be costly and take a long time to settle. During bankruptcy proceedings, the value of a company's assets could deteriorate due to loss of customers and key employees, while legal expenses mount. A bankruptcy reorganization plan is confirmed by a vote among all classes of investors with less than 100% recovery rate. To avoid unnecessary delays, negotiation and compromise among various claimholders may result in a reorganization plan that does not strictly conform to the original priority of claims. By such a vote or by order of the bankruptcy court, the final plan may differ from absolute priority.

LOS 59.c: Distinguish between corporate issuer credit ratings and issue credit ratings and describe the rating agency practice of "notching".

CFA® Program Curriculum, Volume 5, page 616

Credit rating agencies assign ratings to categories of bonds with similar credit risk. Rating agencies rate both the issuer (i.e., the company issuing the bonds) and the debt issues, or the bonds themselves. Issuer credit ratings are called **corporate family ratings** (CFR), while issue-specific ratings are called **corporate credit ratings** (CCR). Issuer ratings are based on the overall creditworthiness of the company. The issuers are rated on their senior unsecured debt.

Figure 1 shows ratings scales used by Standard & Poor's, Moody's, and Fitch, three of the major credit rating agencies.

Figure 1: Credit Rating Categories

(a) Investment grade ratings		(b) Non-investment grade ratings	
Moody's	*Standard &Poor's, Fitch*	*Moody's*	*Standard &Poor's, Fitch*
Aaa	AAA	Ba1	BB+
Aa1	AA+	Ba2	BB
Aa2	AA	Ba3	BB–
Aa3	AA–	B1	B+
A1	A+	B2	B
A2	A	B3	B–
A3	A–	Caa1	CCC+
Baa1	BBB+	Caa2	CCC
Baa2	BBB	Caa3	CCC–
Baa3	BBB–	Ca	CC
		C	C
		C	D

Study Session 16

Triple A (AAA or Aaa) is the highest rating. Bonds with ratings of Baa3/BBB– or higher are considered **investment grade**. Bonds rated Ba1/BB+ or lower are considered **non-investment grade** and are often called *high yield bonds* or *junk bonds*.

Bonds in default are rated D by Standard & Poor's and Fitch and are included in Moody's lowest rating category, C. When a company defaults on one of its several outstanding bonds, provisions in bond indentures may trigger default on the remaining issues as well. Such a provision is called a *cross default provision*.

A borrower can have multiple debt issues that vary not only by maturities and coupons but also by credit rating. Issue credit ratings depend on the seniority of a bond issue and its covenants. **Notching** is the practice by rating agencies of assigning different ratings to bonds of the same issuer. Notching is based on several factors, including seniority of the bonds and its impact on potential loss severity.

An example of a factor that rating agencies consider when notching an issue credit rating is **structural subordination**. In a holding company structure, both the parent company and the subsidiaries may have outstanding debt. A subsidiary's debt covenants may restrict the transfer of cash or assets "upstream" to the parent company before the subsidiary's debt is serviced. In such a case, even though the parent company's bonds are not junior to the subsidiary's bonds, the subsidiary's bonds have a priority claim to the subsidiary's cash flows. Thus the parent company's bonds are effectively subordinated to the subsidiary's bonds.

Notching is less common for highly rated issuers than for lower-rated issuers. For lower-rated issuers, higher default risk leads to significant differences between recovery rates of debt with different seniority, leading to more notching.

LOS 59.d: Explain risks in relying on ratings from credit rating agencies.

CFA® Program Curriculum, Volume 5, page 618

Relying on ratings from credit rating agencies has some risks. Four specific risks are:

1. **Credit ratings are dynamic.** Credit ratings change over time. Rating agencies may update their default risk assessments during the life of a bond. Higher credit ratings tend to be more stable than lower credit ratings.

2. **Rating agencies are not perfect.** Ratings mistakes occur from time to time. For example, subprime mortgage securities were assigned much higher ratings than they deserved.

3. **Event risk is difficult to assess.** Risks that are specific to a company or industry are difficult to predict and incorporate into credit ratings. Litigation risk to tobacco companies is one example. Events that are difficult to anticipate, such as natural disasters, acquisitions, and equity buybacks using debt, are not easily captured in credit ratings.

4. **Credit ratings lag market pricing.** Market prices and credit spreads change much faster than credit ratings. Additionally, two bonds with same rating can trade at different yields. Market prices reflect expected losses, while credit ratings only assess default risk.

LOS 59.e: Explain the components of traditional credit analysis.

CFA® Program Curriculum, Volume 5, page 623

A common way to categorize the key components of credit analysis is by the **four Cs of credit analysis**: capacity, collateral, covenants, and character.

Capacity

Capacity refers to a corporate borrower's ability repay its debt obligations on time. Analysis of capacity is similar to the process used in equity analysis. Capacity analysis entails three levels of assessment: (1) industry structure, (2) industry fundamentals, and (3) company fundamentals.

Industry Structure

The first level of a credit analyst's assessment is industry structure. Industry structure can be described by Porter's five forces: rivalry among existing competitors, threat of new entrants, threat of substitute products, bargaining power of buyers, and bargaining power of suppliers.

 Professor's Note: We describe industry analysis based on Porter's five forces in the Study Session on equity valuation.

Industry Fundamentals

The next level of a credit analyst's assessment is industry fundamentals, including the influence of macroeconomic factors on an industry's growth prospects and profitability. Industry fundamentals evaluation focuses on:

- **Industry cyclicality.** Cyclical industries are sensitive to economic performance. Cyclical industries tend to have more volatile earnings, revenues, and cash flows, which make them more risky than noncyclical industries.
- **Industry growth prospects.** Creditworthiness is most questionable for the weaker companies in a slow-growing or declining industry.
- **Industry published statistics.** Industry statistics provided by rating agencies, investment banks, industry periodicals, and government agencies can be a source for industry performance and fundamentals.

Company Fundamentals

The last level of credit analysts' assessment is company fundamentals. A corporate borrower should be assessed on:

- **Competitive position.** Market share changes over time and cost structure relative to peers are some of the factors to analyze.
- **Operating history.** The performance of the company over different phases of business cycle, trends in margins and revenues, and current management's tenure.
- **Management's strategy and execution.** This includes the soundness of the strategy, the ability to execute the strategy, and the effects of management's decisions on bondholders.
- **Ratios and ratio analysis.** As we will discuss later in this topic review, leverage and coverage ratios are important tools for credit analysis.

Collateral

Collateral analysis is more important for less creditworthy companies. The market value of a company's assets can be difficult to observe directly. Issues to consider when assessing collateral values include:

- **Intangible assets.** Patents are considered high-quality intangible assets because they can be more easily sold to generate cash flows than other intangibles. Goodwill is not considered a high-quality intangible asset and is usually written down when company performance is poor.
- **Depreciation.** High depreciation expense relative to capital expenditures may signal that management is not investing sufficiently in the company. The quality of the company's assets may be poor, which may lead to reduced operating cash flow and potentially high loss severity.
- **Equity market capitalization.** A stock that trades below book value may indicate that company assets are of low quality.
- **Human and intellectual capital.** These are difficult to value, but a company may have intellectual property that can function as collateral.

Covenants

Covenants are the terms and conditions the borrowers and lenders have agreed to as part of a bond issue. Covenants protect lenders while leaving some operating flexibility to the borrowers to run the company. There are two types of covenants: (1) *affirmative covenants* and (2) *negative covenants*.

Affirmative covenants require the borrower to take certain actions, such as paying interest, principal, and taxes; carrying insurance on pledged assets; and maintaining certain financial ratios within prescribed limits.

Negative covenants restrict the borrower from taking certain actions, such as incurring additional debt or directing cash flows to shareholders in the form of dividends and stock repurchases.

Covenants that are overly restrictive of an issuer's operating activities may reduce the issuer's ability to repay. On the other hand, covenants create a legally binding contractual framework for repayment of the debt obligation, which reduces uncertainty for the debt holders. A careful credit analysis should include an assessment of whether the covenants protect the interests of the bondholders without unduly constraining the borrower's operating activities.

Character

Character refers to management's integrity and its commitment to repay the loan. Factors such as management's business qualifications and operating record are important for evaluating character. Character analysis includes an assessment of:

- **Soundness of strategy.** Management's ability to develop a sound strategy.
- **Track record.** Management's past performance in executing its strategy and operating the company without bankruptcies, restructurings, or other distress situations that led to additional borrowing.
- **Accounting policies and tax strategies.** Use of accounting policies and tax strategies that may be hiding problems, such as revenue recognition issues, frequent restatements, and frequently changing auditors.
- **Fraud and malfeasance record.** Any record of fraud or other legal and regulatory problems.
- **Prior treatment of bondholders.** Benefits to equity holders at the expense of debt holders, through actions such as debt-financed acquisitions and special dividends, especially if they led to credit rating downgrades.

LOS 59.f: Calculate and interpret financial ratios used in credit analysis.

CFA® Program Curriculum, Volume 5, page 628

Ratio analysis is part of capacity analysis. Two primary categories of ratios for credit analysis are *leverage ratios* and *coverage ratios*. Credit analysts calculate company ratios to assess the viability of a company, to find trends over time, and to compare companies to industry averages and peers.

Profits and Cash Flows

Profits and cash flows are needed to service debt. Here we examine four profit and cash flow metrics commonly used in ratio analysis by credit analysts.

1. **Earnings before interest, taxes, depreciation, and amortization (EBITDA).** EBITDA is a commonly used measure that is calculated as operating income plus depreciation and amortization. A drawback to using this measure for credit analysis is that it does not adjust for capital expenditures and changes in working capital, which are necessary uses of funds for a going concern. Cash needed for these uses is not available to debt holders.

2. **Funds from operations (FFO).** Funds from operations are net income from continuing operations plus depreciation, amortization, deferred taxes, and noncash items. FFO is similar to cash flow from operations (CFO) except that FFO excludes changes in working capital.

3. **Free cash flow before dividends.** Free cash flow before dividends is net income plus depreciation and amortization minus capital expenditures minus increase in working capital. Free cash flow before dividends excludes non-recurring items.

4. **Free cash flow after dividends.** This is free cash flow before dividends minus the dividends. If free cash flow after dividends is greater than zero, it represents cash that could pay down debt or accumulate on the balance sheet. Either outcome is a form of deleveraging, a positive indicator for creditworthiness.

Leverage Ratios

Analysts should adjust debt reported on the financial statements by including the firm's obligations such as underfunded pension plans (net pension liabilities) and off-balance-sheet liabilities such as operating leases.

The three most common measures of leverage used by credit analysts are the debt-to-capital ratio, the debt-to-EBITDA ratio, and the FFO-to-debt ratio.

1. **Debt/capital.** Capital is the sum of total debt and shareholders' equity. The debt-to-capital ratio is the percentage of the capital structure financed by debt. A lower ratio indicates less credit risk. If the financial statements list high values for intangible assets such as goodwill, an analyst should calculate a second debt-to-capital ratio adjusted for a writedown of these assets' after-tax value.

2. **Debt/EBITDA.** A higher ratio indicates higher leverage and higher credit risk. This ratio is more volatile for firms in cyclical industries or with high operating leverage because of their high variability of EBITDA.

3. **FFO/debt.** Because this ratio divides a cash flow measure by the value of debt, a higher ratio indicates lower credit risk.

Coverage Ratios

Coverage ratios measure the borrower's ability to generate cash flows to meet interest payments. The two most commonly used are EBITDA-to-interest and EBIT-to-interest.

1. **EBITDA/interest expense.** A higher ratio indicates lower credit risk. This ratio is used more often than the EBIT-to-interest expense ratio. Because depreciation and amortization are still included as part of the cash flow measure, this ratio will be higher than the EBIT version.

2. **EBIT/interest expense.** A higher ratio indicates lower credit risk. This ratio is the more conservative measure because depreciation and amortization are subtracted from earnings.

Example: Credit analysis with financial ratios (Part 1)

A credit analyst is assessing Saxor, a U.S. multimedia company with the following selected financial information:

In $ millions	20X1	20X2	20X3
Operating income	5,205	6,456	7,726
Revenue	36,149	38,063	40,893
Depreciation and amortization	1,631	1,713	1,841
Capital expenditures	1,753	2,110	3,559
Cash flow from operations	5,319	6,578	6,994
Total debt	12,701	12,480	13,977
Total equity	33,734	37,519	37,385
Dividends paid	648	653	756
Interest expense	300	330	360

Calculate the cash flows and ratios listed below. Free cash flow (FCF) is after dividends for all calculations.

	20X1	20X2	20X3
EBITDA			
FCF after dividends			
Operating margin			
Debt/EBITDA			
EBITDA/interest			
FCF/debt			
Debt/capital			

Answer:

EBITDA = operating income + depreciation and amortization:
20X1: 5,205 + 1,631 = $6,836 million
20X2: 6,456 + 1,713 = $8,169 million
20X3: 7,726 + 1,841 = $9,567 million

FCF = cash flow from operations – capital expenditures – dividends:
20X1: 5,319 – 1,753 – 648 = $2,918 million
20X2: 6,578 – 2,110 – 653 = $3,815 million
20X3: 6,994 – 3,559 – 756 = $2,679 million

Operating margin = operating income / revenue:
20X1: 5,205 / 36,149 = 14.4%
20X2: 6,456 / 38,063 = 17.0%
20X3: 7,726 / 40,893 = 18.9%

Debt/EBITDA:
20X1: 12,701 / 6,836 = 1.9x
20X2: 12,480 / 8,169 = 1.5x
20X3: 13,977 / 9,567 = 1.5x

EBITDA/interest:
20X1: 6,836 / 300 = 22.8x
20X2: 8,169 / 330 = 24.8x
20X3: 9,567 / 360 = 26.6x

FCF/debt:
20X1: 6,836 / 12,701 = 23.0%
20X2: 8,169 / 12,480 = 30.6%
20X3: 9,567 / 13,977 = 19.2%

Debt/capital:
20X1: 12,701 / (12,701 + 33,734) = 27.4%
20X2: 12,480 / (12,480 + 37,519) = 25.0%
20X3: 13,977 / (13,977 + 37,385) = 27.2%

	20X1	20X2	20X3
EBITDA	6,836	8,169	9,567
FCF after dividends	2,918	3,815	2,679
Operating margin	14.4%	17.0%	18.9%
Debt/EBITDA	1.9×	1.5×	1.5×
EBITDA/interest	22.8×	24.8×	26.6×
FCF/debt	23.0%	30.6%	19.2%
Debt/capital	27.4%	25.0%	27.2%

Example: Credit analysis with financial ratios (Part 2)

2. Coyote Media is also a multimedia company and is a rival of Saxor. Given the following ratios for Coyote over the same period, calculate the 3-year averages for both Saxor and Coyote and comment on which multimedia company is expected to have a better credit rating.

Coyote Media	20X1	20X2	20X3
Operating margin	18.0%	7.0%	9.5%
Debt/EBITDA	1.9×	3.0×	2.0×
EBITDA/interest	27.5×	12.7×	18.3×
FCF/debt	15.0%	28.0%	26.6%
Debt/capital	28.7%	41.2%	42.6%

Answer:

3-Year Averages	Saxor	Coyote
Operating margin	16.8%	11.5%
Debt/EBITDA	1.6x	2.3x
EBITDA/interest	24.7x	19.5x
FCF/debt	24.2%	23.2%
Debt/capital	26.5%	37.5%

All ratios support a higher credit rating for Saxor. Saxor has a better operating margin and better coverage for interest (EBITDA/interest) and for debt (FCF/debt). Lower leverage as measured by debt-to-capital and debt-to-EBITDA also favor Saxor.

LOS 59.g: Evaluate the credit quality of a corporate bond issuer and a bond of that issuer, given key financial ratios for the issuer and the industry.

CFA® Program Curriculum, Volume 5, page 631

Ratings agencies publish benchmark values for financial ratios that are associated with each ratings classification. Credit analysts can evaluate the potential for upgrades and downgrades based on subject company ratios relative to these benchmarks.

Example: Credit ratings based on ratios (Part 1)

A credit rating agency publishes the following benchmark ratios for bond issues of multimedia companies in each of the investment grade ratings, based on 3-year averages over the period 20X1 to 20X3:

Credit Ratings	AAA	AA	A	BBB
Operating margin	24.5%	16.5%	10.0%	7.5%
Debt/EBITDA	1.3x	1.8x	2.2x	2.5x
EBITDA/interest	25.0x	20.0x	17.5x	15.0x
FCF/debt	30.0%	24.0%	20.0%	17.0%
Debt/capital	25.0%	30.0%	35.0%	40.0%

Based on the ratios calculated in the previous example and the industry standards in the table above, what are the expected issuer credit ratings for Coyote and Saxor?

Answer:

3-Year Averages	Saxor	Coyote
Operating margin	16.8%	11.5%
Debt/EBITDA	1.6×	2.3×
EBITDA/interest	24.7×	19.5×
FCF/debt	24.3%	23.2%
Debt/capital	26.6%	37.5%

Based on the ratio averages, it is most likely that Saxor's issuer rating is AA and Coyote's issuer rating is A.

Example: Credit ratings based on ratios (Part 2)

Coyote Media decides to spin off its television division. The new company, CoyTV, will issue new debt and will not be a restricted subsidiary of Coyote Media. CoyTV is more profitable and generates higher and less volatile cash flows. Describe possible notching for the new CoyTV issue and the potential credit rating change to Coyote Media.

Answer:

Because CoyTV may be a better credit risk due to a better profit potential, the new issue may have a credit rating one notch above Coyote Media.

Coyote Media may now be less profitable and could have more volatile cash flows. This suggests an increase in credit risk that could lead to a credit rating downgrade.

LOS 59.h: Describe factors that influence the level and volatility of yield spreads.

CFA® Program Curriculum, Volume 5, page 642

We can think of the yield on an option-free corporate bond as the sum of the real risk-free interest rate, the expected inflation rate, a maturity premium, a liquidity premium, and a credit spread. All bond prices and yields are affected by changes in the first three of these components. The last two components are the yield spread:

yield spread = liquidity premium + credit spread

Yield spreads on corporate bonds are affected primarily by five interrelated factors:

1. **Credit cycle.** The market's perception of overall credit risk is cyclical. At the top of the credit cycle, the bond market perceives low credit risk and is generally bullish. Credit spreads narrow as the credit cycle improves. Credit spreads widen as the credit cycle deteriorates.

2. **Economic conditions.** Credit spreads narrow as the economy strengthens and investors expect firms' credit metrics to improve. Conversely, credit spreads widen as the economy weakens.

3. **Financial market performance.** Credit spreads narrow in strong-performing markets overall, including the equity market. Credit spreads widen in weak-performing markets. In steady-performing markets with low volatility of returns, credit spreads also tend to narrow as investors reach for yield.

4. **Broker-dealer capital.** Because most bonds trade over the counter, investors need broker-dealers to provide market-making capital for bond markets to function. Yield spreads are narrower when broker-dealers provide sufficient capital but can widen when market-making capital becomes scarce.

5. **General market demand and supply.** Credit spreads narrow in times of high demand for bonds. Credit spreads widen in times of low demand for bonds. Excess supply conditions, such as large issuance in a short period of time, can lead to widening spreads.

Yield spreads on lower-quality issues tend to be more volatile than spreads on higher-quality issues.

LOS 59.i: Calculate the return impact of spread changes.

CFA® Program Curriculum, Volume 5, page 646

The return impact of spread changes is a combination of two factors: (1) the magnitude of the spread change (Δspread) and (2) the price sensitivity of the bond to interest rate changes (i.e., the bond's modified duration).

For small spread changes, the return impact (percent change in bond price) can be approximated by:

$$\text{return impact} \approx -\text{ modified duration} \times \Delta\text{spread}$$

The negative sign in the equation reflects the inverse relationship between prices and yields. As spreads widen (the change in spread is positive), bond prices decrease and the impact on return is negative. As spreads narrow (the change in spread is negative), bond prices increase and the impact on return is positive.

For larger spread changes, incorporating convexity improves the accuracy of return impact measurement.

$$\text{return impact} \approx -\text{ modified duration} \times \Delta\text{spread} + \frac{1}{2}\text{convexity} \times (\Delta\text{spread})^2$$

> *Professor's Note: Make sure the value of convexity is scaled correctly. For option-free bonds, convexity should be on the same order of magnitude as <u>modified duration squared</u>. For example, if you are given that duration is 6.0 and convexity is 0.562, duration squared is 36.0 and the correctly scaled convexity is 56.2.*

> *Also notice that convexity is divided in half here, but was not divided in half when we adjusted for convexity in an earlier topic review. This is because different authors calculate convexity differently. For the exam, use one-half times convexity if a question asks for the return impact of a change in spread.*

Longer maturity bonds have higher duration and consequently higher spread sensitivity; their prices and returns are more sensitive to changes in spread. The longer the maturity, the higher the uncertainty of the future creditworthiness of the debt issuer, implying higher credit spreads for longer maturity bonds. Longer maturity bonds also tend to have larger bid-ask spreads (i.e., higher transaction costs), implying investors in longer maturity bonds would require higher spreads.

Credit curves or *spread curves* show the relationship between spread and maturity. Because longer maturity bonds tend to have wider spreads, credit curves are typically upward sloping.

Bond performance is positively affected by narrowing credit spreads and negatively affected by widening credit spreads. To enhance bond portfolio performance, active bond managers need to forecast spread changes and expected credit losses for individual issues held and for the overall bond portfolio.

Example: Impact on return

An 8-year semiannual-pay corporate bond with a 5.75% coupon is priced at $108.32. This bond's duration and reported convexity are 6.4 and 0.5. The bond's credit spread narrows by 75 basis points due to a credit rating upgrade. Estimate the return impact with and without the convexity adjustment.

Answer:

$$\text{return impact (without convexity adjustment)} \approx -\text{ modified duration} \times \Delta\text{spread}$$
$$\approx -6.4 \times -0.0075$$
$$\approx 0.0480$$
$$\approx 0.048 \text{ or } \mathbf{4.80\%}$$

return impact with convexity adjustment

$$\approx -\text{ modified duration} \times \Delta\text{spread} + \frac{1}{2}\text{convexity} \times (\Delta\text{spread})^2$$
$$\approx -6.4 \times -0.0075 + \frac{1}{2}(50.0) \times (-0.0075)^2$$
$$\approx 0.0480 + 0.0014$$
$$\approx 0.0494 \text{ or } \mathbf{4.94\%}$$

Notice that convexity needed to be corrected to match the scale of duration.

We can calculate the actual change in the bond's price from the information given to illustrate the need for the convexity adjustment.

Beginning yield to maturity:

N = 16; PMT = 5.75 / 2 = 2.875; FV = 100; PV = −108.32;
CPT → I/Y = 2.25 × 2 = 4.50

Yield to maturity after upgrade: 4.50 − 0.75 = 3.75%

Price after upgrade:

I/Y = 3.75 / 2 = 1.875; CPT → PV = −113.71

The calculated bond price of $113.71 is an increase of (113.71 / 108.32) − 1 = 4.98%. The approximation is closer with the convexity adjustment.

LOS 59.j: Explain special considerations when evaluating the credit of high yield, sovereign, and municipal debt issuers and issues.

CFA® Program Curriculum, Volume 5, page 650

High Yield Debt

High yield or *non-investment grade* corporate bonds are rated below Baa3/BBB by credit rating agencies. These bonds are also called *junk bonds* because of their higher perceived credit risk.

Reasons for non-investment grade ratings may include:

- High leverage.
- Unproven operating history.
- Low or negative free cash flow.
- High sensitivity to business cycles.
- Low confidence in management.
- Unclear competitive advantages.
- Large off-balance-sheet liabilities.
- Industry in decline.

Because high yield bonds have higher default risk than investment grade bonds, credit analysts must pay more attention to loss severity. Special considerations for high yield bonds include their liquidity, financial projections, debt structure, corporate structure, and covenants.

Liquidity. Liquidity or availability of cash is critical for high yield issuers. High yield issuers have limited access to additional borrowings, and available funds tend to be more expensive for high yield issuers. Bad company-specific news and difficult financial market conditions can quickly dry up the liquidity of debt markets. Many high yield issuers are privately owned and cannot access public equity markets for needed funds.

Analysts focus on six sources of liquidity (in order of reliability):

1. Balance sheet cash.

2. Working capital.

3. Operating cash flow (CFO).

4. Bank credit.

5. Equity issued.

6. Sales of assets.

For a high yield issuer with few or unreliable sources of liquidity, significant amounts of debt coming due within a short time frame may indicate potential default. Running out of cash with no access to external financing to refinance or service existing debt is the primary reason why high yield issuers default. For high yield financial firms that are highly levered and depend on funding long-term assets with short-term liabilities, liquidity is critical.

Financial projections. Projecting future earnings and cash flows, including stress scenarios and accounting for changes in capital expenditures and working capital, are important for revealing potential vulnerabilities to the inability to meet debt payments.

Debt structure. High yield issuers' capital structures often include different types of debt with several levels of seniority and hence varying levels of potential loss severity. Capital structures typically include secured bank debt, second lien debt, senior unsecured debt, subordinated debt, and preferred stock. Some of these, especially subordinated debt, may be convertible to common shares.

A credit analyst will need to calculate leverage for each level of the debt structure when an issuer has multiple layers of debt with a variety of expected recovery rates.

High yield companies for which secured bank debt is a high proportion of the capital structure are said to be *top heavy* and have less capacity to borrow from banks in financially stressful periods. Companies that have top-heavy capital structures are more likely to default and have lower recovery rates for unsecured debt issues.

Example: Debt structure and leverage

Two European high yield companies in the same industry have the following financial information:

In € million	A	B
Cash	100.0	50.0
Interest expense	40.0	20.0
EBITDA	85.0	42.5
Secured bank debt	500.0	125.0
Senior unsecured debt	200.0	50.0
Convertible bonds	50.0	200.0

1. Calculate total leverage through each level of debt for both companies.

2. Calculate net leverage for both companies.

3. Comment on which company is more attractive to an unsecured debt investor.

Answer:

	A	B
Secured debt leverage: secured debt/EBITDA	500.0 / 85.0 = 5.9x	125.0 / 42.5 = 2.9x
Senior unsecured leverage: (secured + senior unsecured debt)/EBITDA	(500.0 + 200.0) / 85.0 = 8.2x	(125.0 + 50.0) / 42.5 = 4.1x
Total debt leverage: total debt/EBITDA	(500.0 + 200.0 + 50.0) / 85.0 = 8.8x	(125.0 + 50.0 + 200.0) / 42.5= 8.8x
Net leverage: (total debt – cash)/ EBITDA	(750.0 – 100.0) / 85.0 = 7.6x	(375.0 – 50.0) / 42.5 = 7.6x

Company B has a lower secured debt leverage ratio than Company A, while total and net leverage ratios are about the same. Company B is more attractive to unsecured debt holders because it is less top heavy and may have some capacity to borrow from banks, which suggests a lower probability of default. If it does default, Company B may have a higher percentage of assets available to unsecured debt holders than Company A, especially if holders of convertible bonds have exercised their options.

Corporate structure. Many high-yield companies use a holding company structure. A parent company receives dividends from the earnings of subsidiaries as its primary source of operating income. Because of structural subordination, subsidiaries' dividends paid upstream to a parent company are subordinate to interest payments. These dividends can be insufficient to pay the debt obligations of the parent, thus reducing the recovery rate for debt holders of the parent company.

Despite structural subordination, a parent company's credit rating may be superior to subsidiaries' ratings because the parent can benefit from having access to multiple cash flows from diverse subsidiaries.

Some complex corporate structures have intermediate holding companies that carry their own debt and do not own 100% of their subsidiaries' stock. These companies are typically a result of mergers, acquisitions, or leveraged buyouts.

Default of one subsidiary may not necessarily result in cross default. Analysts need to scrutinize bonds' indentures and other legal documents to fully understand the impact of complex corporate structures. To analyze these companies, analysts should calculate leverage ratios at each level of debt issuance and on a consolidated basis.

Covenants. Important covenants for high yield debt include:

- **Change of control put.** This covenant gives debt holders the right to require the issuer to buy back debt (typically for par value or a value slightly above par) in the event of an acquisition. For investment grade bonds, a change of control put typically applies only if an acquisition of the borrower results in a rating downgrade to below investment grade.

- **Restricted payments.** The covenant protects lenders by limiting the amount of cash that may be paid to equity holders.
- **Limitations on liens.** The covenant limits the amount of secured debt that a borrower can carry. Unsecured debt holders prefer the issuer to have less secured debt, which increases the recovery amount available to them in the event of default.
- **Restricted versus unrestricted subsidiaries.** Issuers can classify subsidiaries as restricted or unrestricted. Restricted subsidiaries' cash flows and assets can be used to service the debt of the parent holding company. This benefits creditors of holding companies because their debt is pari passu with the debt of restricted subsidiaries, rather than structurally subordinated. Restricted subsidiaries are typically the holding company's larger subsidiaries that have significant assets. Tax and regulatory issues can factor into the classification of subsidiary's restriction status. A subsidiary's restriction status is found in the bond indenture.

Bank covenants are often more restrictive than bond covenants, and when covenants are violated, banks can block additional loans until the violation is corrected. If a violation is not remedied, banks can trigger a default by accelerating the full repayment of a loan.

In terms of the factors that affect their return, high yield bonds may be viewed as a hybrid of investment grade bonds and equity. Compared to investment grade bonds, high yield bonds show greater price and spread volatility and are more highly correlated with the equity market.

High yield analysis can include some of the same techniques as equity market analysis, such as enterprise value. **Enterprise value** (EV) is equity market capitalization plus total debt minus excess cash. For high yield companies that are not publicly traded, comparable public company equity data can be used to estimate EV. Enterprise value analysis can indicate a firm's potential for additional leverage, or the potential credit damage that might result from a leveraged buyout. An analyst can compare firms based on the differences between their EV/EBITDA and debt/EBITDA ratios. Firms with a wider difference between these ratios have greater equity relative to their debt and therefore have less credit risk.

Sovereign Debt

Sovereign debt is issued by national governments. Sovereign credit analysis must assess both the government's ability to service debt and its willingness to do so. The assessment of willingness is important because bondholders usually have no legal recourse if a national government refuses to pay its debts.

A basic framework for evaluating and assigning a credit rating to sovereign debt includes five key areas:

1. **Institutional effectiveness** includes successful policymaking, absence of corruption, and commitment to honor debts.

2. **Economic prospects** include growth trends, demographics, income per capita, and size of government relative to the private economy.

3. **International investment position** includes the country's foreign reserves, its external debt, and the status of its currency in international markets.

4. **Fiscal flexibility** includes the government's willingness and ability to increase revenue or cut expenditures to ensure debt service, as well as trends in debt as a percentage of GDP.

5. **Monetary flexibility** includes the ability to use monetary policy for domestic economic objectives (this might be lacking with exchange rate targeting or membership in a monetary union) and the credibility and effectiveness of monetary policy.

Credit rating agencies assign each national government two ratings: (1) a local currency debt rating and (2) a foreign currency debt rating. The ratings are assigned separately because defaults on foreign currency denominated debt have historically exceeded those on local currency debt. Foreign currency debt typically has a higher default rate and a lower credit rating because the government must purchase foreign currency in the open market to make interest and principal payments, which exposes it to the risk of significant local currency depreciation. In contrast, local currency debt can be repaid by raising taxes, controlling domestic spending, or simply printing more money. Ratings can differ as much as two notches for local and foreign currency bonds.

Sovereign defaults can be caused by events such as war, political instability, severe devaluation of the currency, or large declines in the prices of the country's export commodities. Access to debt markets can be difficult for sovereigns in bad economic times.

Municipal Debt

Municipal bonds are issued by state and local governments or their agencies. Municipal bonds usually have lower default rates than corporate bonds with same credit ratings.

Most municipal bonds can be classified as *general obligation bonds* or *revenue bonds*. **General obligation** (GO) bonds are unsecured bonds backed by the full faith credit of the issuing governmental entity, which is to say they are supported by its taxing power.

Unlike sovereigns, municipalities cannot use monetary policy to service their debt and usually must balance their operating budgets. Municipal governments' ability to service their general obligation debt depends ultimately on the local economy (i.e., the tax base). Economic factors to assess include employment, trends in per capita income and per capita debt, tax base dimensions (depth, breadth and stability), demographics, and ability to attract new jobs (location, infrastructure). Credit analysts must also observe revenue variability through economic cycles. Relying on highly variable taxes that are subject to economic cycles, such as capital gains and sales taxes, can signal higher credit risk. Municipalities may have long-term obligations such as underfunded pensions and post-retirement benefits. Inconsistent reporting requirements for municipalities are also an issue.

Revenue bonds finance specific projects. Revenue bonds often have higher credit risk than GO bonds because the project is the sole source of funds to service the debt.

Analysis of revenue bonds combines analysis of the project, using techniques similar to those for analyzing corporate bonds, with analysis of the financing of the project.

A key metric for revenue bonds is the **debt service coverage ratio** (DSCR), which is the ratio of the project's net revenue to the required interest and principal payments on the bonds. Many revenue bonds include a covenant requiring a minimum debt service coverage ratio to protect the lenders' interests. Lenders prefer higher debt service coverage ratios, as this represents lower default risk (better creditworthiness).

KEY CONCEPTS

LOS 59.a

Credit risk refers to the possibility that a borrower fails to make the scheduled interest payments or return of principal. Credit risk is composed of default risk, which is the probability of default, and loss severity, which is the portion of the value of a bond or loan a lender or investor will lose if the borrower defaults. The expected loss is the probability of default multiplied by the loss severity.

Spread risk is the possibility that a bond loses value because its credit spread widens relative to its benchmark. Spread risk includes credit migration or downgrade risk and market liquidity risk.

LOS 59.b

Corporate debt is ranked by seniority or priority of claims. Secured debt is a direct claim on specific firm assets and has priority over unsecured debt. Secured or unsecured debt may be further ranked as senior or subordinated. Priority of claims may be summarized as follows:

- First mortgage or first lien.
- Second or subsequent lien.
- Senior secured debt.
- Senior subordinated debt.
- Senior unsecured debt.
- Subordinated debt.
- Junior subordinated debt.

LOS 59.c

Issuer credit ratings, or corporate family ratings, reflect a debt issuer's overall creditworthiness and typically apply to a firm's senior unsecured debt.

Issue credit ratings, or corporate credit ratings, reflect the credit risk of a specific debt issue. Notching refers to the practice of adjusting an issue credit rating upward or downward from the issuer credit rating to reflect the seniority and other provisions of a debt issue.

LOS 59.d

Lenders and bond investors should not rely exclusively on credit ratings from rating agencies for the following reasons:

- Credit ratings can change during the life of a debt issue.
- Rating agencies cannot always judge credit risk accurately.
- Firms are subject to risk of unforeseen events that credit ratings do not reflect.
- Market prices of bonds often adjust more rapidly than credit ratings.

LOS 59.e

Components of traditional credit analysis are known as the four Cs:

- Capacity: The borrower's ability to make timely payments on its debt.
- Collateral: The value of assets pledged against a debt issue or available to creditors if the issuer defaults.
- Covenants: Provisions of a bond issue that protect creditors by requiring or prohibiting actions by an issuer's management.
- Character: Assessment of an issuer's management, strategy, quality of earnings, and past treatment of bondholders.

LOS 59.f

Credit analysts use profitability, cash flow, and leverage and coverage ratios to assess debt issuers' capacity.

- Profitability refers to operating income and operating profit margin, with operating income typically defined as earnings before interest and taxes (EBIT).
- Cash flow may be measured as earnings before interest, taxes, depreciation, and amortization (EBITDA); funds from operations (FFO); free cash flow before dividends; or free cash flow after dividends.
- Leverage ratios include debt-to-capital, debt-to-EBITDA, and FFO-to-debt.
- Coverage ratios include EBIT-to-interest expense and EBITDA-to-interest expense.

LOS 59.g

Lower leverage, higher interest coverage, and greater free cash flow imply lower credit risk and a higher credit rating for a firm. When calculating leverage ratios, analysts should include in a firm's total debt its obligations such as underfunded pensions and off-balance-sheet financing.

For a specific debt issue, secured collateral implies lower credit risk compared to unsecured debt, and higher seniority implies lower credit risk compared to lower seniority.

LOS 59.h

Corporate bond yields comprise the real risk-free rate, expected inflation rate, credit spread, maturity premium, and liquidity premium. An issue's yield spread to its benchmark includes its credit spread and liquidity premium.

The level and volatility of yield spreads are affected by the credit and business cycles, the performance of financial markets as a whole, availability of capital from broker-dealers, and supply and demand for debt issues. Yield spreads tend to narrow when the credit cycle is improving, the economy is expanding, and financial markets and investor demand for new debt issues are strong. Yield spreads tend to widen when the credit cycle, the economy, and financial markets are weakening, and in periods when the supply of new debt issues is heavy or broker-dealer capital is insufficient for market making.

LOS 59.i
Analysts can use duration and convexity to estimate the impact on return (the percentage change in bond price) of a change in credit spread.

For small spread changes:

$$\text{return impact} \approx -\text{duration} \times \Delta\text{spread}$$

For larger spread changes:

$$\text{return impact} \approx -\text{duration} \times \Delta\text{spread} + \frac{1}{2}\text{convexity} \times (\Delta\text{spread})^2$$

LOS 59.j
High yield bonds are more likely to default than investment grade bonds, which increases the importance of estimating loss severity. Analysis of high yield debt should focus on liquidity, projected financial performance, the issuer's corporate and debt structures, and debt covenants.

Credit risk of sovereign debt includes the issuing country's ability and willingness to pay. Ability to pay is greater for debt issued in the country's own currency than for debt issued in a foreign currency. Willingness refers to the possibility that a country refuses to repay its debts.

Analysis of general obligation municipal debt is similar to analysis of sovereign debt, focusing on the strength of the local economy and its effect on tax revenues. Analysis of municipal revenue bonds is similar to analysis of corporate debt, focusing on the ability of a project to generate sufficient revenue to service the bonds.

CONCEPT CHECKERS

1. Expected loss can decrease with an increase in a bond's:
    A. default risk.
    B. loss severity.
    C. recovery rate.

2. Absolute priority of claims in a bankruptcy might be violated because:
    A. of the *pari passu* principle.
    B. creditors negotiate a different outcome.
    C. available funds must be distributed equally among creditors.

3. "Notching" is *best* described as a difference between a(n):
    A. issuer credit rating and an issue credit rating.
    B. company credit rating and an industry average credit rating.
    C. investment grade credit rating and a non-investment grade credit rating.

4. Which of the following statements is *least likely* a limitation of relying on ratings from credit rating agencies?
    A. Credit ratings are dynamic.
    B. Firm-specific risks are difficult to rate.
    C. Credit ratings adjust quickly to changes in bond prices.

5. Ratio analysis is *most likely* used to assess a borrower's:
    A. capacity.
    B. character.
    C. collateral.

6. Higher credit risk is indicated by a higher:
    A. FFO/debt ratio.
    B. debt/EBITDA ratio.
    C. EBITDA/interest expense ratio.

7. Compared to other firms in the same industry, an issuer with a credit rating of AAA should have a lower:
    A. FFO/debt ratio.
    B. operating margin.
    C. debt/capital ratio.

8. Credit spreads tend to widen as:
    A. the credit cycle improves.
    B. economic conditions worsen.
    C. broker-dealers become more willing to provide capital.

9. Compared to shorter duration bonds, longer duration bonds:
    A. have smaller bid-ask spreads.
    B. are less sensitive to credit spreads.
    C. have less certainty regarding future creditworthiness.

10. One key difference between sovereign bonds and municipal bonds is that sovereign issuers:
    A. can print money.
    B. have governmental taxing power.
    C. are affected by economic conditions.

CHALLENGE PROBLEM

Woden, Inc., is a high yield bond issuer with a credit rating of Ba2/BB. Woden presents the following balance sheet for the most recent year (in millions of dollars):

Cash	10	Accounts payable	10
Accounts receivable	15	Short-term debt	5
Inventories	55	Current portion of long-term debt	3
Current assets	80	Current liabilities	18
Land	10	Long-term bank loans	30
Property, plant, and equipment, net	85	Secured bonds	10
Goodwill	25	Unsecured bonds	20
Non-current assets	120	Total long-term debt	60
Total assets	200	Net pension liability	22
		Total liabilities	100
		Paid-in capital	10
		Retained earnings	90
		Total shareholders' equity	100
		Total liabilities and equity	200

For the year, Woden's earnings before interest, taxes, depreciation, and amortization (EBITDA) were $45 million.

For firms in Woden's industry, credit rating standards for an investment grade (Baa3/BBB–) credit rating include a debt-to-EBITDA ratio less than 1.8× and a debt-to-capital ratio (based on all sources of financing) less than 40%. On a conference call with analysts, Woden's management states that they believe Woden should be upgraded to investment grade, based on its debt-to-EBITDA ratio of 1.5× and its debt-to-capital ratio of 34%.

Why might a credit analyst disagree with management's assessment?

ANSWERS – CONCEPT CHECKERS

1. **C** An increase in the recovery rate means that the loss severity has decreased, which decreases expected loss.

2. **B** A negotiated bankruptcy settlement does not always follow the absolute priority of claims.

3. **A** Notching refers to the credit rating agency practice of distinguishing between the credit rating of an issuer (generally for its senior unsecured debt) and the credit rating of particular debt issues from that issuer, which may differ from the issuer rating because of provisions such as seniority.

4. **C** Bond prices and credit spreads change much faster than credit ratings.

5. **A** Ratio analysis is used to assess a corporate borrower's capacity to repay its debt obligations on time.

6. **B** A higher debt/EBITDA ratio is sign of higher leverage and higher credit risk. Higher FFO/debt and EBITDA/interest expense ratios indicate lower credit risk.

7. **C** A low debt/capital ratio is an indicator of low leverage. An issuer rated AAA is likely to have a high operating margin and a high FFO/debt ratio compared to its industry group.

8. **B** Credit spreads widen as economic conditions worsen. Spreads narrow as the credit cycle improves and as broker-dealers provide more capital to bond markets.

9. **C** Longer duration bonds usually have longer maturities and carry more uncertainty of future creditworthiness.

10. **A** Sovereign entities can print money to repay debt, while municipal borrowers cannot. Both sovereign and municipal entities have taxing powers, and both are affected by economic conditions.

ANSWERS – CHALLENGE PROBLEM

The debt ratios calculated by management are based on the firm's short-term and long-term debt:

Total debt = 5 + 3 + 30 + 10 + 20 = 68

Debt/EBITDA = 68 / 45 = 1.5×

Debt/capital = 68 / 200 = 34%

A credit analyst, however, should add Woden's net pension liability to its total debt:

Debt + net pension liability = 68 + 22 = 90

Adjusted debt/EBITDA = 90 / 45 = 2.0×

Adjusted debt/capital = 90 / 200 = 45%

Additionally, a credit analyst may calculate what the debt-to-capital ratio would be if Woden wrote down the value of its balance sheet goodwill and reduced retained earnings by the same amount:

Adjusted capital = 200 – 25 = 175

Adjusted debt / adjusted capital = 90 / 175 = 51%

These adjustments suggest Woden does not meet the requirements for an investment grade credit rating.

14 questions, 21 minutes

1. An estimate of the price change for an option-free bond caused by a 1% decline in its yield to maturity based only on its modified duration will result in an answer that:
   A. is too small.
   B. is too large.
   C. may be too small or too large.

2. Three companies in the same industry have exhibited the following average ratios over a 5-year period:

5-Year Averages	Alden	Barrow	Collison
Operating margin	13.3%	15.0%	20.7%
Debt/EBITDA	4.6×	0.9×	2.8×
EBIT/Interest	3.6×	8.9×	5.7×
FFO/Debt	12.5%	14.6%	11.5%
Debt/Capital	60.8%	23.6%	29.6%

   Based only on the information given, the company that is expected to have the highest credit rating is:
   A. Alden.
   B. Barrow.
   C. Collison.

3. Which statement about the theories of the term structure of interest rates is *most accurate*?
   A. Under the liquidity preference theory, the yield curve will be positively sloped.
   B. A yield curve that slopes up and then down (humped) is consistent with the market segmentation theory but not with the pure expectations theory.
   C. Evidence that life insurance companies have a strong preference for 30-year bonds supports the market segmentation theory.

4. Which of the following is *least likely* a common form of external credit enhancement?
   A. Portfolio insurance.
   B. A corporate guarantee.
   C. A letter of credit from a bank.

5. A bond with an embedded put option has a modified duration of 7, an effective duration of 6 and a convexity of 62.5. If interest rates rise 25 basis points, the bond's price will change by *approximately*:
   A. 1.46%.
   B. 1.50%.
   C. 1.54%.

6. Which of the following bonds would be the best one to own if the yield curve shifts down by 50 basis points at all maturities?
    A. 4-year 8%, 8% YTM.
    B. 5-year 8%, 7.5% YTM.
    C. 5-year 8.5%, 8% YTM.

7. Which of the following provisions would *most likely* decrease the yield to maturity on a debt security?
    A. Call option.
    B. Conversion option.
    C. Cap on a floating-rate security.

8. Other things equal, a corporate bond's yield spread is likely to be *most* volatile if the bond is rated:
    A. AA with 5 years to maturity.
    B. AAA with 3 years to maturity.
    C. BBB with 15 years to maturity.

9. The effects of a decrease in interest rate (yield) volatility on the market yield of a debt security with a prepayment option and on a debt security with a put option are *most likely* a(n):

	Prepayment option	Put option
A.	Increase	Decrease
B.	Decrease	Increase
C.	Decrease	Decrease

10. Bond A has an embedded option, a nominal yield spread to Treasuries of 1.6%, a zero-volatility spread of 1.4%, and an option-adjusted spread of 1.2%. Bond B is identical to Bond A except that it does not have the embedded option, has a nominal yield spread to Treasuries of 1.4%, a zero-volatility spread of 1.3%, and an option-adjusted spread of 1.3%. The *most likely* option embedded in Bond A, and the bond that is the better value, are:

	Embedded option	Better value
A.	Put	Bond A
B.	Call	Bond A
C.	Call	Bond B

11. A bank loan department is trying to determine the correct rate for a 2-year loan to be made two years from now. If current implied Treasury effective annual spot rates are: 1-year = 2%, 2-year = 3%, 3-year = 3.5%, 4-year = 4.5%, the base (risk-free) forward rate for the loan before adding a risk premium is *closest* to:
    A. 4.5%.
    B. 6.0%.
    C. 9.0%.

12. Compared to mortgage passthrough securities, CMOs created from them *most likely* have:
    A. less prepayment risk.
    B. greater average yields.
    C. a different claim to the mortgage cash flows.

13. The arbitrage-free approach to bond valuation *most likely*:
    A. can only be applied to Treasury securities.
    B. requires each cash flow to be discounted at a rate specific to its time period.
    C. shows that discounting each cash flow at the yield to maturity must result in the correct value for a bond.

14. Which of the following statements *least accurately* describes a form of risk associated with investing in fixed income securities?
    A. Credit risk has only two components, default risk and downgrade risk.
    B. Other things equal, a bond is more valuable to an investor when it has less liquidity risk.
    C. Bonds that are callable, prepayable, or amortizing have more reinvestment risk than otherwise equivalent bonds without these features.

SELF-TEST ANSWERS: FIXED INCOME INVESTMENTS

1. **A** Duration is a linear measure, but the relationship between bond price and yield for an option-free bond is convex. For a given decrease in yield, the estimated price increase using duration alone will be smaller than the actual price increase.

2. **B** Four of the five credit metrics given indicate that Barrow should have the highest credit rating of these three companies. Barrow has higher interest coverage and lower leverage than Alden or Collison.

3. **C** The market segmentation theory is based on the idea that different market participants (both borrowers and lenders) have strong preferences for different segments of the yield curve. If expectations are that future short-term interest rates will be falling enough, then the yield curve could be downward sloping even given that there is an increasing premium for lack of liquidity at longer maturities. A humped yield curve is consistent with expectations that short-term rates will rise over the near term and then decline.

4. **A** External credit enhancements are financial guarantees from third parties that generally support the performance of the bond. Portfolio insurance is not a third party guarantee.

5. **A** Effective duration must be used with bonds that have embedded options.

   $$\Delta P = (-)(ED)(\Delta y) + (C)(\Delta y)^2$$

   $$\Delta P = (-)(6)(0.0025) + (62.5)(0.0025)^2 = -0.015 + 0.00039 = -0.014610\% \text{ or } -1.461\%$$

6. **B** The bond with the highest duration will benefit the most from a decrease in rates. The lower the coupon, lower the yield to maturity, and longer the time to maturity, the higher will be the duration.

7. **B** A conversion provision is an embedded option that favors the buyer, not the issuer, so buyers will accept a lower YTM with a conversion option. Call options and caps favor the issuer and increase the YTM that buyers will require.

8. **C** Spread volatility is typically greatest for lower quality and longer maturities. The BBB rated 15-year corporate bond has the lowest credit quality and longest maturity of the three choices.

9. **B** A decrease in yield volatility will decrease the values of embedded options. The security holder is short the prepayment option. The decrease in the value of the prepayment option increases the value of the security, and the required yield will decrease. The security holder is long the put option so the value of a putable bond will decrease with a decrease in yield volatility and the required yield will increase.

10. **C** Since the OAS is less than the *Z*-spread for Bond A, the effect of the embedded option is to increase the required yield, so it must be a call option and not a put option. The OAS is the spread after taking out the effect of the embedded option. Since the OAS is higher for Bond B, it represents the better value after adjusting for the value of the call in Bond A.

11. **B**   The forward rate is $[1.045^4 / 1.03^2]^{1/2} - 1 = 6.02\%$, or use the approximation $[4.5(4) - 3(2)]/2 = 6$.

12. **C**   CMOs are created to have different claims to the cash flows (principal, scheduled repayments, prepayments) than those of the underlying mortgage passthrough securities. On average, the yield will likely be lower on the CMO, since the reason to create them is to lower overall funding costs. They can have more or less prepayment risk, but on average will have the same prepayment risk as the underlying MBS.

13. **B**   The arbitrage-free valuation approach discounts each cash flow at a discount rate specific to its maturity. For Treasury securities these discount rates are theoretical Treasury spot rates. For non-Treasury securities, these discount rates are Treasury spot rates plus a spread to account for liquidity risk, credit risk, and any other relevant risks that differ from those of a Treasury bond of similar maturity.

14. **A**   Even if a bond does not default and is not downgraded, it still faces credit spread risk as the premium in the market for the bond's credit risk may increase. Lower liquidity risk (i.e., higher liquidity) is preferred by investors, reduces a bond's required rate of return, and increases its value, other things equal. Reinvestment risk is higher for callable, prepayable, or amortizing bonds as all these features lead to a greater probability of receiving principal repayment earlier, which means there are more funds to be reinvested over the life of the bond.

DERIVATIVE MARKETS AND INSTRUMENTS

Study Session 17

EXAM FOCUS

This topic review contains introductory material for the upcoming reviews of specific types of derivatives. Derivatives-specific definitions and terminology are presented along with information about derivatives markets. Upon completion of this review, candidates should be familiar with the basic concepts that underlie derivatives and the general arbitrage framework. There is little contained in this review that will not be elaborated upon in the five reviews that follow.

LOS 60.a: Define a derivative and distinguish between exchange-traded and over-the-counter derivatives.

CFA® Program Curriculum, Volume 6, page 5

A **derivative** is a security that *derives* its value from the value or return of another asset or security.

A physical exchange exists for many options contracts and futures contracts. **Exchange-traded derivatives** are standardized and backed by a clearinghouse.

Forwards and *swaps* are custom instruments and are traded/created by dealers in a market with no central location. A dealer market with no central location is referred to as an **over-the-counter** market. They are largely unregulated markets and each contract is with a counterparty, which may expose the owner of a derivative to default risk (when the counterparty does not honor their commitment).

Some *options* trade in the over-the-counter market, notably bond options.

LOS 60.b: Contrast forward commitments and contingent claims.

CFA® Program Curriculum, Volume 6, page 6

A **forward commitment** is a legally binding promise to perform some action in the future. Forward commitments include forward contracts, futures contracts, and swaps. Forward contracts and futures contracts can be written on equities, indexes, bonds, physical assets, or interest rates.

A **contingent claim** is a claim (to a payoff) that depends on a particular event. **Options** are contingent claims that depend on a stock price at some future date. While forwards, futures, and swaps have payments that are made based on a price or rate outcome whether the movement is up or down, contingent claims only require a payment if a certain threshold price is broken (e.g., if the price is above X or the rate is below Y). It takes two options to replicate a future or forward.

LOS 60.c: Define forward contracts, futures contracts, options (calls and puts), and swaps and compare their basic characteristics.

CFA® Program Curriculum, Volume 6, page 6

In a **forward contract**, one party agrees to buy, and the counterparty to sell, a physical asset or a security at a specific price on a specific date in the future. If the future price of the asset increases, the buyer (at the older, lower price) has a gain, and the seller a loss.

A **futures contract** is a forward contract that is standardized and exchange-traded. The main differences with forwards are that futures are traded in an active secondary market, are regulated, backed by the clearinghouse, and require a daily settlement of gains and losses.

A **swap** is a series of forward contracts. In the simplest swap, one party agrees to pay the short-term (floating) rate of interest on some principal amount, and the counterparty agrees to pay a certain (fixed) rate of interest in return. Swaps of different currencies and equity returns are also common.

An option to buy an asset at a particular price is termed a **call option**. The seller of the option has an *obligation* to sell the asset at the agreed-upon price, if the call buyer chooses to exercise the right to buy the asset.

An option to sell an asset at a particular price is termed a **put option**. The seller of the option has an *obligation* to purchase the asset at the agreed-upon price, if the put buyer chooses to exercise the right to sell the asset.

 Professor's Note: To remember these terms, note that the owner of a call can "call the asset in" (i.e., buy it); the owner of a put has the right to "put the asset to" the writer of the put.

LOS 60.d: Describe purposes of and controversies related to derivative markets.

CFA® Program Curriculum, Volume 6, page 17

The *criticism of derivatives* is that they are "too risky," especially to investors with limited knowledge of sometimes complex instruments. Because of the high leverage involved in derivatives payoffs, they are sometimes likened to gambling.

The *benefits of derivatives* markets are that they:

- Provide price information.
- Allow risk to be managed and shifted among market participants.
- Reduce transactions costs.

LOS 60.e: Explain arbitrage and the role it plays in determining prices and promoting market efficiency.

CFA® Program Curriculum, Volume 6, page 20

Arbitrage is an important concept in valuing (pricing) derivative securities. In its purest sense, arbitrage is riskless. If a return greater than the risk-free rate can be earned by holding a portfolio of assets that produces a certain (riskless) return, then an arbitrage opportunity exists.

Arbitrage opportunities arise when assets are mispriced. Trading by arbitrageurs will continue until they affect supply and demand enough to bring asset prices to efficient (no-arbitrage) levels.

There are two arbitrage arguments that are particularly useful in the study and use of derivatives.

The first is based on the **law of one price**. Two securities or portfolios that have identical cash flows in the future, regardless of future events, should have the same price. If A and B have the identical future payoffs, and A is priced lower than B, buy A and sell B. You have an immediate profit, and the payoff on A will satisfy the (future) liability of being short on B.

The second type of arbitrage is used where two securities with uncertain returns can be combined in a portfolio that will have a certain payoff. If a portfolio consisting of A and B has a certain payoff, the portfolio should yield the risk-free rate. If this no-arbitrage condition is violated in that the certain return of A and B together is higher than the risk-free rate, an arbitrage opportunity exists. An arbitrageur could borrow at the risk-free rate, buy the A + B portfolio, and earn arbitrage profits when the certain payoff occurs. The payoff will be more than is required to pay back the loan at the risk-free rate.

 Professor's Note: We will discuss arbitrage further in our review of options.

KEY CONCEPTS

LOS 60.a
A derivative has a value that is derived from the value of another asset or interest rate.

Exchange-traded derivatives, notably futures and some options, are traded in centralized locations and are standardized, regulated, and default risk free.

Forwards and swaps are customized contracts (over-the-counter derivatives) created by dealers and by financial institutions. There is very limited trading of these contracts in secondary markets and default (counterparty) risk must be considered.

LOS 60.b
A forward commitment is a binding promise to buy or sell an asset or make a payment in the future. Forward contracts, futures contracts, and swaps are all forward commitments.

A contingent claim is an asset that has value only if some future event takes place (e.g., asset price is greater than a specified price). Options are contingent claims.

LOS 60.c
Forward contracts obligate one party to buy, and another to sell, a specific asset at a predetermined price at a specific time in the future.

Swaps contracts are equivalent to a series of forward contracts on interest rates, currencies, or equity returns.

Futures contracts are much like forward contracts, but are exchange-traded, quite liquid, and require daily settlement of any gains or losses.

A call option gives the holder the right, but not the obligation, to buy an asset at a predetermined price at some time in the future.

A put option gives the holder the right, but not the obligation, to sell an asset at a predetermined price at some time in the future.

LOS 60.d
Derivative markets are criticized for their risky nature. However, many market participants use derivatives to manage and reduce existing risk exposures.

Derivative securities play an important role in promoting efficient market prices and reducing transaction costs.

LOS 60.e
Riskless arbitrage refers to earning more than the risk-free rate of return with no risk, or earning an immediate gain with no possible future liability.

Arbitrage can be expected to force the prices of two securities or portfolios of securities to be equal if they have the same future cash flows regardless of future events.

CONCEPT CHECKERS

1. Which of the following *most accurately* describes a derivative security?
    A derivative:
    A. always increases risk.
    B. has no expiration date.
    C. has a payoff based on another asset.

2. Which of the following statements about exchange-traded derivatives is *least accurate*?
    A. They are liquid.
    B. They are standardized contracts.
    C. They carry significant default risk.

3. A customized agreement to purchase a certain T-bond next Thursday for $1,000 is:
    A. an option.
    B. a futures contract.
    C. a forward commitment.

4. A swap is:
    A. highly regulated.
    B. a series of forward contracts.
    C. the exchange of one asset for another.

5. A call option gives the holder:
    A. the right to sell at a specific price.
    B. the right to buy at a specific price.
    C. an obligation to sell at a certain price.

6. Arbitrage prevents:
    A. market efficiency.
    B. profit higher than the risk-free rate of return.
    C. two assets with identical payoffs from selling at different prices.

7. Derivatives are *least likely* to provide or improve:
    A. liquidity.
    B. price information.
    C. inflation reduction.

ANSWERS – CONCEPT CHECKERS

1. **C** A derivative's value is derived from another asset.

2. **C** Exchange-traded derivatives have relatively low default risk because the clearinghouse stands between the counterparties involved in most contracts.

3. **C** This non-standardized type of contract is a forward commitment.

4. **B** A swap is an agreement to buy or sell an underlying asset periodically over the life of the swap contract. It is equivalent to a series of forward contracts.

5. **B** A call gives the owner the right to call an asset away (buy it) from the seller.

6. **C** Arbitrage forces two assets with the same expected future value to sell for the same current price. If this were not the case, you could simultaneously buy the cheaper asset and sell the more expensive one for a guaranteed riskless profit.

7. **C** Inflation is a monetary phenomenon, unaffected by derivatives.

The following is a review of the Derivatives principles designed to address the learning outcome statements set forth by CFA Institute. This topic is also covered in:

FORWARD MARKETS AND CONTRACTS

Study Session 17

EXAM FOCUS

This topic review introduces forward contracts in general and covers the characteristics of forward contracts on various financial securities, as well as interest rates. It is not easy material, and you should take the time to learn it well. This material on forward contracts provides a good basis for futures contracts and many of the characteristics of both types of contracts are the same. Take the time to understand the intuition behind the valuation of forward rate agreements.

FORWARD CONTRACTS

A **forward contract** is a bilateral contract that obligates one party to buy and the other to sell a specific quantity of an asset, at a set price, on a specific date in the future. Typically, neither party to the contract pays anything to get into the contract. If the expected future price of the asset increases over the life of the contract, the right to buy at the contract price will have positive value, and the obligation to sell will have an equal negative value. If the future price of the asset falls below the contract price, the result is opposite and the right to sell (at an above-market price) will have the positive value. The parties may enter into the contract as a speculation on the future price. More often, a party seeks to enter into a forward contract to hedge a risk it already has. The forward contract is used to eliminate uncertainty about the future price of an asset it plans to buy or sell at a later date. Forward contracts on physical assets, such as agricultural products, have existed for centuries. The Level I CFA curriculum, however, focuses on their (more recent) use for financial assets, such as T-bills, bonds, equities, and foreign currencies.

LOS 61.a: Explain delivery/settlement and default risk for both long and short positions in a forward contract.

CFA® Program Curriculum, Volume 6, page 28

The party to the forward contract that agrees to buy the financial or physical asset has a **long forward position** and is called the *long*. The party to the forward contract that agrees to sell or deliver the asset has a **short forward position** and is called the *short*.

We will illustrate the mechanics of the basic forward contract through an example based on the purchase and sale of a Treasury bill. Note that while forward and futures contracts on T-bills are usually quoted in terms of a discount percentage from face value, we will use dollar prices to make the example easy to follow. Actual pricing conventions and calculations are among the contract characteristics covered later in this review.

Consider a contract under which Party A agrees to buy a $1,000 face value, 90-day Treasury bill from Party B 30 days from now at a price of $990. Party A is the long and Party B is the short. Both parties have removed uncertainty about the price they will pay/receive for the T-bill at the future date. If 30 days from now T-bills are trading at $992, the short must deliver the T-bill to the long in exchange for a $990 payment. If T-bills are trading at $988 on the future date, the long must purchase the T-bill from the short for $990, the contract price.

Each party to a forward contract is exposed to **default risk** (or **counterparty risk**), the probability that the other party (the counterparty) will not perform as promised. It is unusual for any cash to actually be exchanged at the inception of a forward contract, unlike futures contracts in which each party posts an initial deposit (margin) as a guarantee of performance.

At any point in time, including the settlement date, only one party to the forward contract will owe money, meaning that side of the contract has a negative value. The other side of the contract will have a positive value of an equal amount. Following the example, if the T-bill price is $992 at the (future) settlement date and the short does not deliver the T-bill for $990 as promised, the short has defaulted.

LOS 61.b: Describe the procedures for settling a forward contract at expiration, and how termination prior to expiration can affect credit risk.

CFA® Program Curriculum, Volume 6, page 29

The previous example was for a **deliverable forward contract**. The short contracted to deliver the actual instrument, in this case a $1,000 face value, 90-day T-bill.

This is one procedure for settling a forward contract at the *settlement date* or expiration date specified in the contract.

An alternative settlement method is **cash settlement**. Under this method, the party that has a position with negative value is obligated to pay that amount to the other party. In the previous example, if the price of the T-bill were $992 on the expiration date, the short would satisfy the contract by paying $2 to the long. Ignoring transactions costs, this method yields the same result as asset delivery. If the short had the T-bill, it could be sold in the market for $992. The short's net proceeds, however, would be $990 after subtracting the $2 payment to the long. If the T-bill price at the settlement date were $988, the long would make a $2 payment to the short. Purchasing a T-bill at the market price of $988, together with this $2 payment, would make the total cost $990, just as it would be if it were a deliverable contract.

On the expiration (or settlement) date of the contract, the long receives a payment if the price of the asset is above the agreed-upon (forward) price; the short receives a payment if the price of the asset is below the contract price.

Terminating a Position Prior to Expiration

A party to a forward contract can **terminate the position** prior to expiration by entering into an opposite forward contract with an expiration date equal to the time remaining on the original contract.

Recall our example and assume that ten days after inception (it was originally a 30-day contract), the 20-day forward price of a $1,000 face value, 90-day T-bill is $992. The short, expecting the price to be even higher by the delivery date, wishes to terminate the contract. Since the short is obligated to sell the T-bill 20 days in the future, he can effectively exit the contract by entering into a new (20-day) forward contract to buy an identical T-bill (a long position) at the current forward price of $992.

The position of the original short now is two-fold, an obligation to sell a T-bill in 20 days for $990 (under the original contract) and an obligation to purchase an identical T-bill in 20 days for $992. He has locked in a $2 loss, but has effectively exited the contract since the amount owed at settlement is $2, regardless of the market price of the T-bill at the settlement date. No matter what the price of a 90-day T-bill is 20 days from now, he has the contractual right and obligation to buy one at $992 and to sell one at $990.

However, if the short's new forward contract is with a different party than the first forward contract, some **credit risk** remains. If the price of the T-bill at the expiration date is above $992, and the counterparty to the second forward contract fails to perform, the short's losses could exceed $2.

An alternative is to enter into the second (offsetting) contract with the same party as the original contract. This would avoid credit risk since the short could make a $2 payment to the counterparty at contract expiration, the amount of his net exposure. In fact, if the original counterparty were willing to take the short position in the second (20-day) contract at the $992 price, a payment of the present value of the $2 (discounted for the 20 days until the settlement date) would be an equivalent transaction. The original counterparty would be willing to allow termination of the original contract for an immediate payment of that amount.

If the original counterparty requires a payment larger than the present value of $2 to exit the contract, the short must weight this additional cost to exit the contract against the default risk he bears by entering into the offsetting contract with a different counterparty at a forward price of $992.

LOS 61.c: Distinguish between a dealer and an end user of a forward contract.

CFA® Program Curriculum, Volume 6, page 30

The **end user of a forward contract** is typically a corporation, government unit, or nonprofit institution that has existing risk they wish to avoid by locking in the future price of an asset. A U.S. corporation that has an obligation to make a payment in Euros 60 days from now can eliminate its exchange rate risk by entering into a forward contract to purchase the required amount of Euros for a certain dollar-denominated payment with a settlement date 60 days in the future.

Dealers are often banks, but can also be nonbank financial institutions such as securities brokers. Ideally, dealers will balance their overall long positions with their overall short positions by entering forward contracts with end users who have opposite existing risk exposures. A dealer's quote desk will quote a buying price (at which they will assume a long position) and a slightly higher selling price (at which they will assume a short position). The bid/ask spread between the two is the dealer's compensation for administrative costs as well as bearing default risk and any asset price risk from unbalanced (unhedged) positions. Dealers will also enter into contracts with other dealers to hedge a net long or net short position.

LOS 61.d: Describe the characteristics of equity forward contracts and forward contracts on zero-coupon and coupon bonds.

CFA® Program Curriculum, Volume 6, page 32

Equity forward contracts where the underlying asset is a single stock, a portfolio of stocks, or a stock index, work in much the same manner as other forward contracts. An investor who wishes to sell 10,000 shares of IBM stock 90 days from now and wishes to avoid the uncertainty about the stock price on that date, could do so by taking a short position in a forward contract covering 10,000 IBM shares. (We will leave the motivation for this and the pricing of such a contract aside for now.)

A dealer might quote a price of $100 per share, agreeing to pay $1 million for the 10,000 shares 90 days from now. The contract may be deliverable or settled in cash as described above. The stock seller has locked in the selling price of the shares and will get no more if the price (in 90 days) is actually higher, and will get no less if the price actually lower.

A portfolio manager who wishes to sell a portfolio of several stocks 60 days from now can similarly request a quote, giving the dealer the company names and the number of shares of each stock in the portfolio. The only difference between this type of forward contract and several forward contracts each covering a single stock, is that the pricing would be better (a higher total price) for the portfolio because overall administration/ origination costs would be less for the portfolio forward contract.

A forward contract on a stock index is similar except that the contract will be based on a notional amount and will very likely be a cash-settlement contract.

Example: Equity index forward contracts

A portfolio manager desires to generate $10 million 100 days from now from a portfolio that is quite similar in composition to the S&P 100 index. She requests a quote on a short position in a 100-day forward contract based on the index with a notional amount of $10 million and gets a quote of 525.2. If the index level at the settlement date is 535.7, calculate the amount the manager will pay or receive to settle the contract.

Answer:

The actual index level is 2% *above* the contract price, or:

535.7 / 525.2 − 1 = 0.02 = 2%

As the short party, the portfolio manager must pay 2% of the $10 million notional amount, $200,000, to the long.

Alternatively, if the index were 1% below the contract level, the portfolio manager would receive a payment from the long of $100,000, which would approximately offset any decrease in the portfolio value.

Dividends are usually not included in equity forward contracts, as the uncertainty about dividend amounts and payment dates is small compared to the uncertainty about future equity prices. Since forward contracts are custom instruments, the parties could specify a total return value (including dividends) rather than simply the index value. This would effectively remove dividend uncertainty as well.

Forward Contracts on Zero-Coupon and Coupon Bonds

Forward contracts on short-term, zero-coupon bonds (T-bills in the United States) and coupon interest-paying bonds are quite similar to those on equities. However, while equities do not have a maturity date, bonds do, and the forward contract must settle before the bond matures.

As we noted earlier, T-bill prices are often quoted as a percentage discount from face value. The percentage discount for T-bills is annualized so that a 90-day T-bill quoted at a 4% discount will be priced at a (90 / 360) × 4% = 1% discount from face value. This is equivalent to a price quote of (1 − 0.01) × $1,000 = $990 per $1,000 of face value.

Example: Bond forwards

A forward contract covering a $10 million face value of T-bills that will have 100 days to maturity at contract settlement is priced at 1.96 on a discount yield basis. Compute the dollar amount the long must pay at settlement for the T-bills.

Answer

The 1.96% annualized discount must be "unannualized" based on the 100 days to maturity.

$$0.0196 \times (100 / 360) = 0.005444 \text{ is the actual discount.}$$

The dollar settlement price is $(1 - 0.005444) \times \$10$ million $= \$9,945,560$.

Please note that when market interest rates increase, discounts increase, and T-bill prices fall. A long, who is obligated to purchase the bonds, will have losses on the forward contract when interest rates rise, and gains on the contract when interest rates fall. The outcomes for the short will be opposite.

The price specified in forward contracts on coupon-bearing bonds is typically stated as a yield to maturity as of the settlement date, exclusive of accrued interest. If the contract is on bonds with the possibility of default, there must be provisions in the contract to define default and specify the obligations of the parties in the event of default. Special provisions must also be included if the bonds have embedded options such as call features or conversion features. Forward contracts can be constructed covering individual bonds or portfolios of bonds.

LOS 61.e: Describe the characteristics of the Eurodollar time deposit market, and define LIBOR and Euribor.

CFA® Program Curriculum, Volume 6, page 36

Eurodollar deposit is the term for deposits in large banks outside the United States denominated in U.S. dollars. The lending rate on dollar-denominated loans between banks is called the London Interbank Offered Rate (LIBOR). It is quoted as an annualized rate based on a 360-day year. In contrast to T-bill discount yields, LIBOR is an add-on rate, like a yield quote on a short-term certificate of deposit. LIBOR is used as a reference rate for floating rate U.S. dollar-denominated loans worldwide.

> **Example: LIBOR-based loans**
>
> Compute the amount that must be repaid on a $1 million loan for 30 days if 30-day LIBOR is quoted at 6%.
>
> **Answer:**
>
> The add-on interest is calculated as $1 million × 0.06 × (30 / 360) = $5,000. The borrower would repay $1,000,000 + $5,000 = $1,005,000 at the end of 30 days.

LIBOR is published daily by the British Banker's Association and is compiled from quotes from a number of large banks; some are large multinational banks based in other countries that have London offices.

There is also an equivalent Euro lending rate called **Euribor**, or Europe Interbank Offered Rate. Euribor, established in Frankfurt, is published by the European Central Bank.

The floating rates are for various periods and are quoted as such. For example, the terminology is 30-day LIBOR (or Euribor), 90-day LIBOR, and 180-day LIBOR, depending on the term of the loan. For longer-term floating-rate loans, the interest rate is reset periodically based on the then-current LIBOR for the relevant period.

LOS 61.f: Describe forward rate agreements (FRAs) and calculate the gain/loss on a FRA.

LOS 61.g: Calculate and interpret the payoff of a FRA and explain each of the component terms of the payoff formula.

CFA® Program Curriculum, Volume 6, page 35

A **forward rate agreement** (FRA) can be viewed as a forward contract to borrow/lend money at a certain rate at some future date. In practice, these contracts settle in cash, but no actual loan is made at the settlement date. This means that the creditworthiness of the parties to the contract need not be considered in the forward interest rate, so an essentially riskless rate, such as LIBOR, can be specified in the contract. (The parties to the contract may still be exposed to default risk on the amount owed at settlement.)

The long position in an FRA is the party that would borrow the money (long the loan with the contract price being the interest rate on the loan). If the floating rate at contract expiration (LIBOR or Euribor) is above the rate specified in the forward agreement, the long position in the contract can be viewed as the right to borrow at below market rates and the long will receive a payment. If the reference rate at the expiration date is below the contract rate, the short will receive a cash payment from the long. (The right to lend at rates *higher than* market rates would have a positive value.)

To calculate the cash payment at settlement for a forward rate agreement, we need to calculate the value as of the settlement date of making a loan at a rate that is either above or below the market rate. Since the interest savings would come at the end of the loan period, the cash payment at settlement of the forward is the present value of the interest savings. We need to calculate the discounted value at the settlement date of the interest savings or excess interest at the end of the loan period. An example will illustrate the calculation of the payment at expiration and some terminology of FRAs.

Example: FRAs

Consider an FRA that:

- Expires/settles in 30 days.
- Is based on a notional principal amount of $1 million.
- Is based on 90-day LIBOR.
- Specifies a forward rate of 5%.

Assume that the actual 90-day LIBOR 30-days from now (at expiration) is 6%. Compute the cash settlement payment at expiration, and identify which party makes the payment.

Answer:

If the long could borrow at the contract rate of 5%, rather than the market rate of 6%, the interest saved on a 90-day $1 million loan would be:

$$(0.06 - 0.05)(90 / 360) \times 1 \text{ million} = 0.0025 \times 1 \text{ million} = \$2,500$$

The $2,500 in interest savings would not come until the end of the 90-day loan period. The value at settlement is the present value of these savings. The correct discount rate to use is the actual rate at settlement, 6%, not the contract rate of 5%.

The payment at settlement from the short to the long is:

$$\frac{2,500}{1 + [(0.06) \times (90 / 360)]} = \$2,463.05$$

In doing the calculation of the settlement payment, remember that the term of the FRA and the term of the underlying "loan" need not be the same and are *not* interchangeable. While the settlement date can be any future date, in practice it is usually some multiple of 30 days. The specific market rate on which we calculate the value of the contract will typically be similar, 30-day, 60-day, 90-day, or 180-day LIBOR. If we describe an FRA as a 60-day FRA on 90-day LIBOR, settlement or expiration is 60 days from now and the payment at settlement is based on 90-day LIBOR 60 days from now. Such an FRA could be quoted in (30-day) months, and would be described as a 2-by-5 FRA (or 2 × 5 FRA). The 2 refers to the number of months until contract expiration and the 5 refers to the total time until the end of the interest rate period (2 + 3 = 5).

The general formula for the payment to the long at settlement is:

$$\left(\text{notional principal}\right)\frac{\left(\text{floating} - \text{forward}\right)\left(\dfrac{\text{days}}{360}\right)}{1 + \left[\left(\text{floating}\right)\left(\dfrac{\text{days}}{360}\right)\right]}$$

where:

days = number of days in the loan term

The numerator is the interest savings in percent, and the denominator is the discount factor.

Note that if the *floating* rate underlying the agreement turns out to be below the *forward* rate specified in the contract, the numerator in the formula is negative and the short receives a payment from the long.

FRAs for non-standard periods (e.g., a 45-day FRA on 132-day LIBOR) are termed off-the-run FRAs.

LOS 61.h: Describe the characteristics of currency forward contracts.

CFA® Program Curriculum, Volume 6, page 38

Under the terms of a **currency forward contract**, one party agrees to exchange a certain amount of one currency for a certain amount of another currency at a future date. This type of forward contract in practice will specify an exchange rate at which one party can buy a fixed amount of the currency underlying the contract. If we need to exchange 10 million Euros for U.S. dollars 60 days in the future, we might receive a quote of USD0.95. The forward contract specifies that we (the long) will purchase USD9.5 million for EUR10 million at settlement. Currency forward contracts can be deliverable or settled in cash. As with other forward contracts, the cash settlement amount is the amount necessary to compensate the party who would be disadvantaged by the actual change in market rates as of the settlement date. An example will illustrate this.

Example: Currency forwards

Gemco expects to receive EUR50 million three months from now and enters into a cash settlement currency forward to exchange these euros for U.S. dollars at USD1.23 per euro. If the market exchange rate is USD1.25 per euro at settlement, what is the amount of the payment to be received or paid by Gemco?

Answer:

Under the terms of the contract Gemco would receive:

$$\text{EUR50 million} \times \frac{\text{USD}}{\text{EUR}} 1.23 = \text{USD61.5 million}$$

Without the forward contract, Gemco would receive:

$$\text{EUR50 million} \times \frac{\text{USD}}{\text{EUR}} 1.25 = \text{USD62.5 million}$$

The counterparty would be disadvantaged by the difference between the contract rate and the market rate in an amount equal to the advantage that would have accrued to Gemco had they not entered into the currency forward.

Gemco must make a payment of USD1.0 million to the counterparty.

A direct calculation of the value of the long (USD) position at settlement is:

$$\left(\frac{\text{USD}}{\text{EUR}} 1.23 - \frac{\text{USD}}{\text{EUR}} 1.25 \right) \times \text{EUR50 million} = -\text{USD1.0 million}$$

KEY CONCEPTS

LOS 61.a

A deliverable forward contract on an asset specifies that the long (the buyer) will pay a certain amount at a future date to the short, who will deliver a certain amount of an asset.

Default risk in a forward contract is the risk that the other party to the contract will not perform at settlement, because typically no money changes hands at the initiation of the contract.

LOS 61.b

A forward contract with cash settlement does not require delivery of the underlying asset, but a cash payment at the settlement date from one counterparty to the other, based on the contract price and the market price of the asset at settlement.

Early termination of a forward contract can be accomplished by entering into a new forward contract with the opposite position, at the then-current expected forward price. This early termination will fix the amount of the gain or loss at the settlement date. If this new forward is with a different counterparty than the original, there is credit or default risk to consider since one of the two counterparties may fail to honor its obligation under the forward contract.

LOS 61.c

An end user of a forward contract is most often a corporation hedging an existing risk.

Forward dealers, large banks, or brokerages originate forward contracts and take the long side in some contracts and the short side in others, with a spread in pricing to compensate them for actual costs, bearing default risk, and any unhedged price risk they must bear.

LOS 61.d

An equity forward contract may be on a single stock, a customized portfolio, or an equity index, and is used to hedge the risk of equity prices at some future date.
- Equity forward contracts can be written on a total return basis (including dividends), but are typically based solely on an index value.
- Index forwards settle in cash based on the notional amount and the percentage difference between the index value in the forward contract and the actual index level at settlement.

Forward contracts in which bonds are the underlying asset may be quoted in terms of the discount on zero-coupon bonds (e.g., T-bills) or in terms of the yield to maturity on coupon bonds. Forwards on corporate bonds must contain special provisions to deal with the possibility of default as well as with any call or conversion features. Forward contracts may also be written on portfolios of fixed income securities or on bond indexes.

LOS 61.e
Eurodollar time deposits are USD-denominated short-term unsecured loans to large money-center banks outside the United States.

The London Interbank Offered Rate (LIBOR) is an international reference rate for Eurodollar deposits and is quoted for 30-day, 60-day, 90-day, 180-day, or 360-day (1-year) terms.

Euribor is the equivalent for short-term Euro-denominated bank deposits (loans to banks).

For both LIBOR and Euribor, rates are expressed as annual rates and actual interest is based on the loan term as a proportion of a 360-day year.

LOS 61.f
Forward rate agreements (FRAs) serve to hedge the uncertainty about short-term rates (e.g., 30- or 90-day LIBOR) that will prevail in the future. If rates rise, the long receives a payment at settlement. The short receives a payment if the specified rate falls to a level below the contract rate.

LOS 61.g
The payment to the long at settlement on an FRA is:

$$\text{notional principal amount} \left\{ \frac{(\text{reference rate at settlement} - \text{FRA rate})\left[\dfrac{\text{days in loan term}}{360}\right]}{1 + \text{reference rate at settlement} \times \left[\dfrac{\text{days in loan term}}{360}\right]} \right\}$$

The numerator is the difference between the rate on a loan for the specified period at the forward contract rate and the rate at settlement, and the denominator is to discount this interest differential back to the settlement date at the market rate at settlement.

LOS 61.h
Currency forward contracts specify that one party will deliver a certain amount of one currency at the settlement date in exchange for a certain amount of another currency.

Under cash settlement, a single cash payment is made at settlement based on the difference between the exchange rate fixed in the contract and the market exchange rate at the settlement date.

CONCEPT CHECKERS

1. The short in a deliverable forward contract:
    A. has no default risk.
    B. is obligated to deliver the specified asset.
    C. makes a cash payment to the long at settlement.

2. On the settlement date of a forward contract:
    A. the short may be required to sell the asset.
    B. the long must sell the asset or make a cash payment.
    C. at least one party must make a cash payment to the other.

3. Which of the following statements regarding early termination of a forward contract is *most accurate*?
    A. A party who enters into an offsetting contract to terminate has no risk.
    B. A party who terminates a forward contract early must make a cash payment.
    C. Early termination through an offsetting transaction with the original counterparty eliminates default risk.

4. A dealer in the forward contract market:
    A. cannot be a bank.
    B. may enter into a contract with another dealer.
    C. gets a small payment for each contract at initiation.

5. Which of the following statements regarding equity forward contracts is *least accurate*?
    A. Equity forwards may be settled in cash.
    B. Dividends are never included in index forwards.
    C. A short position in an equity forward could not hedge the risk of a purchase of that equity in the future.

6. Which of the following statements regarding forward contracts on 90-day T-bills is *most accurate*?
    A. The face value must be paid by the long at settlement.
    B. There is no default risk on these forwards because T-bills are government-backed.
    C. If short-term yields increase unexpectedly after contract initiation, the short will profit on the contract.

7. A Eurodollar time deposit:
    A. is priced on a discount basis.
    B. may be issued by a Japanese bank.
    C. is a certificate of deposit denominated in Euros.

8. One difference between LIBOR and Euribor is that:
    A. LIBOR is for London deposits.
    B. they are for different currencies.
    C. LIBOR is slightly higher due to default risk.

9. Which of the following statements regarding a LIBOR-based FRA is *most accurate*?
    A. The short will settle the contract by making a loan.
    B. FRAs can be based on interest rates for 30-, 60-, or 90-day periods.
    C. If LIBOR increases unexpectedly over the contract term, the long will be required to make a cash payment at settlement.

10. Consider a $2 million FRA with a contract rate of 5% on 60-day LIBOR. If 60-day LIBOR is 6% at settlement, the long will:
    A. pay $3,333.
    B. receive $3,300.
    C. receive $3,333.

11. Party A has entered a currency forward contract to purchase €10 million at an exchange rate of $0.98 per euro. At settlement, the exchange rate is $0.97 per euro. If the contract is settled in cash, Party A will:
    A. make a payment of $100,000.
    B. receive a payment of $100,000.
    C. receive a payment of $103,090.

12. If the quoted discount yield on a 128-day, $1 million T-bill decreases from 3.15% to 3.07%, how much has the holder of the T-bill gained or lost?
    A. Lost $284.
    B. Gained $284.
    C. Gained $800.

13. 90-day LIBOR is quoted as 3.58%. How much interest would be owed at maturity for a 90-day loan of $1.5 million at LIBOR + 1.3%?
    A. $17,612.
    B. $18,300.
    C. $32,925.

14. A company treasurer needs to borrow 10 million euros for 180 days, 60 days from now. The type of FRA and the position he should take to hedge the interest rate risk of this transaction are:

	FRA	Position
A.	2 × 6	Short
B.	2 × 8	Long
C.	2 × 8	Short

ANSWERS – CONCEPT CHECKERS

1. **B**   The short in a forward contract is obligated to deliver the specified asset at the contract price on the settlement date. Either party may have default risk if there is any probability that the counterparty may not perform under the terms of the contract.

2. **A**   A forward contract may call for settlement in cash or for delivery of the asset. Under a deliverable contract, the short is required to deliver the asset at settlement, not to make a cash payment.

3. **C**   Terminating a forward contract early by entering into an offsetting forward contract with a different counterparty exposes a party to default risk. If the offsetting transaction is with the original counterparty, default risk is eliminated. No cash payment is required if an offsetting contract is used for early termination.

4. **B**   Forward contracts dealers are commonly banks and large brokerage houses. They frequently enter into forward contracts with other dealers to offset long or short exposure. No payment is typically made at contract initiation.

5. **B**   Index forward contracts may be written as total return contracts, which include dividends. Contracts may be written to settle in cash, or to be deliverable. A *long* position is used to reduce the price risk of an expected future purchase.

6. **C**   When short-term rates increase, T-bill prices fall and the short position will profit. The price of a T-bill prior to maturity is always less than its face value. The deliverable security is a T-bill with 90 days to maturity. There is default risk on the *forward*, even though the underlying asset is considered risk free.

7. **B**   Eurodollar time deposits are U.S. dollar-denominated accounts with banks outside the United States and are quoted as an add-on yield rather than on a discount basis.

8. **B**   LIBOR is for U.S. dollar-denominated accounts while Euribor is for euro-denominated accounts. Neither is location-specific. Differences in these rates are due to the different currencies involved, not differences in default risk.

9. **B**   A LIBOR-based contract can be based on LIBOR for various terms. They are settled in cash. The long will receive a payment when LIBOR is higher than the contract rate at settlement.

10. **B** $(0.06 - 0.05) \times (60 / 360) \times \$2$ million $\times 1 / (1 + 0.06 / 6) = \$3,300.33$.

11. **A** $(\$0.98 - \$0.97) \times 10$ million $= \$100,000$ loss. The long, Party A, is obligated to buy euros at \$0.98 when they are only worth \$0.97 and must pay $\$0.01 \times 10$ million $= \$100,000$.

12. **B**   The actual discount has decreased by:

$$(0.0315 - 0.0307) \times \frac{128}{360} = 0.0284\% \text{ of } \$1,000,000, \text{ or } \$284.$$

A decrease in the discount is an increase in value.

13. **B** $(0.0358 + 0.013)\left(\dfrac{90}{360}\right)1.5$ million $= \$18,300$. Both LIBOR and any premium to LIBOR are quoted as annualized rates.

14. **B** This requires a long position in a 2 × 8 FRA.

FUTURES MARKETS AND CONTRACTS

EXAM FOCUS

Candidates should focus on the terminology of futures markets, how futures differ from forwards, the mechanics of margin deposits, and the process of marking to market. Other important concepts here include limit price moves, delivery options, and the characteristics of the basic types of financial futures contracts. Learn the ways a futures position can be terminated prior to contract expiration and understand how cash settlement is accomplished by the final mark-to-market at contract expiration.

LOS 62.a: Describe the characteristics of futures contracts.

LOS 62.b: Compare futures contracts and forward contracts.

CFA® Program Curriculum, Volume 6, page 43

Futures contracts are very much like the forward contracts we learned about in the previous topic review. They are *similar* in that both:

- Can be either deliverable or cash settlement contracts.
- Are priced to have zero value at the time an investor enters into the contract.

Futures contracts *differ* from forward contracts in the following ways:

- Futures contracts trade on organized exchanges. Forwards are private contracts and do not trade.
- Futures contracts are highly standardized. Forwards are customized contracts satisfying the needs of the parties involved.
- A single clearinghouse is the counterparty to all futures contracts. Forwards are contracts with the originating counterparty.
- The government regulates futures markets. Forward contracts are usually not regulated.

Characteristics of Futures Contracts

Standardization. A major difference between forwards and futures is that futures contracts have standardized contract terms. Futures contracts specify the quality and quantity of goods that can be delivered, the delivery time, and the manner of delivery. The exchange also sets the minimum price fluctuation (which is called the tick size). For example, the basic price movement, or tick, for a 5,000-bushel grain contract is a quarter of a point (1 point = $0.01) per bushel, or $12.50 per contract. Contracts also have a daily price limit, which sets the maximum price movement allowed in a single day. For example, wheat cannot move more than $0.20 from its close the preceding day.

The maximum price limits expand during periods of high volatility and are not in effect during the delivery month. The exchange also sets the trading times for each contract.

It would appear that these rules would restrict trading activity, but in fact, they stimulate trading. Why? Standardization tells traders exactly what is being traded and the conditions of the transaction. *Uniformity promotes market liquidity.*

The purchaser of a futures contract is said to have gone long or taken a *long position*, while the seller of a futures contract is said to have gone short or taken a *short position*. For each contract traded, there is a buyer and a seller. The long has contracted to buy the asset at the contract price at contract expiration, and the short has an obligation to sell at that price. Futures contracts are used by *speculators* to gain exposure to changes in the price of the asset underlying a futures contract. A *hedger*, in contrast, will use futures contracts to reduce exposure to price changes in the asset (hedge their asset price risk). An example is a wheat farmer who sells wheat futures to reduce the uncertainty about the price of wheat at harvest time.

Clearinghouse. Each exchange has a *clearinghouse*. The clearinghouse guarantees that traders in the futures market will honor their obligations. The clearinghouse does this by splitting each trade once it is made and acting as the opposite side of each position. The clearinghouse acts as the buyer to every seller and the seller to every buyer. By doing this, the clearinghouse allows either side of the trade to reverse positions at a future date without having to contact the other side of the initial trade. This allows traders to enter the market knowing that they will be able to reverse their position. Traders are also freed from having to worry about the counterparty defaulting since the counterparty is now the clearinghouse. In the history of U.S. futures trading, the clearinghouse has never defaulted on a trade.

 Professor's Note: The terminology is that you "bought" bond futures if you entered into the contract with the long position. In my experience, this terminology has caused confusion for many candidates. You don't purchase the contract, you enter into it. You are contracting to buy an asset on the long side. "Buy" means take the long side, and "sell" means take the short side in futures.

LOS 62.c: Distinguish between margin in the securities markets and margin in the futures markets, and explain the role of initial margin, maintenance margin, variation margin, and settlement in futures trading.

CFA® Program Curriculum, Volume 6, page 48

In securities markets, margin on a stock or bond purchase is a percentage of the market value of the asset. Initially, 50% of the stock purchase amount may be borrowed, and the remaining amount, the equity in the account, must be paid in cash. There is interest charged on the borrowed amount, the margin loan. The margin percentage, the percent of the security value that is owned, will vary over time and must be maintained at some minimum percentage of market value.

In the futures markets, margin is a performance guarantee. It is money deposited by both the long and the short. There is no loan involved and, consequently, no interest charges.

Each futures exchange has a clearinghouse. To safeguard the clearinghouse, the exchange requires traders to post margin and settle their accounts on a daily basis. Before trading, the trader must deposit funds (called margin) with a broker (who, in turn, will post margin with the clearinghouse).

In securities markets, the cash deposited is paid to the seller of the security, with the balance of the purchase price provided by the broker. This is why the unpaid balance is a loan, with interest charged to the buyer who purchased on margin.

Initial margin is the money that must be deposited in a futures account before any trading takes place. It is set for each type of underlying asset. Initial margin per contract is relatively low and equals about one day's maximum price fluctuation on the total value of the contract's underlying asset.

Maintenance margin is the amount of margin that must be maintained in a futures account. If the margin balance in the account falls below the maintenance margin due to a change in the contract price for the underlying asset, additional funds must be deposited to bring the margin balance back up to the initial margin requirement.

This is in contrast to equity account margins, which require investors only to bring the margin percentage up to the maintenance margin, not back to the initial margin level.

Variation margin is the funds that must be deposited into the account to bring it back to the initial margin amount. If account margin exceeds the initial margin requirement, funds can be withdrawn or used as initial margin for additional positions.

The **settlement price** is analogous to the closing price for a stock but is not simply the price of the last trade. It is an average of the prices of the trades during the last period of trading, called the closing period, which is set by the exchange. This feature of the settlement price prevents manipulation by traders. The settlement price is used to make margin calculations at the end of each trading day.

Initial and minimum margins in securities accounts are set by the Federal Reserve, although brokerage houses can require more. Initial and maintenance margins in the futures market are set by the clearinghouse and are based on historical daily price volatility of the underlying asset since margin is resettled daily in futures accounts. Margin in futures accounts is typically *much lower* as a percentage of the value of the assets covered by the futures contract. This means that the leverage, based on the actual cash required, is much higher for futures accounts.

How a Futures Trade Takes Place

In contrast to forward contracts in which a bank or brokerage is usually the counterparty to the contract, there is a buyer and a seller on each side of a futures trade. The futures exchange selects the contracts that will trade. The asset, the amount of the asset, and the settlement/delivery date are standardized in this manner (e.g., a June futures contract on 90-day T-bills with a face amount of $1 million). Each time there is a trade, the delivery price for that contract is the equilibrium price at that point in time, which depends on supply (by those wishing to be short) and demand (by those wishing to be long).

The mechanism by which supply and demand determine this equilibrium is open outcry at a particular location on the exchange floor called a *pit*. Each trade is reported to the exchange so that the equilibrium price, at any point in time, is known to all traders.

LOS 62.d: Describe price limits and the process of marking to market, and calculate and interpret the margin balance, given the previous day's balance and the change in the futures price.

CFA® Program Curriculum, Volume 6, page 48

Many futures contracts have **price limits**, which are exchange-imposed limits on how much the contract price can change from the previous day's settlement price. Exchange members are prohibited from executing trades at prices outside these limits. If the (equilibrium) price at which traders would willingly trade is above the upper limit or below the lower limit, trades cannot take place.

Consider a futures contract that has daily price limits of two cents and settled the previous day at $1.04. If, on the following trading day, traders wish to trade at $1.07 because of changes in market conditions or expectations, no trades will take place. The settlement price will be reported as $1.06 (for the purposes of marking-to-market). The contract will be said to have made a **limit move**, and the price is said to be **limit up** (from the previous day). If market conditions had changed such that the price at which traders are willing to trade is below $1.02, $1.02 will be the settlement price, and the price is said to be **limit down**. If trades cannot take place because of a limit move, either up or down, the price is said to be **locked limit** since no trades can take place and traders are locked into their existing positions.

Marking-to-market is the process of adjusting the margin balance in a futures account each day for the change in the value of the contract assets from the previous trading day, based on the new settlement price.

The futures exchanges can require a mark-to-market more frequently (than daily) under extraordinary circumstances.

Study Session 17

Computing the Margin Balance

Example: Margin balance

Consider a long position of five July wheat contracts, each of which covers 5,000 bushels. Assume that the contract price is $2.00 and that each contract requires an initial margin deposit of $150 and a maintenance margin of $100. The total initial margin required for the 5-contract trade is $750. The maintenance margin for the account is $500. Compute the margin balance for this position after a 2-cent decrease in price on Day 1, a 1-cent increase in price on Day 2, and a 1-cent decrease in price on Day 3.

Answer:

Each contract is for 5,000 bushels so that a price change of $0.01 per bushel changes the contract value by $50, or $250 for the five contracts: $(0.01)(5)(5,000) = 250.00.

The following figure illustrates the change in the margin balance as the price of this contract changes each day. Note that the initial balance is the initial margin requirement of $750 and that the required deposit is based on the previous day's price change.

Margin Balances

Day	Required Deposit	Price/Bushel	Daily Change	Gain/Loss	Balance
0 (Purchase)	$750	$2.00	0	0	$750
1	0	$1.98	−$0.02	−$500	$250
2	$500	$1.99	+$0.01	+$250	$1,000
3	0	$1.98	−$0.01	−$250	$750

At the close on Day 1, the margin balance has gone below the minimum or maintenance margin level of $500. Therefore, a deposit of $500 is required to bring the margin back to the initial margin level of $750. We can interpret the margin balance at any point as the amount the investor would realize if the position were closed out by a reversing trade at the most recent settlement price used to calculate the margin balance.

LOS 62.e: Describe how a futures contract can be terminated at or prior to expiration.

CFA® Program Curriculum, Volume 6, page 53

There are **four ways to terminate a futures contract**:

1. A short can terminate the contract by delivering the goods, and a long can terminate the contract by accepting delivery and paying the contract price to the short. This is called **delivery**. The location for delivery (for physical assets), terms of delivery, and details of exactly what is to be delivered are all specified in the contract. Deliveries represent less than 1% of all contract terminations.

2. In a **cash-settlement contract**, delivery is not an option. The futures account is marked-to-market based on the settlement price on the last day of trading.

3. You may make a **reverse**, or **offsetting**, trade in the futures market. This is similar to the way we described exiting a forward contract prior to expiration. With futures, however, the other side of your position is held by the clearinghouse—if you make an exact opposite trade (maturity, quantity, and good) to your current position, the clearinghouse will net your positions out, leaving you with a zero balance. This is how most futures positions are settled. The contract price can differ between the two contracts. If you initially are long one contract at $370 per ounce of gold and subsequently sell (take the short position in) an identical gold contract when the price is $350/oz., $20 times the number of ounces of gold specified in the contract will be deducted from the margin deposit(s) in your account. The sale of the futures contract ends the exposure to future price fluctuations on the first contract. Your position has been *reversed*, or **closed out**, by a *closing* trade.

4. A position may also be settled through an **exchange for physicals**. Here, you find a trader with an opposite position to your own and deliver the goods and settle up between yourselves, off the floor of the exchange (called an ex-pit transaction). This is the sole exception to the federal law that requires that all trades take place on the floor of the exchange. You must then contact the clearinghouse and tell them what happened. An exchange for physicals differs from a delivery in that the traders actually exchange the goods, the contract is not closed on the floor of the exchange, and the two traders privately negotiate the terms of the transaction. Regular delivery involves only one trader and the clearinghouse.

Delivery Options in Futures Contracts

Some futures contracts grant **delivery options** to the short; options on what, where, and when to deliver. Some Treasury bond contracts give the short a choice of several bonds that are acceptable to deliver and options as to when to deliver during the expiration month. Physical assets, such as gold or corn, may offer a choice of delivery locations to the short. These options can be of significant value to the holder of the short position in a futures contract.

LOS 62.f: Describe the characteristics of the following types of futures contracts: Treasury bill, Eurodollar, Treasury bond, stock index, and currency.

CFA® Program Curriculum, Volume 6, page 57

Let's introduce financial futures by first examining the mechanics of a T-bill futures contract. **Treasury bill futures contracts** are based on a $1 million face value 90-day (13-week) T-bill and settle in cash. The price quotes are 100 minus the annualized discount in percent on the T-bills.

A price quote of 98.52 represents an annualized discount of 1.48%, an actual discount from face of $0.0148 \times (90 / 360) = 0.0037$, and a delivery price of $(1 - 0.0037) \times 1$ million = $996,300.

T-bill futures contracts are not as important as they once were. Their prices are heavily influenced by U.S. Federal Reserve operations and overall monetary policy. T-bill futures have lost importance in favor of Eurodollar futures contracts, which represent a more free-market and more global measure of short-term interest rates to top quality borrowers for U.S. dollar-denominated loans.

Eurodollar futures are based on 90-day LIBOR, which is an add-on yield, rather than a discount yield. By convention, however, the price quotes follow the same convention as T-bills and are calculated as (100 – annualized LIBOR in percent). These contracts settle in cash, and the minimum price change is one *tick*, which is a price change of 0.0001 = 0.01%, representing $25 per $1 million contract. A quote of 97.60 corresponds to an annualized LIBOR of (100 – 97.6) = 2.4% and an effective 90-day yield of 2.4 / 4 = 0.6%.

> *Professor's Note: Eurodollar futures are priced such that the long position gains value when interest rates decrease. This is different from forward rate agreements and interest rate call options, where the long position gains when interest rates increase.*

> *One of the first things a new T-bill futures trader learns is that each change in price of 0.01 in the price of a T-bill futures contract is worth $25. If you took a long position at 98.52 and the price fell to 98.50, your loss is $50 per contract. Because Eurodollar contracts on 90-day LIBOR are the same size and priced in a similar fashion, a price change of 0.01 represents a $25 change in value for these as well.*

Treasury bond futures contracts:

- Are traded for Treasury bonds with maturities greater than 15 years.
- Are a deliverable contract.
- Have a face value of $100,000.
- Are quoted as a percent and fractions of 1% (measured in 1/32nds) of face value.

The short in a Treasury bond futures contract has the option to deliver any of several bonds that will satisfy the delivery terms of the contract. This is called a delivery option and is valuable to the short because at expiration, one particular Treasury bond will be the **cheapest-to-deliver** bond.

Each bond is given a *conversion factor*, which is used to adjust the long's payment at delivery so that the more valuable bonds receive a higher payment. These factors are multipliers for the futures price at settlement. The long pays the futures price at expiration times the conversion factor.

Stock index futures. The most popular stock index future is the S&P 500 Index Future that trades in Chicago. Settlement is in cash and is based on a multiplier of 250.

The value of a contract is 250 times the level of the index stated in the contract. With an index level of 1,000, the value of each contract is $250,000. Each index point in the futures price represents a gain or loss of $250 per contract. A long stock index futures position on S&P 500 index futures at 1,051 would show a gain of $1,750 in the trader's account if the index were 1,058 at the settlement date ($250 × 7 = $1,750). A smaller contract is traded on the same index and has a multiplier of 50.

Futures contracts covering several other popular indices are traded, and the pricing and contract valuation are the same, although the multiplier can vary from contract to contract.

Currency futures. The currency futures market is smaller in volume than the forward currency market we described in the previous topic review. In the United States, currency contracts trade on the euro (EUR), Mexican peso (MXP), and yen (JPY), among others. Contracts are set in units of the foreign currency, and the price is stated in USD/unit. The size of the peso contract is MXP500,000, and the euro contract is on EUR125,000. A change in the price of the currency unit of USD0.0001 translates into a gain or loss of USD50 on a MXP500,000 unit contract and USD12.50 on a EUR125,000 unit contract.

KEY CONCEPTS

LOS 62.a
Like forward contracts, futures contracts are most commonly for delivery of commodities and financial assets at a future date and can require delivery or settlement in cash.

LOS 62.b
Compared to forward contracts, futures contracts:
- Are more liquid, trade on exchanges, and can be closed out by an offsetting trade.
- Do not have counterparty risk; the clearinghouse acts as counterparty to each side of the contract.
- Have lower transactions costs.
- Require margin deposits and are marked to market daily.
- Are standardized contracts as to asset quantity, quality, settlement dates, and delivery requirements.

LOS 62.c
Futures margin deposits are not loans, but deposits to ensure performance under the terms of the contract.

Initial margin is the deposit required to initiate a futures position.

Maintenance margin is the minimum margin amount. When margin falls below this amount, it must be brought back up to its initial level by depositing variation margin.

Margin calculations are based on the daily settlement price, the average of the prices for trades during a closing period set by the exchange.

LOS 62.d
Trades cannot take place at prices that differ from the previous day's settlement prices by more than the price limit and are said to be limit down (up) when the new equilibrium price is below (above) the minimum (maximum) price for the day.

Marking-to-market is the process of adding gains to or subtracting losses from the margin account daily, based on the change in settlement prices from one day to the next.

The mark-to-market adjustment either adds the day's gains in contract value to the long's margin balance and subtracts them from the short's margin balance, or subtracts the day's loss in contract value from the long's margin balance and adds them to the short's margin balance.

LOS 62.e
A futures position can be terminated in the following ways:
- An offsetting trade, entering into an opposite position in the same contract.
- Cash payment at expiration (cash-settlement contract).
- Delivery of the asset specified in the contract.
- An exchange for physicals (asset delivery off the exchange).

LOS 62.f

Eurodollar futures contracts are for a face value of $1,000,000, are quoted as 100 minus annualized 90-day LIBOR in percent, and settle in cash.

Treasury bond contracts are for a face value of $100,000, give the short a choice of bonds to deliver, and use conversion factors to adjust the contract price for the bond that is delivered.

Stock index futures have a multiplier that is multiplied by the index to calculate the contract value, and settle in cash.

Currency futures are for delivery of standardized amounts of foreign currency.

CONCEPT CHECKERS

1. Which of the following statements about futures markets is *least accurate*?
    A. Hedgers trade to reduce some preexisting risk exposure.
    B. The clearinghouse guarantees that traders in the futures market will honor their obligations.
    C. If an account rises to or exceeds the maintenance margin, the trader must deposit variation margin.

2. The daily process of adjusting the margin in a futures account is called:
    A. variation margin.
    B. marking-to-market.
    C. maintenance margin.

3. A trader buys (takes a long position in) a Eurodollar futures contract ($1 million face value) at 98.14 and closes it out at a price of 98.27. On this contract, the trader has:
    A. lost $325.
    B. gained $325.
    C. gained $1,300.

4. In the futures market, a contract does not trade for two days because trades are not permitted at the equilibrium price. The market for this contract is:
    A. limit up.
    B. limit down.
    C. locked limit.

5. The existence of a delivery option with respect to Treasury bond futures means that the:
    A. short can choose which bond to deliver.
    B. short has the option to settle in cash or by delivery.
    C. long chooses which of a number of bonds will be delivered.

6. Assume the holder of a long futures position negotiates privately with the holder of a short futures position to accept delivery to close out both the long and short positions. Which of the following statements about the transaction is *most accurate*? The transaction is:
    A. also known as delivery.
    B. also known as an exchange for physicals.
    C. the most common way to close a futures position.

7. A conversion factor in a Treasury bond contract is:
    A. used to adjust the number of bonds to be delivered.
    B. multiplied by the face value to determine the delivery price.
    C. multiplied by the futures price to determine the delivery price.

8.   Three 125,000 euro futures contracts are sold at a price of $1.0234. The next day the price settles at $1.0180. The mark-to-market for this account changes the previous day's margin by:
A.   +$675.
B.   −$675.
C.   +$2,025.

9.   In the futures market, the clearinghouse is *least likely* to:
A.   decide which contracts will trade.
B.   set initial and maintenance margins.
C.   act as the counterparty to every trade.

10.   Funds deposited to meet a margin call are termed:
A.   daily margin.
B.   settlement costs.
C.   variation margin.

11.   Compared to forward contracts, futures contracts are *least likely* to be:
A.   standardized.
B.   larger in size.
C.   less subject to default risk.

Study Session 17

ANSWERS – CONCEPT CHECKERS

1. **C**   If an account rises to or exceeds the maintenance margin, no payment needs to be made, and the trader has the option to remove the excess funds from the account. Only if an account falls below the maintenance margin does variation margin need to be paid to bring the level of the account back up to the level of the initial margin.

2. **B**   The *process* is called marking-to-market. Variation margin is the funds that must be deposited when marking-to-market draws the margin balance below the maintenance margin.

3. **B**   The price is quoted as 100 minus the annualized discount in percent. Remember that the gains and losses on T-bill and Eurodollar futures are $25 per basis point of the price quote. The price is up 13 ticks, and 13 × $25 is a gain of $325 for a long position.

4. **C**   This describes the situation when the equilibrium price is either above or below the prior day's settle price by more than the permitted (limit) daily price move. We do not know whether it is limit up or limit down.

5. **A**   The short has the option to deliver any of a number of permitted bonds. The delivery price is adjusted by a conversion factor that is calculated for each permitted bond.

6. **B**   When the holder of a long position negotiates directly with the holder of the short position to accept delivery of the underlying commodity to close out both positions, this is called an *exchange for physicals*. (This is a private transaction that occurs *ex-pit* and is one exception to the federal law that all trades take place on the exchange floor.) Note that the exchange for physicals differs from an offsetting trade in which no delivery takes place and also differs from delivery in which the commodity is simply delivered as a result of the futures expiration with no secondary agreement. Most futures positions are settled by an *offsetting trade*.

7. **C**   It adjusts the delivery price based on the futures price at contract expiration.

8. **C**   (1.0234 − 1.0180) × 125,000 × 3 = $2,025. The contracts were sold and the price declined, so the adjustment is an addition to the account margin.

9. **A**   The exchange determines which contracts will trade.

10. **C**   When insufficient funds exist to satisfy margin requirements, a variation margin must be posted.

11. **B**   Size is not one of the things that distinguishes forwards and futures, although the contract size of futures is standardized, whereas forwards are customized for each party.

OPTION MARKETS AND CONTRACTS

EXAM FOCUS

This derivatives review introduces options, describes their terms and trading, and provides derivations of several options valuation results. Candidates should spend some time understanding how the payoffs on several types of options are determined. This includes options on stocks, bonds, stock indices, interest rates, currencies, and futures. The assigned material on establishing upper and lower bounds is extensive, so it should not be ignored. Candidates must learn at least one of the put-call parity relations and how to construct an arbitrage strategy. The notation, formulas, and relations may seem daunting, but if you put in the time to understand what the notation is saying (and why), you can master the important points.

LOS 63.a: Describe call and put options.

CFA® Program Curriculum, Volume 6, page 72

An **option contract** gives its owner the right, but not the legal obligation, to conduct a transaction involving an underlying asset at a predetermined future date (the exercise date) and at a predetermined price (the **exercise price** or **strike price**). Options give the option buyer the right to decide whether or not the trade will eventually take place. The seller of the option has the obligation to perform if the buyer exercises the option.

- The owner of a **call option** has the right to purchase the underlying asset at a specific price for a specified time period.
- The owner of a **put option** has the right to sell the underlying asset at a specific price for a specified time period.

For every owner of an option, there must be a seller. The seller of the option is also called the **option writer**. There are four possible options positions:

1. Long call: the buyer of a call option—has the right to buy an underlying asset.

2. Short call: the writer (seller) of a call option—has the obligation to sell the underlying asset.

3. Long put: the buyer of a put option—has the right to sell the underlying asset.

4. Short put: the writer (seller) of a put option—has the obligation to buy the underlying asset.

To acquire these rights, owners of options must buy them by paying a price called the **option premium** to the seller of the option.

Listed stock option contracts trade on exchanges and are normally for 100 shares of stock. After issuance, stock option contracts are adjusted for stock splits but not cash dividends.

To see how an option contract works, consider the stock of ABC Company. It sells for $55 and has a call option available on it that sells for a premium of $10. This call option has an exercise price of $50 and has an expiration date in five months.

 Professor's Note: The option premium is simply the price of the option. Please do not confuse this with the exercise price of the option, which is the price at which the underlying asset will be bought/sold if the option is exercised.

If the ABC call option is purchased for $10, the buyer can purchase ABC stock from the option seller over the next five months for $50. The seller, or writer, of the option gets to keep the $10 premium no matter what the stock does during this time period. If the option buyer exercises the option, the seller will receive the $50 strike price and must deliver to the buyer a share of ABC stock. If the price of ABC stock falls to $50 or below, the buyer is not obligated to exercise the option. Note that option holders will only exercise their right to act if it is profitable to do so. The option writer, however, has an obligation to act at the request of the option holder.

A put option on ABC stock is the same as a call option, except the buyer of the put (long position) has the right to sell a share of ABC for $50 at any time during the next five months. The put writer (short position) has the obligation to buy ABC stock at the exercise price in the event that the option is exercised.

The owner of the option is the one who decides whether or not to exercise the option. If the option has value, the buyer may either exercise the option or sell the option to another buyer in the secondary options market.

LOS 63.b: Distinguish between European and American options.

CFA® Program Curriculum, Volume 6, page 73

American options may be exercised at any time up to and including the contract's expiration date.

European options can be exercised only on the contract's expiration date.

 Professor's Note: The name of the option does not imply where the option trades— they are just names.

At expiration, an American option and a European option on the same asset with the same strike price are identical. They may either be exercised or allowed to expire. Before expiration, however, they are different and may have different values, so you must distinguish between the two.

If two options are identical (maturity, underlying stock, strike price, etc.) in all ways, except that one is a European option and the other is an American option, the value of the American option will equal or exceed the value of the European option. Why? The early exercise feature of the American option gives it more flexibility, so it should be worth at least as much and possibly more.

LOS 63.c: Define the concept of moneyness of an option.

CFA® Program Curriculum, Volume 6, page 75

Moneyness refers to whether an option is *in the money* or *out of the money*. If immediate exercise of the option would generate a positive payoff, it is in the money. If immediate exercise would result in a loss (negative payoff), it is out of the money. When the current asset price equals the exercise price, exercise will generate neither a gain nor loss, and the option is *at the money*.

The following describe the conditions for a **call option** to be in, out of, or at the money.

- *In-the-money call options.* If $S - X > 0$, a call option is in the money. $S - X$ is the amount of the payoff a call holder would receive from immediate exercise, buying a share for X and selling it in the market for a greater price S.
- *Out-of-the-money call options.* If $S - X < 0$, a call option is out of the money.
- *At-the-money call options.* If $S = X$, a call option is said to be at the money.

The following describe the conditions for a **put option** to be in, out of, or at the money.

- *In-the-money put options.* If $X - S > 0$, a put option is in the money. $X - S$ is the amount of the payoff from immediate exercise, buying a share for S and exercising the put to receive X for the share.
- *Out-of-the-money put options.* When the stock's price is greater than the strike price, a put option is said to be out of the money. If $X - S < 0$, a put option is out of the money.
- *At-the-money put options.* If $S = X$, a put option is said to be at the money.

Example: Moneyness

Consider a July 40 call and a July 40 put, both on a stock that is currently selling for $37/share. Calculate how much these options are in or out of the money.

 Professor's Note: A July 40 call is a call option with an exercise price of $40 and an expiration date in July.

Answer:

The call is $3 out of the money because $S - X = -\$3.00$. The put is $3 in the money because $X - S = \$3.00$.

LOS 63.d: Compare exchange-traded options and over-the-counter options.

CFA® Program Curriculum, Volume 6, page 76

Exchange-traded or **listed options** are regulated, standardized, liquid, and backed by the Options Clearing Corporation for Chicago Board Options Exchange transactions. Most exchange-listed options have expiration dates within two to four months of the current date. Exchanges also list **long-term equity anticipatory securities** (LEAPS), which are equity options with expiration dates longer than one year.

Over-the-counter (OTC) options on stocks for the retail trade all but disappeared with the growth of the organized exchanges in the 1970s. There is now, however, an active market in OTC options on currencies, swaps, and equities, primarily for institutional buyers. Like the forward market, the OTC options market is largely unregulated, consists of custom options, involves counterparty risk, and is facilitated by dealers in much the same way forwards markets are.

LOS 63.e: Identify the types of options in terms of the underlying instruments.

CFA® Program Curriculum, Volume 6, page 80

The three types of options we consider are (1) financial options, (2) options on futures, and (3) commodity options.

Financial options include equity options and other options based on stock indices, Treasury bonds, interest rates, and currencies. The strike price for financial options can be in terms of yield-to-maturity on bonds, an index level, or an exchange rate for *foreign currency options*. LIBOR-based *interest rate options* have payoffs based on the difference between LIBOR at expiration and the strike rate in the option.

Bond options are most often based on Treasury bonds because of their active trading. There are relatively few listed options on bonds—most are over-the-counter options. Bond options can be deliverable or settle in cash. The mechanics of bond options are like those of equity options, but are based on bond prices and a specific face value of the bond. The buyer of a call option on a bond will gain if interest rates fall and bond prices rise. A put buyer will gain when rates rise and bond prices fall.

Index options settle in cash, nothing is delivered, and the payoff is made directly to the option holder's account. The payoff on an index call (long) is the amount (if any) by which the index level at expiration exceeds the index level specified in the option (the strike price), multiplied by the *contract multiplier*. An equal amount will be deducted from the account of the index call option writer.

Example: Index options

Assume that you own a call option on the S&P 500 Index with an exercise price equal to 950. The multiplier for this contract is 250. Compute the payoff on this option assuming that the index is 962 at expiration.

Answer:

This is a call, so the expiration date payoff is $(962 - 950) \times \$250 = \$3,000$.

Options on futures, sometimes called futures options, give the holder the right to buy or sell a specified futures contract on or before a given date at a given futures price, the strike price.

- *Call options* on futures contracts give the holder the right to enter into the long side of a futures contract at a given futures price. Assume that you hold a call option on a bond future at 98 (percent of face) and at expiration the futures price on the bond contract is 99. By exercising the call, you take on a long position in the futures contract, and the account is immediately marked to market based on the settlement price. Your account would be credited with cash in an amount equal to 1% (99 – 98) of the face value of the bonds covered by the contract. The seller of the exercised call will take on the short position in the futures contract, and the mark-to-market value of this position will generate the cash deposited to your account.
- *Put options* on futures contracts give the holder the option to take on a short futures position at a futures price equal to the strike price. The writer has the obligation to take on the opposite (long) position if the option is exercised.

Commodity options give the holder the right to either buy or sell a fixed quantity of some physical asset at a fixed (strike) price.

Some capital investment projects have provisions that give the company flexibility to adjust the project's cash flows while it is in progress (for example, an option to abandon the project before completion). Such **real options** have value that should be considered when evaluating a project's NPV.

 Professor's Note: Evaluating projects with real options is covered in the Study Session on corporate finance at Level II.

LOS 63.f: Compare interest rate options with forward rate agreements (FRAs).

CFA® Program Curriculum, Volume 6, page 81

Interest rate options are similar to the stock options except that the exercise price is an interest rate and the underlying asset is a reference rate such as LIBOR. Interest rate options are also similar to FRAs because there is no deliverable asset. Instead they are settled in cash, in an amount that is based on a notional amount and the spread between the strike rate and the reference rate. Most interest rate options are European options.

To see how interest rate options work, consider a long position in a 1-year LIBOR-based interest rate call option with a notional amount of $1,000,000 and a strike rate of 5%. For our example, let's assume that this option is costless for simplicity. If at expiration, LIBOR is greater than 5%, the option can be exercised and the owner will receive $1,000,000 × (LIBOR – 5%). If LIBOR is less than 5%, the option expires worthless and the owner receives nothing.

Now, let's consider a short position in a LIBOR-based interest rate put option with the same features as the call that we just discussed. Again, the option is assumed to be costless, with a strike rate of 5% and notional amount of $1,000,000. If at expiration, LIBOR falls below 5%, the option writer (short) must pay the put holder an amount equal to $1,000,000 × (5% – LIBOR). If at expiration, LIBOR is greater than 5%, the option expires worthless and the put writer makes no payments. If the rate is for less than one year, the payoff is adjusted. For example, if the reference rate for the option is 60-day LIBOR, the payoff would be $1,000,000 × (5% – LIBOR)(60/360) because the actual LIBOR rate and the strike rate are annualized rates.

Notice the one-sided payoff on these interest rate options. The long call receives a payoff when LIBOR exceeds the strike rate and receives nothing if LIBOR is below the strike rate. On the other hand, the short put position makes payments if LIBOR is below the strike rate, and makes no payments when LIBOR exceeds the strike rate.

The combination of the long interest rate call option plus a short interest rate put option has the same payoff as a forward rate agreement (FRA). To see this, consider the fixed-rate payer in a 5% fixed-rate, $1,000,000 notional, LIBOR-based FRA. Like our long call position, the fixed-rate payer will receive $1,000,000 × (LIBOR – 5%). And, like our short put position, the fixed-rate payer will pay $1,000,000 × (5% – LIBOR).

 Professor's Note: For the exam, you need to know that a long interest rate call combined with a short interest rate put can have the same payoff as a long position in an FRA.

LOS 63.g: Define interest rate caps, floors, and collars.

CFA® Program Curriculum, Volume 6, page 83

An **interest rate cap** is a series of interest rate call options, having expiration dates that correspond to the reset dates on a floating-rate loan. Caps are often used to protect a floating-rate borrower from an increase in interest rates. Caps place a maximum (upper limit) on the interest payments on a floating-rate loan.

Caps pay when rates rise above the cap rate. In this regard, a cap can be viewed as a series of interest rate call options with strike rates equal to the cap rate. Each option in a cap is called a *caplet*.

An **interest rate floor** is a series of interest rate put options, having expiration dates that correspond to the reset dates on a floating-rate loan. Floors are often used to protect a floating-rate lender from a decline in interest rates. Floors place a minimum (lower limit) on the interest payments that are received from a floating-rate loan.

An interest rate floor on a loan operates just the opposite of a cap. The floor rate is a minimum rate on the payments on a floating-rate loan.

Floors pay when rates fall below the floor rate. In this regard, a floor can be viewed as a series of interest rate put options with strike rates equal to the floor rate. Each option in a floor is called a *floorlet*.

An **interest rate collar** combines a cap and a floor. A borrower with a floating-rate loan may *buy* a cap for protection against rates above the cap and *sell* a floor in order to defray some of the cost of the cap.

Let's review the information in Figure 1, which illustrates the payments from a cap and a floor. On each reset date of a floating-rate loan, the interest for the next period (e.g., 90 days) is determined on the basis of some reference rate. Here, we assume that LIBOR is the reference rate and that we have quarterly payment dates on the loan.

The figure shows the effect of a cap that is set at 10%. In the event that LIBOR rises above 10%, the cap will make a payment to the cap buyer to offset any interest expense in excess of an annual rate of 10%. A cap may be structured to cover a certain number of periods or for the entire life of a loan. The cap will make a payment at any future interest payment due date whenever the reference rate (LIBOR in our example) exceeds the cap rate. As indicated in the figure, the cap's payment is based on the difference between the reference rate and the cap rate. The amount of the payment will equal the notional amount specified in the cap contract times the difference between the cap rate and the reference rate. When used to hedge a loan, the notional amount is usually equal to the loan amount.

Figure 1 also illustrates a floor of 5% for our LIBOR-based loan. For any payment where the reference rate on the loan falls below 5%, there is an additional payment required by the floor to bring the total payment to 5% (1.25% quarterly on a 90-day LIBOR-based loan). Note that the issuer of a floating-rate note with both a cap and a floor (a collar) is long a cap and *short* (has sold) a floor. The note issuer receives a payment when rates are above the cap, and makes an additional payment when rates are below the floor (compared to just paying the reference rate).

Figure 1: Interest Rate Caps and Floors

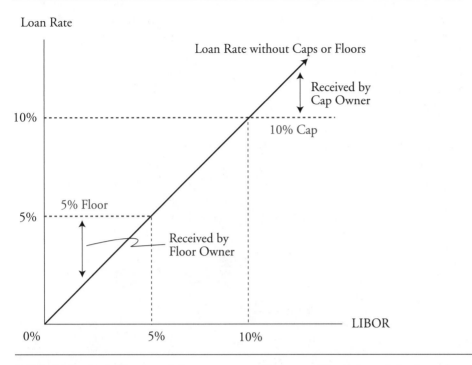

LOS 63.h: Calculate and interpret option payoffs and explain how interest rate options differ from other types of options.

CFA® Program Curriculum, Volume 6, page 83

Calculating the payoff for a stock option, or other type of option with a monetary-based exercise price, is straightforward. At expiration, a call owner receives any amount by which the asset price exceeds the strike price, and zero otherwise. The holder of a put will receive any amount that the asset price is below the strike price at expiration, and zero otherwise.

While bonds are quoted in terms of yield-to-maturity, T-bills in discount yield, indices in index points, and currencies as an exchange rate, the same principle applies. That is, in each case, to get the payoff per unit of the relevant asset, we need to translate the asset value to a dollar value and the strike price (or rate, or yield) to a dollar strike price. We can then multiply this payoff times however many units of the asset are covered by the options contract.

- For a stock index option, we saw that these dollar values were obtained from multiplying the index level and the strike level by the multiplier specified in the contract. The resulting dollar payoffs are per contract.
- The payoff on options on futures is the cash the option holder receives when he exercises the option and the resulting futures position is marked to market.

The **payoffs on interest rate options** are different. For example, a call option based on 90-day LIBOR makes a payment based on a stated notional amount and the difference between 90-day LIBOR and the option's strike rate, times 90 / 360 to adjust for the interest rate period. The payment is made, not at option expiration, but at a future date corresponding to the term of the reference rate. For example, an option based on 90-day LIBOR will make a payment 90 days after the expiration date of the option. This payment date often corresponds to the date on which a LIBOR-based borrower would make the next interest payment on a loan.

Example: Computing the payoff for an interest rate option

Assume you bought a 60-day call option on 90-day LIBOR with a notional principal of $1 million and a strike rate of 5%. Compute the payment that you will receive if 90-day LIBOR is 6% at contract expiration, and determine when the payment will be received.

Answer:

The interest savings on a $1 million 90-day loan at 5% versus 6% is:

$$1 \text{ million} \times (0.06 - 0.05)(90 / 360) = \$2,500$$

This is the amount that will be paid by the call writer 90 days after expiration.

LOS 63.i: Define intrinsic value and time value, and explain their relationship.

CFA® Program Curriculum, Volume 6, page 88

An option's **intrinsic value** is the amount by which the option is in-the-money. It is the amount that the option owner would receive if the option were exercised. An option has zero intrinsic value if it is at the money or out of the money, regardless of whether it is a call or a put option.

Let's look at the value of a call option *at expiration*. If the expiration date price of the stock exceeds the strike price of the option, the call owner will exercise the option and receive S – X. If the price of the stock is less than or equal to the strike price, the call holder will let the option expire and get nothing.

The *intrinsic value of a call* option is the greater of (S – X) or 0. That is:

$$C = \max[0, S - X]$$

Similarly, the *intrinsic value of a put* option is (X – S) or 0, whichever is greater. That is:

$$P = \max[0, X - S]$$

Example: Intrinsic value

Consider a call option with a strike price of $50. Compute the intrinsic value of this option for stock prices of $55, $50, and $45.

Answer:

stock price = $55: C = max[0, S – X] = max[0, (55 – 50)] = $5

stock price = $50: C = max[0, S – X] = max[0, (50 – 50)] = $0

stock price = $45: C = max[0, S – X] = max[0, (45 – 50)] = $0

Notice that at expiration, if the stock is worth $50 or below, the call option is worth $0. Why? Because a rational option holder will not exercise the call option and take the loss. This one-sided feature of call options is illustrated in the option payoff diagram presented in Figure 2 for the call option we have used in this example.

 Professor's Note: Option payoff diagrams are commonly used tools to illustrate the value of an option at expiration.

Figure 2: Call Option Payoff Diagram

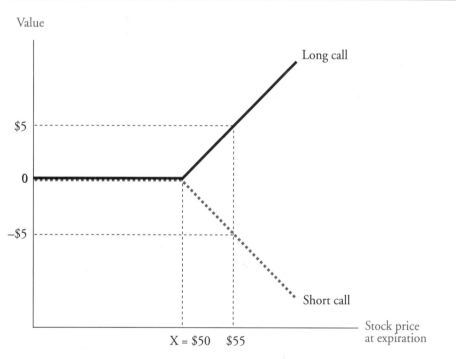

As indicated in Figure 2, the expiration date payoff to the owner is either zero or the amount that the option is in the money. For a call option writer (seller), the payoff is either zero or minus the amount it is in the money. There are no positive payoffs for an option writer. The option writer receives the premium and takes on the obligation to pay whatever the call owner gains.

With reference to Figure 2, you should make the following observations:

- The payoff to a long call position (the solid line) is a flat line which angles upward to the right at a 45 degree angle from the strike price, X.
- The payoff to the writer of a call (dotted line), is a flat line which angles downward to the right at a 45 degree angle from the strike price, X.
- Options are a zero-sum game. If you add the long call option's payoff to the short option's payoff, you will get a net payoff of zero.
- At a stock price of $55, the payoff to the long is $5, which is a $5 loss to the short.

Similar to our payoff diagram for a call option, Figure 3 illustrates the at-expiration payoff values for a put option. As indicated here, if the price of the stock is less than the strike price, the put owner will exercise the option and receive $(X – S)$. If the price of the stock is greater than or equal to the strike price, the put holder will let the put option expire and get nothing (0). At a stock price of $40, the payoff on a long put is $10; the seller of the put (the short) would have a negative payoff because he must buy the stock at $50 and receive stock worth $40.

Figure 3: Put Option Payoff Diagram

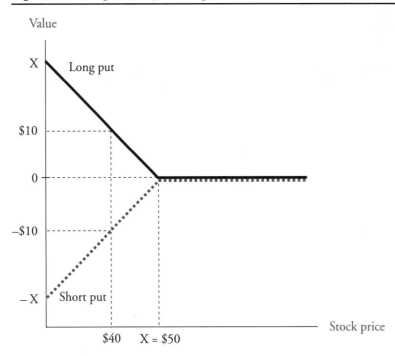

The **time value** of an option is the amount by which the option premium exceeds the intrinsic value and is sometimes called the speculative value of the option. This relationship can be written as:

$$option\ value = intrinsic\ value + time\ value$$

As we discussed earlier, the intrinsic value of an option is the amount by which the option is in the money. At any point during the life of an options contract, its value will typically be greater than its intrinsic value. This is because there is some probability that the stock price will change in an amount that gives the option a positive payoff at expiration greater than the (current) intrinsic value. Recall that an option's intrinsic value (to a buyer) is the amount of the payoff at expiration and is bounded by zero. When an option reaches expiration there is no time remaining and the time value is zero. For American options and in most cases for European options, the longer the time to expiration, the greater the time value and, other things equal, the greater the option's premium (price).

LOS 63.j: Determine the minimum and maximum values of European options and American options.

CFA® Program Curriculum, Volume 6, page 91

The following is some option terminology that we will use when addressing these LOS:

S_t = the price of the underlying stock at time t

X = the exercise price of the option

T = the time to expiration

c_t = the price of a European call at any time t prior to expiration at time = T

C_t = the price of an American call at any time t prior to expiration at time = T

p_t = the price of a European put at any time t prior to expiration at time = T

P_t = the price of an American put at any time t prior to expiration at time = T

RFR = the risk-free rate

 Professor's Note: Please notice that lowercase letters are used to represent European-style options.

Lower bound. Theoretically, no option will sell for less than its intrinsic value and no option can take on a negative value. This means that the lower bound for any option is zero. *The lower bound of zero applies to both American and European options.*

Upper bound for call options. The maximum value of either an American or a European *call* option at any time t is the time-t share price of the underlying stock. This makes sense because no one would pay a price for the right to buy an asset that exceeded the asset's value. It would be cheaper to simply buy the underlying asset. At time t = 0, the upper boundary condition can be expressed respectively for American and European call options as:

$$C_0 \leq S_0 \text{ and } c_0 \leq S_0$$

Upper bound for put options. The price for an American put option cannot be more than its strike price. This is the exercise value in the event the underlying stock price goes to zero. However, since European puts cannot be exercised prior to expiration, the maximum value is the present value of the exercise price discounted at the risk-free rate. Even if the stock price goes to zero, and is expected to stay at zero, the intrinsic value,

X, will not be received until the expiration date. At time t = 0, the upper boundary condition can be expressed for American and European put options, respectively, as:

$$P_0 \leq X \text{ and } p_0 \leq \frac{X}{(1 + RFR)^T}$$

The minimum and maximum boundary conditions for the various types of options at any time t are summarized in Figure 4.

Figure 4: Option Value Limits

Option	Minimum Value	Maximum Value
European call	$c_t \geq 0$	$c_t \leq S_t$
American call	$C_t \geq 0$	$C_t \leq S_t$
European put	$p_t \geq 0$	$p_t \leq X/(1 + RFR)^{(T-t)}$
American put	$P_t \geq 0$	$P_t \leq X$

Professor's Note: The values in the table are the theoretical limits on the value of options. In the next section, we will establish more restrictive limits for option prices.

LOS 63.k: Calculate and interpret the lowest prices of European and American calls and puts based on the rules for minimum values and lower bounds.

CFA® Program Curriculum, Volume 6, page 91

Professor's Note: The option boundary conditions that we discuss below will be important when you study option pricing models. For now, if you follow the logic leading up to the results presented in Figure 5, you will be prepared to deal with these LOS. Knowing and understanding the results in Figure 5 satisfy the requirements of these LOS; the following derivation of those results need not be memorized.

At this point, we know that for **American-style options**, which can be immediately exercised, the minimum price has to be the option's intrinsic value. For at-the-money and out-of-the money options, this minimum is zero, because options cannot have negative values. For in-the-money American options, the minima are simply the intrinsic values $S - X$ for calls, and $X - S$ for puts. If this were not the case, you could buy the option for less than its intrinsic value and immediately exercise it for a guaranteed profit. So, for American options, we can express the *lower bound on the option price* at any time t prior to expiration as:

$$C_t = \max[0, S_t - X]$$
$$P_t = \max[0, X - S_t]$$

For European options, however, the minima are not so obvious because these options are not exercisable immediately. To determine the **lower bounds for European options,** we can examine the value of a portfolio in which the option is combined with a long or short position in the stock and a pure discount bond.

For a *European call option,* construct the following portfolio:

- A long at-the-money European call option with exercise price X, expiring at time $t = T$.
- A long discount bond priced to yield the risk-free rate that pays X at option expiration.
- A short position in one share of the underlying stock priced at $S_0 = X$.

The current value of this portfolio is $c_0 - S_0 + X / (1 + RFR)^T$.

At expiration time, $t = T$, this portfolio will pay $c_T - S_T + X$. That is, we will collect $c_T = \max[0, S_T - X]$ on the call option, pay S_T to cover our short stock position, and collect X from the maturing bond.

- If $S_T \geq X$, the call is in-the-money, and the portfolio will have a zero payoff because the call pays $S_T - X$, the bond pays $+X$, and we pay $-S_T$ to cover our short position. That is, the time $t = T$ payoff is: $S_T - X + X - S_T = 0$.
- If $X > S_T$ the call is out-of-the-money, and the portfolio has a positive payoff equal to $X - S_T$ because the call value, c_T, is zero, we collect X on the bond, and pay $-S_T$ to cover the short position. So, the time $t = T$ payoff is: $0 + X - S_T = X - S_T$.

Note that no matter whether the option expires in-the-money, at-the-money, or out-of-the-money, the portfolio value will be equal to or greater than zero. We will never have to make a payment.

To prevent arbitrage, any portfolio that has no possibility of a negative payoff cannot have a negative value. Thus, we can state the value of the portfolio *at time t = 0* as:

$$c_0 - S_0 + X / (1 + RFR)^T \geq 0$$

which allows us to conclude that:

$$c_0 \geq S_0 - X / (1 + RFR)^T$$

Combining this result with the earlier minimum on the call value of zero, we can write:

$$c_0 \geq \max[0, S_0 - X / (1 + RFR)^T]$$

Note that $X / (1 + RFR)^T$ is the present value of a pure discount bond with a face value of X.

Based on these results, we can now state the **lower bound for the price of an American call** as:

$$C_0 \geq \max[0, S_0 - X / (1 + RFR)^T]$$

How can we say this? This conclusion follows from the following two facts:

1. The early exercise feature on an American call makes it worth at least as much as an equivalent European call (i.e., $C_t \geq c_t$).

2. The lower bound for the value of a European call is equal to or greater than the theoretical lower bound for an American call. For example, $\max[0, S_0 - X / (1 + RFR)^T] \geq \max[0, S_0 - X]$.

 Professor's Note: Don't get bogged down here. We just use the fact that an American call is worth at least as much as a European call to claim that the lower bound on an American call is at least as much as the lower bound on a European call.

Derive the **minimum value of a European put option** by forming the following portfolio at time t = 0:

- A long at-the-money European put option with exercise price X, expiring at t = T.
- A short position on a risk-free bond priced at $X / (1 + RFR)^T$. This is the same as borrowing an amount equal to $X / (1 + RFR)^T$.
- A long position in a share of the underlying stock priced at S_0.

At expiration time t = T, this portfolio will pay $p_T + S_T - X$. That is, we will collect $p_T = \max[0, X - S_T]$ on the put option, receive S_T from the stock, and pay $-X$ on the bond issue (loan).

- If $S_T > X$, the payoff will equal: $p_T + S_T - X = S_T - X$.
- If $S_T \leq X$, the payoff will be zero.

Again, a no-arbitrage argument can be made that the portfolio value must be zero or greater, because there are no negative payoffs to the portfolio.

At time t = 0, this condition can be written as:

$$p_0 + S_0 - X / (1 + RFR)^T \geq 0$$

and rearranged to state the minimum value for a European put option at time t = 0 as:

$$p_0 \geq X / (1 + RFR)^T - S_0$$

We have now established the **minimum bound on the price of a European put option** as:

$$p_0 \geq \max[0, X / (1 + RFR)^T - S_0]$$

Professor's Note: Notice that the lower bound on a European put is below that of an American put option (i.e., max[0, X – S₀]). This is because when it's in the money, the American put option can be exercised immediately for a payoff of X – S₀.

Figure 5 summarizes what we now know regarding the boundary prices for American and European options at any time *t* prior to expiration at time t = T.

Figure 5: Lower and Upper Bounds for Options

Option	Minimum Value	Maximum Value
European call	$c_t \geq \max[0, S_t - X / (1 + RFR)^{T-t}]$	S_t
American call	$C_t \geq \max[0, S_t - X / (1 + RFR)^{T-t}]$	S_t
European put	$p_t \geq \max[0, X / (1 + RFR)^{T-t} - S_t]$	$X / (1 + RFR)^{T-t}$
American put	$P_t \geq \max[0, X - S_t]$	X

Professor's Note: For the exam, know the price limits in Figure 5. You will not be asked to derive them, but you may be expected to use them.

Example: Minimum prices for American vs. European puts

Compute the lowest possible price for 4-month American and European 65 puts on a stock that is trading at 63 when the risk-free rate is 5%.

Answer:

American put: $P_0 \geq \max[0, X - S_0] = \max[0,2] = \$2$

European put: $p_0 \geq \max[0, X / (1 + RFR)^T - S_0] = \max[0, 65 / 1.05^{0.333} - 63] = \$0.95$

Example: Minimum prices for American vs. European calls

Compute the lowest possible price for 3-month American and European 65 calls on a stock that is trading at 68 when the risk-free rate is 5%.

Answer:

$C_0 \geq \max[0, S_0 - X / (1 + RFR)^T] = \max[0, 68 - 65 / 1.05^{0.25}] = \$3.79$

$c_0 \geq \max[0, S_0 - X / (1 + RFR)^T] = \max[0, 68 - 65 / 1.05^{0.25}] = \$3.79$

LOS 63.l: Explain how option prices are affected by the exercise price and the time to expiration.

CFA® Program Curriculum, Volume 6, page 96

The result we are after here is a simple and somewhat intuitive one. That is, given two puts that are identical in all respects except exercise price, the one with the higher exercise price will have at least as much value as the one with the lower exercise price. This is because the underlying stock can be sold at a higher price. Similarly, given two calls that are identical in every respect except exercise price, the one with the lower exercise price will have at least as much value as the one with the higher exercise price. This is because the underlying stock can be purchased at a lower price.

 Professor's Note: The derivation of this result is included here although it is not explicitly required by the LOS.

The method here, for both puts and calls, is to combine two options with different exercise prices into a portfolio and examine the portfolio payoffs at expiration for the three possible stock price ranges. We use the fact that a portfolio with no possibility of a negative payoff cannot have a negative value to establish the pricing relations for options with differing times to expiration.

For $X_1 < X_2$, consider a portfolio at time t that holds the following positions:

$c_t(X_1)$ = a long call with an exercise price of X_1

$c_t(X_2)$ = a short call with an exercise price of X_2

The three expiration date (t = T) conditions and payoffs that need to be considered here are summarized in Figure 6.

Figure 6: Exercise Price vs. Call Price

Expiration Date Condition	Option Value	Portfolio Payoff
$S_T \leq X_1$	$c_T(X_1) = c_T(X_2) = 0$	0
$X_1 < S_T < X_2$	$c_T(X_1) = S_T - X_1$ $c_T(X_2) = 0$	$S_T - X_1 > 0$
$X_2 \leq S_T$	$c_T(X_1) = S_T - X_1$ $c_T(X_2) = S_T - X_2$	$(S_T - X_1) - (S_T - X_2)$ $= X_2 - X_1 > 0$

With no negative payoffs at expiration, the current portfolio of $c_0(X_1) - c_0(X_2)$ must have a value greater than or equal to zero, and we have proven that $c_0(X_1) \geq c_0(X_2)$.

Similarly, consider a portfolio short a put with exercise price X_1 and long a put with exercise price X_2, where $X_1 < X_2$. The expiration date payoffs that we need to consider are summarized in Figure 7.

Figure 7: Exercise Price vs. Put Price

Expiration Date Condition	Option Value	Portfolio Payoff
$S_T \geq X_2$	$p_T(X_1) = p_T(X_2) = 0$	0
$X_2 > S_T > X_1$	$p_T(X_1) = 0$ $p_T(X_2) = X_2 - S_T$	$X_2 - S_T > 0$
$X_1 \geq S_T$	$p_T(X_1) = X_1 - S_T$ $p_T(X_2) = X_2 - S_T$	$(X_2 - S_T) - (X_1 - S_T)$ $= X_2 - X_1 > 0$

Here again, with no negative payoffs at expiration, the current portfolio of $p_0(X_2) - p_0(X_1)$ must have a value greater than or equal to zero, which proves that $p_0(X_2) \geq p_0(X_1)$.

In summary, we have shown that, all else being equal:

- Call prices are inversely related to exercise prices.
- Put prices are directly related to exercise price.

In general, a **longer time to expiration** will increase an option's value. For far out-of-the-money options, the extra time may have no effect, but we can say the longer-term option will be no less valuable that the shorter-term option.

The case that doesn't fit this pattern is the European put. Recall that the minimum value of an in-the-money European put at any time t prior to expiration is $X / (1 + RFR)^{T-t} - S_t$. While longer time to expiration increases option value through increased volatility, it decreases the present value of any option payoff at expiration. For this reason, we cannot state positively that the value of a longer European put will be greater than the value of a shorter-term put.

If volatility is high and the discount rate low, the extra time value will be the dominant factor and the longer-term put will be more valuable. Low volatility and high interest rates have the opposite effect and the value of a longer-term in-the-money put option can be less than the value of a shorter-term put option.

LOS 63.m: Explain put–call parity for European options, and explain how put–call parity is related to arbitrage and the construction of synthetic options.

CFA® Program Curriculum, Volume 6, page 98

Our derivation of **put-call parity** is based on the payoffs of two portfolio combinations, a fiduciary call and a protective put.

A *fiduciary call* is a combination of a pure-discount, riskless bond that pays X at maturity and a call with exercise price X. The payoff for a fiduciary call at expiration is X when the call is out of the money, and $X + (S - X) = S$ when the call is in the money.

A *protective put* is a share of stock together with a put option on the stock. The expiration date payoff for a protective put is $(X - S) + S = X$ when the put is in the money, and S when the put is out of the money.

 Professor's Note: When working with put-call parity, it is important to note that the exercise prices on the put and the call and the face value of the riskless bond are all equal to X.

When the put is in the money, the call is out of the money, and both portfolios pay X at expiration.

Similarly, when the put is out of the money and the call is in the money, both portfolios pay S at expiration.

Put-call parity holds that portfolios with identical payoffs must sell for the same price to prevent arbitrage. We can express the put-call parity relationship as:

$$c + X / (1 + RFR)^T = S + p$$

Equivalencies for each of the individual securities in the put-call parity relationship can be expressed as:

$$S = c - p + X / (1 + RFR)^T$$
$$p = c - S + X / (1 + RFR)^T$$
$$c = S + p - X / (1 + RFR)^T$$
$$X / (1 + RFR)^T = S + p - c$$

The single securities on the left-hand side of the equations all have exactly the same payoffs as the portfolios on the right-hand side. The portfolios on the right-hand side are the **synthetic** equivalents of the securities on the left. Note that the options must be European-style and the puts and calls must have the same exercise price for these relations to hold.

For example, to synthetically produce the payoff for a long position in a share of stock, use the following relationship:

$$S = c - p + X / (1 + RFR)^T$$

This means that the payoff on a long stock can be synthetically created with a long call, a short put, and a long position in a risk-free discount bond.

The other securities in the put-call parity relationship can be constructed in a similar manner.

Professor's Note: After expressing the put-call parity relationship in terms of the security you want to synthetically create, the sign on the individual securities will indicate whether you need a long position (+ sign) or a short position (− sign) in the respective securities.

Example: Call option valuation using put-call parity

Suppose that the current stock price is $52 and the risk-free rate is 5%. You have found a quote for a 3-month put option with an exercise price of $50. The put price is $1.50, but due to light trading in the call options, there was not a listed quote for the 3-month, $50 call. Estimate the price of the 3-month call option.

Answer:

Rearranging put-call parity, we find that the call price is:

$$call = put + stock - present\ value(X)$$

$$call = \$1.50 + \$52 - \frac{\$50}{1.05^{0.25}} = \$4.11$$

This means that if a 3-month, $50 call is available, it should be priced at $4.11 per share.

LOS 63.n: Explain how cash flows on the underlying asset affect put–call parity and the lower bounds of option prices.

CFA® Program Curriculum, Volume 6, page 104

If the asset has positive cash flows over the period of the option, the cost of the asset is less by the present value of the cash flows. You can think of buying a stock for S and simultaneously borrowing the present value of the cash flows, PV_{CF}. The cash flow(s) will provide the payoff of the loan(s), and the loan(s) will reduce the net cost of the asset to $S - PV_{CF}$. Therefore, for assets with positive cash flows over the term of the option, we can **substitute this (lower) net cost, $S - PV_{CF}$,** for S in the lower bound conditions and in all the parity relations.

The lower bounds for European options at time t = 0 can be expressed as:

$$c_0 \geq max[0,\ S_0 - PV_{CF} - X\ /\ (1 + RFR)^T],\ and$$
$$p_0 \geq max[0,\ X\ /\ (1 + RFR)^T - (S_0 - PV_{CF})]$$

The put-call parity relations can be adjusted to account for asset cash flows in the same manner.

$$(S_0 - PV_{CF}) = C - P + X\ /\ (1 + RFR)^T,\ and$$
$$C + X\ /\ (1 + RFR)^T = (S_0 - PV_{CF}) + P$$

LOS 63.o: Determine the directional effect of an interest rate change or volatility change on an option's price.

CFA® Program Curriculum, Volume 6, page 105

When interest rates increase, the value of a call option increases and the value of a put option decreases (holding the price of the underlying security constant). This general result may not apply to interest rate options or to bond or T-bill options, where a change in the risk-free rate may affect the value of the underlying asset.

The no-arbitrage relations for puts and calls make these statements obvious:

$$C = S + P - X / (1 + RFR)^T$$
$$P = C - S + X / (1 + RFR)^T$$

Here we can see that an increase in RFR decreases $X / (1 + RFR)^T$. This will have the effect of increasing the value of the call, and decreasing the value of the put. A decrease in interest rates will decrease the value of a call option and increase the value of a put option.

 Professor's Note: Admittedly, this is a partial analysis of these equations, but it does give the right directions for the effects of interest rate changes and will help you remember them if this relation is tested on the exam.

Greater volatility in the value of an asset or interest rate underlying an option contract increases the values of both puts and calls (and caps and floors). The reason is that options are one-sided. Since an option's value falls no lower than zero when it expires out of the money, the increased upside potential (with no greater downside risk) from increased volatility, increases the option's value.

KEY CONCEPTS

LOS 63.a

A call option on a financial or physical asset gives the option's owner the right, but not the obligation, to buy a specified quantity of the asset from the option writer at the exercise price specified in the option for a given time period. The writer of a call option is obligated to sell the asset at the exercise price if the option's owner chooses to exercise it.

A put option on a financial or physical asset gives the option's owner the right, but not the obligation, to sell a specified quantity of the asset to the option writer at the exercise price specified in the option for a given time period. The writer of a put option is obligated to purchase the asset at the exercise price if the option's owner chooses to exercise it.

The owner (buyer) of an option is said to be long the option, and the writer (seller) of an option is said to be short the option.

LOS 63.b

American options can be exercised at any time up to the option's expiration date.

European options can be exercised only at the option's expiration date.

LOS 63.c

Moneyness for puts and calls is determined by the difference between the strike price (X) and the market price of the underlying stock (S):

Moneyness	Call Option	Put Option
In the money	$S > X$	$S < X$
At the money	$S = X$	$S = X$
Out of the money	$S < X$	$S > X$

LOS 63.d

Exchange-traded options are standardized, regulated, and backed by a clearinghouse. Over-the-counter options are largely unregulated custom options that have counterparty risk.

LOS 63.e

Options are available on financial securities, futures contracts, interest rates, and commodities.

LOS 63.f
Interest rate option payoffs are the difference between the market and strike rates, adjusted for the loan period, multiplied by the principal amount.

At expiration, an interest rate call receives a payment when the reference rate is above the strike rate, and an interest rate put receives a payment when the reference rate is below the strike rate.

An FRA can be replicated with two interest rate options: a long call and a short put.

LOS 63.g
Interest rate caps put a maximum (upper limit) on the payments on a floating-rate loan and are equivalent (from the borrower's perspective) to a series of long interest rate calls at the cap rate.

Interest rate floors put a minimum (lower limit) on the payments on a floating-rate loan and are equivalent (from the borrower's perspective) to a series of short interest rate puts at the floor rate.

An interest rate collar combines a cap and a floor. A borrower can create a collar on a floating-rate loan by buying a cap and selling a floor.

LOS 63.h
The payoff to the holder of a call or put option on a stock is the option's intrinsic value. Payment occurs at expiration of the option.

Payoffs on interest rate options are paid after expiration, at the end of the interest rate (loan) period specified in the contract.

LOS 63.i
The intrinsic value of an option is the payoff from immediate exercise if the option is in the money, and zero otherwise.

The time (speculative) value of an option is the difference between its premium (market price) and its intrinsic value. At expiration, time value is zero.

LOS 63.j,k
Minimum and maximum option values:

Option	Minimum Value	Maximum Value
European call	$c_t \geq \max[0, S_t - X / (1 + RFR)^{T-t}]$	S_t
American call	$C_t \geq \max[0, S_t - X / (1 + RFR)^{T-t}]$	S_t
European put	$p_t \geq \max[0, X / (1 + RFR)^{T-t} - S_t]$	$X / (1 + RFR)^{T-t}$
American put	$P_t \geq \max[0, X - S_t]$	X

LOS 63.l

Calls with lower exercise prices are worth at least as much as otherwise identical calls with higher exercise prices (and typically more).

Puts with higher exercise prices are worth at least as much as otherwise identical puts with lower exercise prices (and typically more).

Otherwise identical options are worth more when there is more time to expiration, with two exceptions:
- Far out-of-the-money options with different expiration dates may be equal in value.
- With European puts, longer time to expiration may decrease an option's value when they are deep in the money.

LOS 63.m

A fiduciary call (a call option and a risk-free zero-coupon bond that pays the strike price X at expiration) and a protective put (a share of stock and a put at X) have the same payoffs at expiration, so arbitrage will force these positions to have equal prices: $c + X / (1 + RFR)^T = S + p$. This establishes put-call parity for European options.

Based on the put-call parity relation, a synthetic security (stock, bond, call, or put) can be created by combining long and short positions in the other three securities.
- $c = S + p - X / (1 + RFR)^T$
- $p = c - S + X / (1 + RFR)^T$
- $S = c - p + X / (1 + RFR)^T$
- $X / (1 + RFR)^T = S + p - c$

LOS 63.n

When the underlying asset has positive cash flows, the minima, maxima, and put-call parity relations are adjusted by subtracting the present value of the expected cash flows from the assets over the life of the option. That is, S can be replaced by (S – PV of expected cash flows).

LOS 63.o

An increase in the risk-free rate will increase call values and decrease put values (for options that do not explicitly depend on interest rates or bond values).

Increased volatility of the underlying asset or interest rate increases both put values and call values.

CONCEPT CHECKERS

1. Which of the following statements about moneyness is *least accurate*? When:
   A. S – X is > 0, a call option is in the money.
   B. S – X = 0, a call option is at the money.
   C. S > X, a put option is in the money.

2. Which of the following statements about American and European options is *most accurate*?
   A. There will always be some price difference between American and European options because of exchange-rate risk.
   B. European options allow for exercise on or before the option expiration date.
   C. Prior to expiration, an American option may have a higher value than an equivalent European option.

3. Which of the following statements about put and call options is *least accurate*?
   A. The price of the option is less volatile than the price of the underlying stock.
   B. Option prices are generally higher the longer the time until the option expires.
   C. For put options, the higher the strike price relative to the stock's underlying price, the more the put is worth.

4. Which of the following statements about options is *most accurate*?
   A. The writer of a put option has the obligation to sell the asset to the holder of the put option.
   B. The holder of a call option has the obligation to sell to the option writer if the stock's price rises above the strike price.
   C. The holder of a put option has the right to sell to the writer of the option.

5. A *decrease* in the risk-free rate of interest will:
   A. increase put and call prices.
   B. decrease put prices and increase call prices.
   C. increase put prices and decrease call prices.

6. A $40 call on a stock trading at $43 is priced at $5. The time value of the option is:
   A. $2.
   B. $5.
   C. $8.

7. Prior to expiration, an American put option on a stock:
   A. is bounded by $S – X / (1 + RFR)^T$.
   B. will never sell for less than its intrinsic value.
   C. can never sell for more than its intrinsic value.

8. The owner of a call option on oil futures with a strike price of $68.70:
   A. can exercise the option and take delivery of the oil.
   B. can exercise the option and take a long position in oil futures.
   C. would never exercise the option when the spot price of oil is less than the strike price.

9. The lower bound for a European put option is:
   A. $\max(0, S - X)$.
   B. $\max[0, X / (1 + RFR)^T - S]$.
   C. $\max[0, S - X / (1 + RFR)^T]$.

10. The lower bound for an American call option is:
    A. $\max(0, S - X)$.
    B. $\max[0, X / (1 + RFR)^T - S]$.
    C. $\max[0, S - X / (1 + RFR)^T]$.

11. To account for positive cash flows from the underlying asset, we need to adjust the put-call parity formula by:
    A. adding the future value of the cash flows to S.
    B. adding the future value of the cash flows to X.
    C. subtracting the present value of the cash flows from S.

12. A forward rate agreement is equivalent to the following interest rate options:
    A. long a call and a put.
    B. short a call and long a put.
    C. long a call and short a put.

13. The payoff on an interest rate option:
    A. comes only at exercise.
    B. is greater the higher the "strike" rate.
    C. comes some period after option expiration.

14. An interest rate floor on a floating-rate note (from the issuer's perspective) is equivalent to a series of:
    A. long interest rate puts.
    B. short interest rate puts.
    C. short interest rate calls.

15. Which of the following relations is *least likely* accurate?
    A. $P = C - S + X / (1 + RFR)^T$.
    B. $C = S - P + X / (1 + RFR)^T$.
    C. $X / (1 + RFR)^T - P = S - C$.

16. A stock is selling at $40, a 3-month put at $50 is selling for $11, a 3-month call at $50 is selling for $1, and the risk-free rate is 6%. How much, if anything, can be made on an arbitrage?
    A. $0 (no arbitrage).
    B. $0.28.
    C. $0.72.

17. Which of the following will *increase* the value of a put option?
    A. An increase in volatility.
    B. A decrease in the exercise price.
    C. A decrease in time to expiration.

ANSWERS – CONCEPT CHECKERS

1. **C**   A put option is out of the money when S > X and in the money when S < X. The other statements are true.

2. **C**   American and European options both give the holder the right to exercise the option at expiration. An American option also gives the holder the right of early exercise, so American options will be worth more than European options when the right to early exercise is valuable, and they will have equal value when it is not, $C_t \geq c_t$ and $P_t \geq p_t$.

3. **A**   Option prices are *more* volatile than the price of the underlying stock. The other statements are true. Options have time value, which means prices are higher the longer the time until the option expires, and a higher strike price increases the value of a put option.

4. **C**   The holder of a put option has the right to sell to the writer of the option. The writer of the put option has the obligation to buy, and the holder of the call option has the right, but not the obligation to buy.

5. **C**   Interest rates are inversely related to put prices and directly related to call prices.

6. **A**   The intrinsic value is S – X = $43 – $40 = $3. So, the time value is $5 – $3 = $2.

7. **B**   At any time *t*, an American put will never sell below intrinsic value, but may sell for more than that. The lower bound is $\max[0, X - S_t]$.

8. **B**   A call on a futures contract gives the holder the right to buy (go long) a futures contract at the exercise price of the call. It is not the current spot price of the asset underlying the futures contract that determines whether a futures option is in the money, it is the futures contract price (which may be higher).

9. **B**   The lower bound for a European put ranges from zero to the present value of the exercise price less the prevailing stock price, where the exercise price is discounted at the risk-free rate.

10. **C**   The lower bound for an American call ranges from zero to the prevailing stock price less the present value of the exercise price discounted at the risk-free rate.

11. **C**   If the underlying asset used to establish the put-call parity relationship generates a cash flow prior to expiration, the asset's value must be reduced by the present value of the cash flow discounted at the risk-free rate.

12. **C**   The payoff to a FRA is equivalent to that of a long interest rate call option and a short interest rate put option.

13. **C**   The payment on a long put increases as the strike rate increases, but not for calls. There is only one payment and it comes after option expiration by the term of the underlying rate.

14. **B**   Short interest rate puts require a payment when the market rate at expiration is below the strike rate, just as lower rates can require a payment from a floor.

15. **B**   The put-call parity relationship is $S + P = C + X / (1 + RFR)^T$. All individual securities can be expressed as rearrangements of this basic relationship.

16. **C** A synthetic stock is: $S = C - P + X / (1 + RFR)^T = \$1 - \$11 + 50 / (1.06)^{0.25} = \$39.28$.
Since the stock is selling for \$40, you can short a share of stock for \$40 and buy the synthetic for an immediate arbitrage profit of \$0.72.

17. **A** Increased volatility of the underlying asset increases both put values and call values.

SWAP MARKETS AND CONTRACTS

EXAM FOCUS

This topic review introduces swaps. The first thing you must learn is the mechanics of swaps so that you can calculate the payments on any of the types of swaps covered. Beyond that, you should be able to recognize that the cash flows of a swap can be duplicated with capital markets transactions (make a loan, issue a bond) or with other derivatives (a series of forward rate agreements or interest rate options). Common mistakes include forgetting that the current-period floating rate determines the next payment, forgetting to adjust the interest rates for the payment period, forgetting to add any margin above the floating rate specified in the swap, and forgetting that currency swaps involve an exchange of currencies at the initiation and termination of the swap. Don't do these things.

SWAP CHARACTERISTICS

Before we get into the details of swaps, a simple introduction may help as you go through the different types of swaps. You can view interest rate swaps as the exchange of one loan for another. If you lend me $10,000 at a floating rate, and I lend you $10,000 at a fixed rate, we have created a swap. There is no reason for the $10,000 to actually change hands. The two equal loans make this pointless. At each payment date, I will make a payment to you based on the floating rate, and you will make one to me based on the fixed rate. Again, it makes no sense to exchange the full amounts; the one with the larger payment liability will make a payment of the difference to the other. This describes the payments of a fixed-for-floating or "plain vanilla" swap.

A currency swap can be viewed the same way. If I lend you 1,000,000 euros at the euro rate of interest, and you lend me the equivalent amount of yen at today's exchange rate at the yen rate of interest, we have done a currency swap. We will "swap" back these same amounts of currency at the maturity date of the two loans. In the interim, I borrowed yen, so I make yen interest payments, and you borrowed euros and must make interest payments in euros.

For other types of swaps, we just need to describe how the payments are calculated on the loans. For an equity swap, I could promise to make quarterly payments on your loan to me equal to the return on a stock index, and you could promise to make fixed-rate (or floating-rate) payments to me. If the stock index goes down, my payments to you are negative (i.e., you make a fixed-rate payment to me *and* a payment equal to the decline in the index over the quarter). If the index went up over the quarter, I would make a payment based on the percentage increase in the index. Again, the payments could be "netted" so that only the difference changes hands.

This intuitive explanation of swaps should make the following a bit easier to understand. Now let's dive into the mechanics and terminology of swaps. We have to specify exactly how the interest payments will be calculated, how often they are made, how much is to be loaned, and how long the loans are for. Swaps are custom instruments, and we can specify any terms both of us can agree on.

LOS 64.a: Describe the characteristics of swap contracts and explain how swaps are terminated.

CFA® Program Curriculum, Volume 6, page 120

Swaps are agreements to exchange a series of cash flows on periodic *settlement dates* over a certain time period (e.g., quarterly payments over two years). In the simplest type of swap, one party makes *fixed-rate* interest payments on the notional principal specified in the swap in return for *floating-rate* payments from the other party. At each settlement date, the two payments are *netted* so that only one (net) payment is made. The party with the greater liability makes a payment to the other party. The length of the swap is termed the *tenor* of the swap and the contract ends on the termination date. A swap can be decomposed into a series of forward contracts (FRAs) that expire on the settlement dates.

In many respects, swaps are similar to forwards:

- Swaps typically require no payment by either party at initiation.
- Swaps are custom instruments.
- Swaps are not traded in any organized secondary market.
- Swaps are largely unregulated.
- Default risk is an important aspect of the contracts.
- Most participants in the swaps market are large institutions.
- Individuals are rarely swaps market participants.

There are swaps facilitators who bring together parties with needs for the opposite sides of swaps. There are also dealers, large banks and brokerage firms, who act as principals in trades just as they do in forward contracts. It is a large business; the total notional principal of swaps contracts is estimated at over $50 trillion.

How Swaps are Terminated

There are **four ways to terminate a swap** prior to its original termination date.

1. *Mutual termination*. A cash payment can be made by one party that is acceptable to the other party. Like forwards, swaps can accumulate value as market prices or interest rates change. If the party that has been disadvantaged by the market movements is willing to make a payment of the swap's value to the counterparty, and the counterparty is willing to accept it, they can mutually terminate the swap.

2. *Offsetting contract*. Just as with forwards, if the terms of the original counterparty offers for early termination are unacceptable, the alternative is to enter an offsetting swap. If our 5-year quarterly-pay floating swap has two years to go, we can seek a current price on a pay-fixed (receive floating) swap that will provide our floating payments and leave us with a fixed-rate liability.

Just as with forwards, exiting a swap may involve taking a loss. Consider the case where we receive 3% fixed on our original 5-year pay floating swap, but must pay 4% fixed on the offsetting swap. We have locked in a loss because we must pay 1% higher rates on the offsetting swap than we receive on the swap we are offsetting. We must make quarterly payments for the next two years, and receive nothing in return. Exiting a swap through an offsetting swap with other than the original counterparty will also expose the investor to default risk, just as with forwards.

3. *Resale*. It is possible to sell the swap to another party, with the permission of the counterparty to the swap. This would be unusual, however, as there is not a functioning secondary market.

4. *Swaption*. A **swaption** is an option to enter into a swap. The option to enter into an offsetting swap provides an option to terminate an existing swap. Consider that, in the case of the previous 5-year pay floating swap, we purchased a 3-year call option on a 2-year pay fixed swap at 3%. Exercising this swap would give us the offsetting swap to exit our original swap. The cost for such protection is the swaption premium.

LOS 64.b: Describe, calculate, and interpret the payments of currency swaps, plain vanilla interest rate swaps, and equity swaps.

CFA® Program Curriculum, Volume 6, page 123

In a **currency swap**, one party makes payments denominated in one currency, while the payments from the other party are made in a second currency. Typically, the notional amounts of the contract, expressed in both currencies at the current exchange rate, are exchanged at contract initiation and returned at the contract termination date in the same amounts.

An example of a currency swap is as follows: Party 1 pays Party 2 $10 million at contract initiation in return for €9.8 million. On each of the settlement dates, Party 1, having received euros, makes payments at a 6% annualized rate in euros on the €9.8 million to Party 2. Party 2 makes payments at an annualized rate of 5% on the $10 million to Party 1. These settlement payments are both made. They are not netted as they are in a single currency interest rate swap.

As an example of what motivates a currency swap, consider that a U.S. firm, Party A, wishes to establish operations in Australia and wants to finance the costs in Australian dollars (AUD). The firm finds, however, that issuing debt in AUD is relatively more expensive than issuing USD-denominated debt, because they are relatively unknown in Australian financial markets. An alternative to issuing AUD-denominated debt is to issue USD debt and enter into a USD/AUD currency swap. Through a swaps facilitator, the U.S. firm finds an Australian firm, Party B, that faces the same situation in reverse. They wish to issue AUD debt and swap into a USD exposure.

There are **four possible types of currency swaps** available.

1. Party A pays a fixed rate on AUD received, and Party B pays a fixed rate on USD received.

2. Party A pays a floating rate on AUD received, and Party B pays a fixed rate on USD received.

3. Party A pays a fixed rate on AUD received, and Party B pays a floating rate on USD received.

4. Party A pays a floating rate on AUD received, and Party B pays a floating rate on USD received.

Following are the steps in a fixed-for-fixed currency swap:

Step 1: The notional principal actually changes hands at the beginning of the swap. Party A gives USD to Party B and gets AUD back. Why? Because the motivation of Party A was to get AUD and the motivation of Party B was to get USD. *Notional principal is swapped at initiation.*

Step 2: Interest payments are made without netting. Party A, who got AUD, pays the Australian interest rate on the notional amount of AUD to Party B. Party B, who got USD, pays the U.S. interest rate on the notional amount of USD received to Party A. Since the payments are made in different currencies, netting is not a typical practice. *Full interest payments are exchanged at each settlement date, each in a different currency.*

Step 3: At the termination of the swap agreement (maturity), the counterparties give each other back the exchanged notional amounts. *Notional principal is swapped again at the termination of the agreement.* The cash flows associated with this currency swap are illustrated in Figure 1.

Figure 1: Fixed-for-Fixed Currency Swap

SWAP INITIATION

SWAP INTEREST PAYMENTS

SWAP TERMINATION

Calculating the Payments on a Currency Swap

Example: Fixed-for-fixed currency swap

BB can borrow in the United States for 9%, while AA has to pay 10% to borrow in the United States. AA can borrow in Australia for 7%, while BB has to pay 8% to borrow in Australia. BB will be doing business in Australia and needs AUD, while AA will be doing business in the United States and needs USD. The exchange rate is 2AUD/USD. AA needs USD1.0 million and BB needs AUD2.0 million. They decide to borrow the funds locally and swap the borrowed funds, charging each other the rate the other party would have paid had they borrowed in the foreign market. The swap period is for five years. Calculate the cash flows for this swap.

Answer:

AA and BB each go to their own domestic bank:

- AA borrows AUD2.0 million, agreeing to pay the bank 7%, or AUD140,000 annually.
- BB borrows USD1.0 million, agreeing to pay the bank 9%, or USD90,000 annually.

AA and BB swap currencies:

- AA gets USD1.0 million, agreeing to pay BB 10% interest in USD annually.
- BB gets AUD2.0 million, agreeing to pay AA 8% interest in AUD annually.

They pay each other the annual interest:

- AA owes BB USD100,000 in interest to be paid on each settlement date.
- BB owes AA AUD160,000 in interest to be paid on each settlement date.

They each owe their own bank the annual interest payment:

- AA pays the Australian bank AUD140,000 (but gets AUD160,000 from BB, an AUD20,000 gain).
- BB pays the U.S. bank USD90,000 (but gets USD100,000 from AA, a USD10,000 gain).
- They both gain by swapping (AA is ahead AUD20,000 and BB is ahead USD 10,000).

In five years, they reverse the swap. They return the notional principal.

- AA gets AUD2.0 million from BB and then pays back the Australian bank.
- BB gets USD1.0 million from AA and then pays back the U.S. bank.

Interest Rate Swaps

The **plain vanilla interest rate swap** involves trading fixed interest rate payments for floating-rate payments. (A **basis swap** involves trading one set of floating rate payments for another.)

The party who wants floating-rate interest payments agrees to pay fixed-rate interest and has the *pay-fixed* side of the swap. The counterparty, who receives the fixed payments and agrees to pay variable-rate interest, has the *pay-floating* side of the swap and is called the *floating-rate payer.*

The floating rate quoted is generally the **London Interbank Offered Rate** (LIBOR), flat or plus a spread.

Let's look at the cash flows that occur in a *plain vanilla interest rate swap.*

- Because the notional principal swapped is the same for both counterparties and is in the same currency units, there is no need to actually exchange the cash. *Notional principal is generally not swapped* in single currency swaps.
- The determination of the variable rate is at the beginning of the settlement period, and the cash interest payment is made at the end of the settlement period. Because the interest payments are in the same currency, there is no need for both counterparties to actually transfer the cash. The difference between the fixed-rate payment and the variable-rate payment is calculated and paid to the appropriate counterparty. *Net interest is paid by the one who owes it.*
- At the conclusion of the swap, since the notional principal was not swapped, there is no transfer of funds.

You should note that swaps are a zero-sum game. What one party gains, the other party loses.

The net formula for the *fixed-rate payer,* based on a 360-day year and a floating rate of LIBOR is:

$$(\text{net fixed-rate payment})_t = \left(\text{swap fixed rate} - \text{LIBOR}_{t-1}\right)\left(\frac{\text{number of days}}{360}\right)(\text{notional principal})$$

If this number is positive, the fixed-rate payer *owes* a net payment to the floating-rate party. If this number is negative, then the fixed-rate payer *receives* a net flow from the floating-rate payer.

 Professor's Note: For the exam, remember that with plain vanilla swaps, one party pays fixed and the other pays a floating rate. Sometimes swap payments are based on a 365-day year. For example, the swap will specify whether 90/360 or 90/365 should be used to calculate a quarterly swap payment. Remember, these are custom instruments.

Example: Interest rate risk

Consider a bank. Its deposits represent liabilities and are most likely short term in nature. In other words, deposits represent floating-rate liabilities. The bank assets are primarily loans. Most loans carry fixed rates of interest. The bank assets are fixed-rate and bank liabilities are floating. Explain the nature of the interest rate risk that the bank faces, and describe how an interest rate swap may be used to hedge this risk.

Answer:

The risk the bank faces is that short-term interest rates will rise, causing cash payment on deposits to increase. This would not be a major problem if cash inflows also increase as interest rates rise, but with a fixed-rate loan portfolio they will not. If the bank remains unhedged as interest rates rise, cash outflows rise and bank profits fall.

The bank can hedge this risk by entering into a fixed-for-floating swap as the fixed-rate payer. The floating-rate payments received would offset any increase in the floating-rate payments on deposits. Note that if rates fall, the bank's costs do not. They still pay fixed for the term of the swap and receive (lower) floating-rate payments that correspond to their lower costs on deposits.

Calculating the Payments on an Interest Rate Swap

Example: Calculating the payments on an interest rate swap

Bank A enters into a $1,000,000 quarterly-pay plain vanilla interest rate swap as the fixed-rate payer at a fixed rate of 6% based on a 360-day year. The floating-rate payer agrees to pay 90-day LIBOR plus a 1% margin; 90-day LIBOR is currently 4%.

90-day LIBOR rates are:	4.5%	90 days from now
	5.0%	180 days from now
	5.5%	270 days from now
	6.0%	360 days from now

Calculate the amounts Bank A pays or receives 90, 270, and 360 days from now.

Answer:

The payment 90 days from now depends on current LIBOR and the fixed rate (don't forget the 1% margin).

Fixed-rate payer pays:

$$\left[0.06\left(\frac{90}{360}\right) - (0.04 + 0.01)\left(\frac{90}{360}\right)\right] \times 1,000,000 = \$2,500$$

270 days from now, the payment is based on LIBOR 180 days from now, which is 5%. Adding the 1% margin makes the floating-rate 6%, which is equal to the fixed rate, so there is no net third quarterly payment.

The bank's "payment" 360 days from now is:

$$\left[0.06\left(\frac{90}{360}\right) - (0.055 + 0.01)\left(\frac{90}{360}\right)\right] \times 1,000,000 = -\$1,250$$

Because the floating-rate payment exceeds the fixed-rate payment, Bank A will *receive* $1,250 at the fourth payment date.

Equity Swaps

In an **equity swap**, the return on a stock, a portfolio, or a stock index is paid each period by one party in return for a fixed-rate or floating-rate payment. The return can be the capital appreciation or the total return including dividends on the stock, portfolio, or index.

In order to reduce equity risk, a portfolio manager might enter into a 1-year quarterly-pay S&P 500 index swap and agree to receive a fixed rate. The percentage increase in the index each quarter is netted against the fixed rate to determine the payment to be made. If the index return is negative, the fixed-rate payer must also pay the percentage decline in the index to the portfolio manager. Uniquely among swaps, equity swap payments can be floating on both sides and the payments are not known until the end of the quarter. With interest rate swaps, both the fixed and floating payments are known at the beginning of period for which they will be paid.

A swap on a single stock can be motivated by a desire to protect the value of a position over the period of the swap. To protect a large capital gain in a single stock, and to avoid a sale for tax or control reasons, an investor could enter into an equity swap as the equity-returns payer and receive a fixed rate in return. Any decline in the stock price would be paid to the investor at the settlement dates, plus the fixed-rate payment. If the stock appreciates, the investor must pay the appreciation less the fixed payment.

Calculating the Payments on an Equity Swap

Example: Equity swap payments

Ms. Smith enters into a 2-year $10 million quarterly swap as the fixed payer and will receive the index return on the S&P 500. The fixed rate is 8%, and the index is currently at 986. At the end of the next three quarters, the index level is: 1030, 968, and 989.

Calculate the net payment for each of the next three quarters and identify the direction of the payment.

Answer:

The percentage change in the index each quarter, Q, is: Q1 = 4.46%, Q2 = –6.02%, and Q3 = 2.17%. The index return payer will receive 0.08 / 4 = 2% each quarter and pay the index return, therefore:

Q1: Index return payer pays 4.46% – 2.00% = 2.46% or $246,000.
Q2: Index return payer receives 6.02% + 2.00% = 8.02% or $802,000.
Q3: Index return payer pays 2.17% – 2.00% = 0.17% or $17,000.

KEY CONCEPTS

LOS 64.a

Swaps are based on a notional amount of principal. Each party is obligated to pay a percentage return on the notional amount at periodic settlement dates over the life (tenor) of the swap. Percentage payments are based on a floating rate, fixed rate, or the return on an equity index or portfolio.

Except in the case of a currency swap, no money changes hands at the inception of the swap and periodic payments are netted (the party that owes the larger amount pays the difference to the other).

Swaps are custom instruments, are largely unregulated, do not trade in secondary markets, and are subject to counterparty (default) risk.

Swaps can be terminated prior to their stated termination dates by:
- Entering into an offsetting swap, sometimes by exercising a swaption (most common).
- Agreeing with the counterparty to terminate (likely involves making or receiving compensation).
- Selling the swap to a third party with the consent of the original counterparty (uncommon).

LOS 64.b

In a plain vanilla (fixed-for-floating) interest-rate swap, one party agrees to pay a floating rate of interest on the notional amount and the counterparty agrees to pay a fixed rate of interest.

The formula for the net payment by the fixed-rate payer, based on a 360-day year and the number of days in the settlement period is:

$$\left(\text{net fixed rate payment}\right)_t$$
$$= \left(\text{swap fixed rate} - \text{LIBOR}_{t-1}\right)\left(\frac{\text{number of days}}{360}\right)\left(\text{notional principal}\right)$$

In an equity swap, the returns payer makes payments based on the return on a stock, portfolio, or index, in exchange for fixed- or floating-rate payments. If the stock, portfolio, or index, declines in value over the period, the returns payer receives the interest payment and a payment based on the percentage decline in value.

In a currency swap, the notional principal (in two different currencies) is exchanged at the inception of the swap, periodic interest payments in two different currencies are exchanged on settlement dates, and the same notional amounts are exchanged (repaid) on the termination date of the swap.

CONCEPT CHECKERS

1. Which of the following statements about swaps is *least likely* correct?
   A. In an interest rate swap, the notional principal is swapped.
   B. The default problem is the most important limitation to the swap market.
   C. In a plain vanilla interest rate swap, fixed rates are traded for variable rates.

2. Which of the following statements about swaps is *least likely* correct?
   A. The time frame of a swap is called its tenor.
   B. In a currency swap, only net interest payments are made.
   C. In a currency swap, the notional principal is actually swapped twice, once at the beginning of the swap and again at the termination of the swap.

3. Which of the following statements is *least likely* an advantage of swaps? Swaps:
   A. have little or no regulation.
   B. minimize default risk.
   C. have customized contracts.

4. In an equity swap:
   A. settlement is made only at swap termination.
   B. shares are exchanged for the notional principal.
   C. returns on an index can be swapped for fixed-rate payments.

5. In a plain vanilla interest rate swap:
   A. the notional principal is swapped.
   B. only the net interest payments are made.
   C. the notional principal is returned at the end of the swap.

6. Which of the following statements about swap markets is *least likely* correct?
   A. In an interest rate swap only the net interest is exchanged.
   B. The notional principal is swapped at inception and at termination of a currency swap.
   C. Only the net difference between the dollar interest and the foreign interest is exchanged in a currency swap.

Use the following data to answer Questions 7 through 10.

Consider a 3-year annual currency swap that takes place between a foreign firm (FF) with FC currency units and a U.S. firm (USF) with $ currency units. USF is the fixed-rate payer and FF is the floating-rate payer. The fixed interest rate at the initiation of the swap is 7%, and 8% at the end of the swap. The variable rate is 5% currently; 6% at the end of year 1; 8% at the end of year 2; and 7% at the end of year 3. At the beginning of the swap, $1.0 million is exchanged at an exchange rate of FC2.0 = $1.0. At the end of the swap period, the exchange rate is FC 1.5 = $1.0.

Note: With this currency swap, end-of-period payments are based on beginning-of-period interest rates.

7. At the initiation of the swap, which of the following statements is *most likely* correct?
    A. FF gives USF $1.0 million.
    B. USF gives FF $1.0 million.
    C. USF gives FF FC2.0 million.

8. At the end of year 2:
    A. USF pays FC140,000; FF pays $60,000.
    B. USF pays FC60,000; FF pays $70,000.
    C. USF pays USD70,000; FF pays FC60,000.

9. At the termination of the swap, FF gives USF which of the following notional amounts?
    A. $1 million.
    B. FC2,000,000.
    C. FC1,500,000.

10. At the end of year 3, FF will pay which of the following total amounts?
    A. $1,080,000.
    B. $1,070,000.
    C. FC2,160,000

Use the following information to answer Questions 11 through 13.

Lambda Corp. has a floating-rate liability and wants a fixed-rate exposure. They enter into a 2-year quarterly-pay $4,000,000 fixed-for-floating swap as the fixed-rate payer. The counterparty is Gamma Corp. The fixed rate is 6% and the floating rate is 90-day LIBOR + 1%, with both calculated based on a 360-day year. Realizations of LIBOR are:

Annualized LIBOR
Current   5.0%
In 1 quarter   5.5%
In 2 quarters   5.4%
In 3 quarters   5.8%
In 4 quarters   6.0%

11. The first swap payment is:
     A. from Gamma to Lambda.
     B. known at the initiation of the swap.
     C. $5,000.

12. The second net swap payment is:
     A. $5,000 from Lambda to Gamma.
     B. $4,000 from Gamma to Lambda.
     C. $5,000 from Gamma to Lambda.

13. The fifth net quarterly payment on the swap is:
     A. 0.
     B. $10,000.
     C. $40,000.

ANSWERS – CONCEPT CHECKERS

1. **A**   In an interest rate swap, the notional principal is only used to calculate the interest payments and does not change hands. The notional principal is only exchanged in a currency swap.

2. **B**   In a currency swap, payments are not netted because they are made in different currencies. Full interest payments are made, and the notional principal is also exchanged.

3. **B**   Swaps do not minimize default risk. Swaps are agreements between two or more parties, and there are no guarantees that one of the parties will not default. Note that swaps do give traders privacy and, being private transactions, have little to no regulation and offer the ability to customize contracts to specific needs.

4. **C**   Equity swaps involve one party paying the return or total return on a stock or index periodically in exchange for a fixed return.

5. **B**   In a plain vanilla interest rate swap, interest payments are netted. Note that notional principal is not exchanged and is only used as a basis for calculating interest payments.

6. **C**   In a currency swap, full interest payments are made, and the notional principal is exchanged.

7. **B**   Because this is a currency swap, we know that the notional principal is exchanged. Because USF holds dollars, it will be handing over dollars to FF.

8. **A**   Remember, the currency swap is pay floating on dollars and pay fixed on foreign. Floating at the end of year 1 is 6% of $1.0 million. Since payments are made in arrears, FF pays $60,000 and USF pays FC140,000 at the end of year 2.

9. **A**   The notional principal is exchanged at termination. FF gives back what it borrowed, $1.0 million, and the terminal exchange rate is not used.

10. **A**   FF is the floating-rate dollar payer. FF will pay the return of $1.0 million in principal at the termination of the swap, plus the floating rate payment (in arrears) of 8% × $1.0 million = $80,000. The total payment will be $1,080,000.

11. **B**   The first payment is based on the fixed rate and current LIBOR + 1%, which are both 6%. There is no net payment made at the first quarterly payment date and this is known at the initiation of the swap.

12. **C**   The second quarter payment is based on the realization of LIBOR at the end of the first quarter, 5.5%. The floating rate is: $(5.5\% + 1\%)\left(\dfrac{90}{360}\right)4,000,000 = \$65,000$. The fixed rate payment is $60,000, making the net payment $5,000 from Gamma to Lambda.

13. **B**   The fifth quarterly floating-rate payment is based on the realization of LIBOR at the end of the fourth quarter, which is 6%. With the 1% margin, the floating rate is 7% compared to 6% fixed, so the net payment is $10,000.

RISK MANAGEMENT APPLICATIONS OF OPTION STRATEGIES

EXAM FOCUS

The most important aspect of this topic review is the interpretation of option profit diagrams. Payoff diagrams for single put or single call positions were covered in our options review. In this review, we introduce profit diagrams and two option strategies that combine stock with options. In a protective put position, we combine a share of stock and a put. With this strategy, we essentially purchase downside protection for the stock (like insurance). A covered call position consists of buying a share of stock and selling a call on it. This strategy equates to selling the upside potential on the stock in return for the added income from the sale of the call. On the Level I CFA® Exam, you will not be required to draw payoff diagrams, but you are expected to know how to interpret them and find the breakeven price, maximum gains and losses, and the gains and losses for any stock price at option expiration.

LOS 65.a: Determine the value at expiration, the profit, maximum profit, maximum loss, breakeven underlying price at expiration, and payoff graph of the strategies of buying and selling calls and puts and determine the potential outcomes for investors using these strategies.

CFA® Program Curriculum, Volume 6, page 144

Call Option Profits and Losses

Consider a call option with a premium of $5 and a strike price of $50. This means the buyer pays $5 to the writer. At expiration, if the price of the stock is less than or equal to the $50 strike price (the option has zero value), the buyer of the option is out $5, and the writer of the option is ahead $5. As the stock's price exceeds $50, the buyer of the option starts to gain (breakeven will come at $55, when the value of the stock equals the strike price and the option premium). However, as the price of the stock moves upward, the seller of the option starts to lose (negative figures will start at $55, when the value of the stock equals the strike price and the option premium).

The profit/loss diagram for the buyer (long) and writer (short) of the call option we have been discussing at expiration is presented in Figure 1. This profit/loss diagram illustrates the following:

- The maximum loss for the buyer of a call is the loss of the $5 premium (at any S ≤ $50).
- The breakeven point for the buyer and seller is the strike price plus the premium (at S = $55).

- The profit potential to the buyer of the option is unlimited, and, conversely, the potential loss to the writer of the call option is unlimited.
- The call holder will exercise the option whenever the stock's price exceeds the strike price at the expiration date.
- The greatest profit the writer can make is the $5 premium (at any $S \leq \$50$).
- The sum of the profits between the buyer and seller of the call option is always zero; thus, options trading is a *zero-sum game*. There are no net profits or losses in the market. The long profits equal the short losses.

 Professor's Note: Please notice that option profit diagrams show the gain or loss to the long and/or short option positions. They differ from the payoff diagrams that we used in our options review in that profit diagrams reflect the cost of the option (i.e., the option premium).

Figure 1: Profit/Loss Diagram for a Call Option

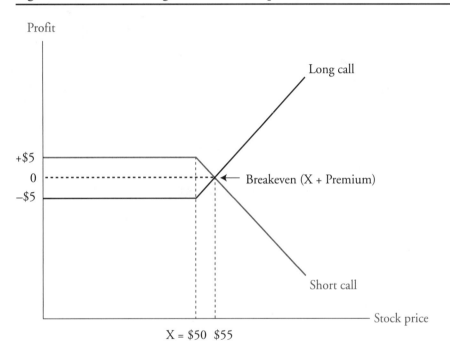

Put Option Profits and Losses

To examine the profits/losses associated with trading put options, consider a put option with a $5 premium. The buyer pays $5 to the writer. When the price of the stock at expiration is greater than or equal to the $50 strike price, the put has zero value. The buyer of the option has a loss of $5, and the writer of the option has a gain of $5. As the stock's price falls below $50, the buyer of the put option starts to gain (breakeven will come at $45, when the value of the stock equals the strike price less the option premium). However, as the price of the stock moves downward, the seller of the option starts to lose (negative profits will start at $45, when the value of the stock equals the strike price less the option premium).

Figure 2 shows the profit/loss diagram for the buyer (long) and seller (short) of the put option that we have been discussing. This profit/loss diagram illustrates that:

- The maximum loss for the buyer of a put is the loss of the $5 premium (at any S ≥ $50).
- The maximum gain to the buyer of a put is limited to the strike price less the premium ($50 – $5 = $45). The potential loss to the writer of the put is the same amount.
- The breakeven price of a put buyer (seller) is at the strike price minus the option premium ($50 – $5 = $45).
- The greatest profit the writer of a put can make is the $5 premium (S ≥ $50).
- The sum of the profits between the buyer and seller of the put option is always zero. Trading put options is a *zero-sum game*. In other words, the buyer's profits equal the writer's losses.

Figure 2: Profit/Loss Diagram for a Put Option

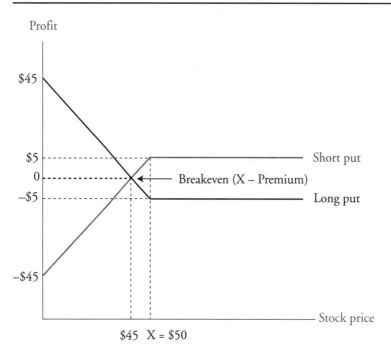

Example: Option profit calculations

Suppose that both a call option and a put option have been written on a stock with an exercise price of $40. The current stock price is $42, and the call and put premiums are $3 and $0.75, respectively.

Calculate the profit to the long and short positions for both the put and the call with an expiration day stock price of $35 and with a price at expiration of $43.

Answer:

Profit will be computed as ending option valuation – initial option cost.

Stock at $35:

- Long call: $0 – $3 = –$3. The option finished out-of-the-money, so the premium is lost.
- Short call: $3 – $0 = $3. Because the option finished out-of-the-money, the call writer's gain equals the premium.
- Long put: $5 – $0.75 = $4.25. You paid $0.75 for an option that is now worth $5.
- Short put: $0.75 – $5 = –$4.25. You received $0.75 for writing the option, but you face a $5 loss because the option is in-the-money.

Stock at $43:

- Long call: –$3 + $3 = $0. You paid $3 for the option, and it is now worth $3. Hence, your net profit is zero.
- Short call: $3 – $3 = $0. You received $3 for writing the option and now face a –$3 valuation for a net profit of zero.
- Long put: –$0.75 – $0 = –$0.75. You paid $0.75 for the put option and the option is now worthless. Your net profit is –$0.75.
- Short put: $0.75 – $0 = $0.75. You received $0.75 for writing the option and keep the premium because the option finished out-of-the-money.

A buyer of puts or a seller of calls will profit when the price of the underlying asset decreases. A buyer of calls or a seller of puts will profit when the price of the underlying asset increases. In general, a put buyer believes the underlying asset is overvalued and will decline in price, while a call buyer anticipates an increase in the underlying asset's price.

LOS 65.b: Determine the value at expiration, profit, maximum profit, maximum loss, breakeven underlying price at expiration, and payoff graph of a covered call strategy and a protective put strategy, and explain the risk management application of each strategy.

CFA® Program Curriculum, Volume 6, page 151

Professor's Note: Whenever we combine options with assets or other options, the net cost of the combined position is simply the sum of the prices paid for the long options/assets minus the proceeds from the option/asset sales (short positions). The profits and losses on a position are simply the value of all the assets/options in the positions at expiration minus the net cost.

In writing **covered calls,** the term *covered* means that owning the stock covers the obligation to deliver stock assumed in writing the call. Why would you write a covered call? You feel the stock's price will not go up any time soon, and you want to increase your income by collecting the call option premium. To add some insurance that the stock won't get called away, the call writer can write out-of-the-money calls. You should know that this strategy for enhancing one's income is not without risk. *The call writer is trading the stock's upside potential for the call premium.*

Figure 3 illustrates the profit/loss of a covered call position at option expiration date. When the call was written, the stock's price was $50. The call's strike price was $55, and the call premium was $4. The call is out-of-the-money. From Figure 3, we can observe that at expiration:

- If the stock closes below $50, the option will expire worthless, and the option writer's loss is offset by the premium income of $4.
- Breakeven *for the position* is at $46 = $50 – $4. Breakeven price = S_0 – call premium.
- If the stock closes between $50 and $55, the option will expire worthless. Because this option was an out-of-the-money call, the option writer will get any stock appreciation above the original stock price and below the strike price. So the gain (premium plus stock appreciation) will be between $4 and $9.
- If stock closes above $55, the strike price, the writer will get nothing more. The maximum gain is $9 on the covered out-of-the-money call.
- The maximum loss occurs if the stock price goes to zero; the net cost of the position ($46 = $50 stock loss offset by $4 premium income) is the maximum loss.

Figure 3: Covered Call Profit and Loss for S = 50, C = 4, X = 55

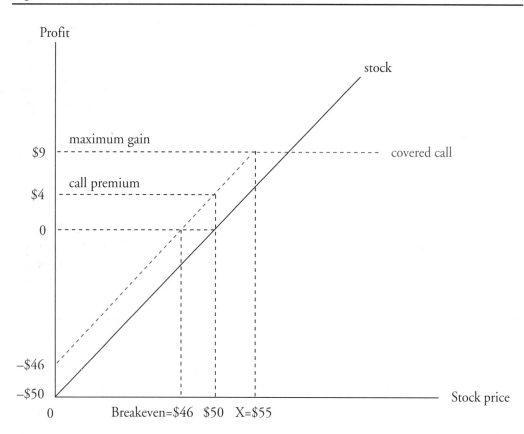

The desirability of writing a covered call to enhance income depends upon the chance that the stock price will exceed the exercise price at which the trader writes the call. In this example, the writer of the call thinks the stock's upside potential is less than the buyer expects. The buyer of the call is paying $4 to get any gain above $55, while the seller has traded the upside potential above $55 for a payment of $4.

A **protective put** is an investment management technique designed to protect a stock from a decline in value. It is constructed by buying a stock and put option on that stock.

Look at the profit/loss diagrams in Figure 4. The diagram on the left is the profit from holding the stock. If the stock's value is up, your profit is positive and if the stock's value is down, your profit is negative. Profit equals the end price, S_T, less the initial price S_t. That is, profit = $S_T – S_t$. The diagram on the right side of Figure 4 is the profit graph from holding a long put. If the market is up, you lose your premium payment, and if the market is down, you have a profit.

The value of the put at termination will be max[0, $X – S_T$]. Your profit will be max[0, $X – S_T$] less the price of the put.

Figure 4: Protective Put Components

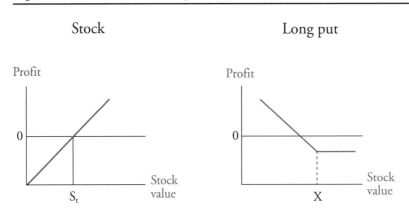

Figure 5 shows the profits from the combination of a long put and a long stock (i.e., a protective put). Here it is assumed that the stock is purchased at $100 and that a put with a strike price of $100 is purchased for $4. Note that the put described in Figure 5 is at the money.

Figure 5: Protective Put

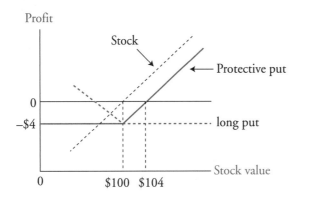

What we should observe in Figure 5 is that:

- A protective put cuts your downside losses (maximum loss = $4) but leaves the upside potential alone (unlimited upside gains).
- Your maximum loss occurs at any price below $100.
- Losses between $0 and $4 occur for stock prices between $100 and $104.
- You will not make a profit until the stock price exceeds $104 (breakeven).
- Breakeven price = S_0 + premium.

Note that *a protective put (stock plus a put) has the same shape profit diagram as a long call.* It could be replicated with a bond that pays (X – premium) at expiration and a call at X.

> *Professor's Note: Recall that this relation was the basis for our derivation of put-call parity. The payoffs at expiration are identical for a protective put (S + P) and a fiduciary call* $\left[\dfrac{X}{(1 + R_f)^{T-t}} + C \right]$, *a call with an exercise price equal to* X *and a pure discount bond that pays* X *at expiration.*

KEY CONCEPTS

LOS 65.a

Call option value at expiration is Max $(0, S - X)$ and profit (loss) is Max $(0, S - X)$ – option cost.

	Call Option	
	Maximum Loss	*Maximum Gain*
Buyer (long)	Option Cost	Unlimited
Seller (short)	Unlimited	Option Cost
Breakeven	X + Option Cost	

Put value at expiration is Max $(0, X - S)$ and profit (loss) is Max $(0, X - S)$ – option cost.

	Put Option	
	Maximum Loss	*Maximum Gain*
Buyer (long)	Option Cost	X – Option Cost
Seller (short)	X – Option Cost	Option Cost
Breakeven	X – Option Cost	

A call buyer (call seller) anticipates an increase (decrease) in the value of the underlying asset.

A put buyer (put seller) anticipates a decrease (increase) in the value of the underlying asset.

LOS 65.b

A covered call position is a share of stock and a short (written) call. Profits and losses are measured relative to the net cost of this combination $(S_0 - \text{premium})$.
- The purpose of selling a covered call is to enhance income by trading the stock's upside potential for the call premium.
- The upside potential on a covered call is limited to $(X - S_0)$ + call premium received. The maximum loss is the net cost $(S_0 - \text{premium})$.

A protective put consists of buying a share of stock and buying a put. Profits and losses are measured relative to the net cost $(S_0 + \text{premium})$.
- A protective put is a strategy to protect against a decline in the value of the stock.
- Maximum gains on a protective put are unlimited, but reduced by the put premium paid. Maximum losses are limited to $(S_0 - X)$ + put premium paid.

CONCEPT CHECKERS

1. A call option sells for $4 on a $25 stock with a strike price of $30. Which of the following statements is *least accurate*?
    A. At expiration, the buyer of the call will not make a profit unless the stock's price exceeds $30.
    B. At expiration, the writer of the call will only experience a net loss if the price of the stock exceeds $34.
    C. A covered call position at these prices has a maximum gain of $9 and the maximum loss of the stock price less the premium.

2. An investor buys a put on a stock selling for $60, with a strike price of $55 for a $5 premium. The maximum gain is:
    A. $50.
    B. $55.
    C. $60.

3. Which of the following is the riskiest single-option transaction?
    A. Writing a call.
    B. Buying a put.
    C. Writing a put.

4. An investor will *likely* exercise a put option when the price of the stock is:
    A. above the strike price.
    B. below the strike price plus the premium.
    C. below the strike price.

5. A put with a strike price of $75 sells for $10. Which of the following statements is *least accurate*? The greatest:
    A. profit the writer of the put option can make is $10.
    B. profit the buyer of a put option can make is $65.
    C. loss the writer of a put option can have is $75.

6. At expiration, the value of a call option must equal:
    A. the larger of the strike price less the stock price or zero.
    B. the stock price minus the strike price, or arbitrage will occur.
    C. the larger of zero, or the stock's price less the strike price.

7. An investor writes a covered call on a $40 stock with an exercise price of $50 for a premium of $2. The investor's maximum:
    A. gain will be $12.
    B. loss will be $40.
    C. loss will be unlimited.

8. Which of the following combinations of options and underlying investments have similarly shaped profit/loss diagrams? A:
    A. covered call, and a short stock combined with a long call.
    B. short put option combined with a long call option, and a protective put.
    C. long call option combined with a short put option, and a long stock position.

ANSWERS – CONCEPT CHECKERS

1. **A** The buyer will not have a net profit unless the stock price exceeds $34 (strike price plus the premium). The other statements are true. At $30 the option will be exercised, but the writer will only lose money in a net sense when the stock's price exceeds $X + C = \$30 + \$4$. The covered call's maximum gain is $4 premium plus $5 appreciation.

2. **A** This assumes the price of the stock falls to zero and you get to sell for $55. Your profit would be $55 – 5 = $50.

3. **A** When buying either a call or a put, the loss is limited to the amount of the premium. When writing a put, the loss is limited to the strike price if the stock falls to zero (however, the writer keeps the premium). When writing an uncovered call, the stock could go up infinitely, and the writer would be forced to buy the stock in the open market and deliver at the strike price—potential losses are unlimited.

4. **C** The owner of a put profits when the stock falls. The put would be exercised when the price of the stock is *below* the strike price. The amount of the premium is used to determine net profits to each party.

5. **C** The greatest loss the put writer can have is the strike price minus the premium received equals $65. The other statements are true. The greatest profit the put writer can make is the amount of the premium. The greatest profit for a put buyer occurs if the stock falls to zero and the buyer makes the strike price minus the premium. Since options are a zero-sum game, the maximum profit to the writer of the put must equal the maximum loss to the buyer of the put.

6. **C** At expiration, the value of a call must be equal to its intrinsic value, which is $\text{Max}[0, S – X]$. If the value of the stock is less than the strike price, the intrinsic value is zero. If the value of the stock is greater than the strike price, the call is in-the-money and the value of the call is the stock price minus the strike price, or $S – X$.

7. **A** As soon as the stock rises to the exercise price, the covered call writer will cease to realize a profit because the short call moves into-the-money. Each dollar gain on the stock is then offset with a dollar loss on the short call. Since the option is $10 out-of-the-money, the covered call writer can gain this amount plus the $2 call premium. Thus, the maximum gain is $2 + $10 = $12. However, because the investor owns the stock, he or she could lose $40 if the stock goes to zero, but gain $2 from the call premium. Maximum loss is $38.

8. **C** A combined long call and a short put, with exercise prices equal to the current stock price, will have profits/losses at expiration nearly identical to those of a long stock position.

 Professor's Note: The easiest way to see this is to draw the payoff diagram for the combined option positions.

The following is a review of the Alternative Investments principles designed to address the learning outcome statements set forth by CFA Institute. This topic is also covered in:

INTRODUCTION TO ALTERNATIVE INVESTMENTS

Study Session 18

EXAM FOCUS

"Alternative investments" collectively refers to the many asset classes that fall outside the traditional definitions of stocks and bonds. This category includes hedge funds, private equity, real estate, commodities, and other alternative investments, primarily collectibles. Each of these alternative investments has unique characteristics that require a different approach by the analyst. You should be aware of the different strategies, fee structures, due diligence, and issues in valuing and calculating returns with each of the alternative investments discussed in this topic review.

LOS 66.a: Compare alternative investments with traditional investments.

CFA® Program Curriculum, Volume 6, page 170

Alternative investments differ from traditional investments (publicly traded stocks, bonds, cash) both in the types of assets and securities included in this asset class and in the structure of the investment vehicles in which these assets are held. Managers of alternative investment portfolios may use derivatives and leverage, invest in illiquid assets, and short securities. Many types of real estate investment are considered alternatives to traditional investment as well. Types of alternative investment structures include hedge funds, private equity funds, various types of real estate investments, and some ETFs. Fee structures for alternative investments are different than those of traditional investments, with higher management fees on average and often with additional incentive fees based on performance. Alternative investments as a group have had low returns correlations with traditional investments. Compared to traditional investments, alternative investments exhibit:

- Less liquidity of assets held.
- More specialization by investment managers.
- Less regulation and transparency.
- More problematic and less available historical return and volatility data.
- Different legal issues and tax treatments.

LOS 66.b: Describe categories of alternative investments.

CFA® Program Curriculum, Volume 6, page 174

We will examine five categories of alternative investments in detail in this topic review. Here we introduce each of those categories.

1. **Hedge funds.** These funds may use leverage, hold long and short positions, use derivatives, and invest in illiquid assets. Managers of hedge funds use a great many different strategies in attempting to generate investment gains. They do not necessarily hedge risk as the name might imply.

2. **Private equity funds.** As the name suggests, private equity funds invest in the equity of companies that are not publicly traded or in the equity of publicly traded firms that the fund intends to take private. Leveraged buyout (LBO) funds use borrowed money to purchase equity in established companies and comprise the majority of private equity investment funds. A much smaller portion of these funds, venture capital funds, invest in or finance young unproven companies at various stages early in their existence. For our purposes here we will also consider investing in the securities of financially distressed companies to be private equity, although hedge funds may hold these also.

3. **Real estate.** Real estate investments include residential or commercial properties as well as real estate backed debt. These investments are held in a variety of structures including full or leveraged ownership of individual properties, individual real estate backed loans, private and publicly traded securities backed by pools of properties or mortgages, and limited partnerships.

4. **Commodities.** To gain exposure to changes in commodities prices, investors can own physical commodities, commodities derivatives, or the equity of commodity producing firms. Some funds seek exposure to the returns on various commodity indices, often by holding derivatives contracts that are expected to track a specific commodity index.

5. **Other.** This category includes investment in tangible collectible assets such as fine wines, stamps, automobiles, antique furniture, and art, as well as patents, an intangible asset.

LOS 66.c: Describe potential benefits of alternative investments in the context of portfolio management.

CFA® Program Curriculum, Volume 6, page 177

Alternative investment returns have had low correlations with those of traditional investments over long periods. The primary motivation for holding alternative investments is their historically low correlation of returns with those of traditional investments, which can reduce an investor's overall portfolio risk. However, the risk measures we use for traditional assets may not be adequate to capture the risk characteristics of alternative investments. Managers often consider measures of risk other than standard deviation of returns, such as worst month or historical frequency of downside returns.

Historical returns for alternative investments have been higher on average than for traditional investments, so adding alternative investments to a traditional portfolio may increase expected returns. The reasons for these higher returns are thought to be that some alternative investments are less efficiently priced than traditional assets (providing opportunities for skilled managers), that alternative investments may offer extra returns for being illiquid, and that alternative investments often use leverage.

While it seems that adding alternative investments to a portfolio will improve both portfolio risk and expected return, choosing the optimal portfolio allocation to alternative investments is complex and there are potential problems with historical returns data and traditional risk measures. *Survivorship bias* refers to the upward bias of returns if data only for currently existing (surviving) firms is included. Since surviving firms tend to be those that had better-than-average returns, excluding the returns data for failed firms results in average returns that are biased upward. *Backfill bias* refers to bias introduced by including the previous performance data for firms recently added to a benchmark index. Since firms that are newly added to an index must be those that have survived and done better than average, including their returns for prior years (without including the previous and current returns for funds that have not been added to the index) tends to bias index returns upward.

LOS 66.d: Describe hedge funds, private equity, real estate, commodities, and other alternative investments, including, as applicable, strategies, sub-categories, potential benefits and risks, fee structures, and due diligence.

LOS 66.e: Describe issues in valuing, and calculating returns on, hedge funds, private equity, real estate, and commodities.

CFA® Program Curriculum, Volume 6, page 178

HEDGE FUNDS

Hedge funds employ a large number of different strategies. Hedge fund managers have more flexibility than managers of traditional investments. Hedge funds can use leverage, take short equity positions, and take long or short positions in derivatives. The complex nature of hedge fund transactions leads managers to trade through **prime brokers**, who provide many services including custodial services, administrative services, money lending, securities lending for short sales, and trading. Hedge fund managers can negotiate various service parameters with the prime brokers, such as margin requirements.

Hedge fund return objectives can be stated on an **absolute basis** (e.g., 10%) or on a **relative basis** (e.g., returns 5% above a specific benchmark return) depending on the fund strategy. Hedge funds are *less regulated* than traditional investments. Like private equity funds, hedge funds are typically set up as limited partnerships, with the investors as the limited (liability) partners. A hedge fund limited partnership may not include more than a proscribed number of investors, who must possess adequate wealth, sufficient liquidity, and an acceptable degree of investment sophistication. The management firm is the general partner and typically receives both a management fee based on the value of assets managed and an incentive fee based on fund returns.

Hedge fund investments are less liquid than traditional, publicly traded investments. Restrictions on redemptions may include a **lockup period** and/or a **notice period**. A lockup period is a time after initial investment during which withdrawals are not allowed. A notice period, typically 30 to 90 days, is the amount of time a fund has after receiving a redemption request to fulfill the request. Additional fees may be charged at redemption. All of these, of course, discourage redemptions. Hedge fund managers often incur significant transactions costs when they redeem shares. Redemption fees can offset these costs. Notice periods allow time for managers to reduce positions in an orderly manner. Redemptions often increase when hedge fund performance is poor over a period, and the costs of honoring redemptions may further decrease the value of partnership interests. This is an additional source of risk for hedge fund investors.

A **fund of funds** is an investment company that invests in hedge funds, giving investors diversification among hedge fund strategies and allowing smaller investors to access hedge funds in which they may not be able to invest directly. Fund of funds managers charge an additional layer of fees beyond the fees charged by the individual hedge funds in the portfolio.

Hedge Fund Strategies

Similar to categorizing alternative investments, classifying hedge funds can also be challenging. According to Hedge Fund Research, Inc., there are four main classifications of hedge fund strategies:

1. **Event-driven strategies** are typically based on a corporate restructuring or acquisition that creates profit opportunities for long or short positions in common equity, preferred equity, or debt of a specific corporation. Subcategories are:
   - **Merger arbitrage:** Buy the shares of a firm being acquired and sell short the firm making the acquisition.
   - **Distressed/restructuring:** Buy the (undervalued) securities of firms in financial distress when analysis indicates value will be increased by a successful restructuring; possibly short overvalued security types at the same time.
   - **Activist shareholder:** Buy sufficient equity shares to influence a company's policies with the goal of increasing company value.
   - **Special situations:** Invest in the securities of firms that are issuing or repurchasing securities, spinning off divisions, selling assets, or distributing capital.

2. **Relative value strategies** involve buying a security and selling short a related security with the goal of profiting when a perceived pricing discrepancy between the two is resolved.
   - **Convertible arbitrage fixed income:** Exploit pricing discrepancies between convertible bonds and the common stock of the issuing companies.
   - **Asset-backed fixed income:** Exploit pricing discrepancies among various mortgage-backed securities (MBS) or asset-backed securities (ABS).
   - **General fixed income:** Exploit pricing discrepancies between fixed income securities of various types.
   - **Volatility:** Exploit pricing discrepancies arising from differences between returns volatility implied by options prices and manager expectations of future volatility.
   - **Multi-strategy:** Exploit pricing discrepancies among securities in asset classes different from those previously listed and across asset classes and markets.

3. **Macro strategies** are based on global economic trends and events and may involve long or short positions in equities, fixed income, currencies, or commodities.

4. **Equity hedge fund strategies** seek to profit from long or short positions in publicly traded equities and derivatives with equities as their underlying assets.
   - **Market neutral:** Use technical or fundamental analysis to select undervalued equities to be held long, and to select overvalued equities to be sold short, in approximately equal amounts to profit from their relative price movements without exposure to market risk.
   - **Fundamental growth:** Use fundamental analysis to find high-growth companies. Identify and buy equities of companies that are expected to sustain relatively high rates of capital appreciation.
   - **Fundamental value:** Buy equity shares that are believed to be undervalued based on fundamental analysis. Here it is the hedge fund structure, rather than the type of assets purchased, that results in classification as an alternative investment.
   - **Quantitative directional:** Buy equity securities believed to be undervalued and short securities believed to be overvalued based on technical analysis. Market exposure may vary depending on relative size of long and short portfolio positions.
   - **Short bias:** Employ predominantly short positions in overvalued equities, possibly with smaller long positions, but with negative market exposure overall.

Many hedge funds tend to specialize in a specific strategy at first and over time may develop or add additional areas of expertise, becoming multi-strategy funds.

Hedge Fund Potential Benefits and Risks

Hedge fund returns have tended to be better than those of global equities in down equity markets and to lag the returns of global equities in up markets. Different hedge fund strategies have the best returns during different time periods. Statements about the performance and diversification benefits of hedge funds are problematic because of the great variety of strategies used. Less-than-perfect correlation with global equity returns may offer some diversification benefits, but correlations tend to increase during periods of financial crisis.

Hedge Fund Valuation

Hedge fund values are based on market values for traded securities in their portfolios, but must use model (estimated) values for non-traded securities. For traded securities it is most conservative to use the prices at which a position could be closed: bid prices for long positions and ask prices for short positions. Some funds use the average of the bid and ask prices instead. In the case of illiquid securities, quoted market prices may be reduced for the degree of illiquidity, based on position size compared to the total value of such securities outstanding and their average trading volume. Some funds calculate a "trading NAV" using such adjustments for illiquidity. Trading NAV is different from the calculated net asset value required by accounting standards, which is based on either market or model prices.

Hedge Fund Due Diligence

Selecting hedge funds (or funds of funds) requires significant investigation of the available funds. This may be somewhat hampered by a lack of transparency by funds that consider their strategies and systems to be proprietary information. The fact that the regulatory requirements for hedge fund disclosures are minimal presents additional challenges. A partial list of factors to consider when selecting a hedge fund or a fund of funds includes an examination of the fund's:

- Investment strategy.
- Investment process.
- Source of competitive advantages.
- Historical returns.
- Valuation and returns calculation methods.
- Longevity.
- Amount of assets under management.
- Management style.
- Key person risk.
- Reputation.
- Growth plans.
- Systems for risk management.
- Appropriateness of benchmarks.

The analysis of these factors is challenging because a lack of persistence in returns may mean that funds with better historical returns will not provide better-than-average returns in the future. Additionally, many of the items for due diligence, such as reputation, risk management systems, and management style, are difficult to quantify in a way that provides clear choices for potential investors. Further, previously profitable strategies to exploit pricing inefficiencies are likely to become less profitable as more funds pursue the same strategy.

PRIVATE EQUITY

The majority of private equity funds invest either in private companies or public companies they intend to take private (leveraged buyout funds), or in early stage companies (venture capital funds). Two additional, but smaller, categories of private equity funds are distressed investment funds and developmental capital funds.

A private equity fund may also charge fees for arranging buyouts, fees for a deal that does not happen, or fees for handling asset divestitures after a buyout.

Private Equity Strategies

Leveraged buyouts (LBOs) are the most common type of private equity fund investment. "Leveraged" refers to the fact that the fund's purchase of the portfolio company is funded primarily by debt. This may be bank debt (leveraged debt), high-yield bonds, or **mezzanine financing**. Mezzanine financing refers to debt or preferred shares that are subordinate to the high-yield bonds issued and carry warrants or conversion features that give investors participation in equity value increases.

Professor's Note: We will use a similar term, "mezzanine-stage financing," when referring to a late-stage investment in a venture capital company that is preparing to go public via an IPO. Here we are referring to a type of security rather than a type of investment.

Two types of LBOs are **management buyouts** (MBOs), in which the existing management team is involved in the purchase, and **management buy-ins** (MBIs), in which an external management team will replace the existing management team.

In an LBO, the private equity firm seeks to increase the value of the firm through some combination of new management, management incentives, restructuring, cost reduction, or revenue enhancement. Firms with high cash flow are attractive LBO candidates because their cash flow can be used to service and eventually pay down the debt taken on for acquisition.

Venture capital (VC) funds invest in companies in the early stages of their development. The investment often is in the form of equity but can be in convertible preferred shares or convertible debt. While the risk of start-up companies is often great, returns on successful companies can be very high. This is often the case when a company has grown to the point where it is sold (at least in part) to the public via an IPO.

The companies in which a venture capital fund is invested are referred to as its **portfolio companies**. Venture capital fund managers are closely involved in the development of portfolio companies, often sitting on their boards or filling key management roles.

Categorization of venture capital investments is based on the company's stage of development. Terminology used to identify venture firm investment at different stages of the company's life includes the following:

1. The **formative stage** refers to investments made during a firm's earliest period and comprises three distinct phases.
   - **Angel investing** refers to investments made very early in a firm's life, often the "idea" stage, and the investment funds are used for business plans and assessing market potential. The funding source is usually individuals ("angels") rather than venture capital funds.
   - The **seed stage** refers to investments made for product development, marketing, and market research. This is typically the stage during which venture capital funds make initial investments, through ordinary or convertible preferred shares.
   - **Early stage** refers to investments made to fund initial commercial production and sales.

2. **Later stage** investment refers to the stage of development where a company already has production and sales and is operating as a commercial entity. Investment funds provided at this stage are typically used for expansion of production and/or increasing sales though an expanded marketing campaign.

3. **Mezzanine-stage financing** refers to capital provided to prepare the firm for an IPO. The term refers to the timing of the financing (between private company and public company) rather than the type of financing.

Other Private Equity Strategies

Developmental capital or **minority equity investing** refers to the provision of capital for business growth or restructuring. The firms financed may be public or private. In the case of public companies, such financing is referred to as **private investment in public equities** (PIPEs).

Distressed investing involves buying debt of mature companies that are experiencing financial difficulties (potentially or currently in default, or in bankruptcy proceedings). Investors in distressed debt often take an active role in the turnaround by working with management on reorganization or to determine the direction the company should take. Distressed debt investors are sometimes referred to as *vulture investors*. Note that although distressed debt investing is included in the private equity category, some hedge funds invest in the debt of financially distressed companies as well.

Private Equity Structure and Fees

Similar to hedge funds, private equity funds are typically structured as limited partnerships. **Committed capital** is the amount of capital provided to the fund by investors. The committed capital amount is typically not all invested immediately but is "drawn down" (invested) as securities are identified and added to the portfolio. Committed capital is usually drawn down over three to five years, but the *drawdown period* is at the discretion of the fund manager. Management fees are typically 1% to 3% of committed capital, rather than invested capital.

Incentive fees for private equity funds are typically 20% of profits, but these fees are not earned until after the fund has returned investors' initial capital. It is possible that incentive fees paid over time may exceed 20% of the profits realized when all portfolio companies have been liquidated. This situation arises when returns on portfolio companies are high early and decline later. A **clawback** provision requires the manager to return any periodic incentive fees to investors that would result in investors receiving less than 80% of the profits generated by portfolio investments as a whole.

Private Equity Exit Strategies

The average holding period for companies in private equity portfolios is five years. There are several primary methods of exiting an investment in a portfolio company:

1. **Trade sale:** Sell a portfolio company to a competitor or another strategic buyer.

2. **IPO:** Sell all or some shares of a portfolio company to the public.

3. **Recapitalization:** The company issues debt to fund a dividend distribution to equity holders (the fund). This is not an exit, in that the fund still controls the company, but is often a step toward an exit.

4. **Secondary sale:** Sell a portfolio company to another private equity firm or a group of investors.

5. **Write-off/liquidation:** Reassess and adjust to take losses from an unsuccessful outcome.

Private Equity Potential Benefits and Risks

There is evidence that over the last 20 years returns on private equity funds have been higher on average than overall stock returns. Less-than-perfect correlation of private equity returns with traditional investment returns suggests that there may be portfolio diversification benefits from including private equity in portfolios. The standard deviation of private equity returns has been higher than the standard deviation of equity index returns, suggesting greater risk. As with hedge fund returns data, private equity returns data may suffer from survivorship bias and backfill bias (both lead to overstated returns). Because portfolio companies are revalued infrequently, reported standard deviations of returns and correlations of returns with equity returns may both be biased downward.

Evidence suggests that choosing skilled fund managers is important. Differences between the returns to top quartile funds and bottom quartile funds are significant and performance rank shows persistence over time.

Private Equity Company Valuation

Valuation for private equity portfolio companies is essentially the same as valuing a publicly traded company, although the discount rate or multiples used may be different for private companies.

*   **Market/comparables approach:** Market or private transaction values of similar companies may be used to estimate multiples of EBITDA, net income, or revenue to use in estimating the portfolio company's value.
*   **Discounted cash flow approach:** A dividend discount model falls into this category, as does calculating the present value of free cash flow to the firm or free cash flow to equity.
*   **Asset-based approach:** Either the liquidation values or fair market values of assets can be used. Liquidation values will be lower as they are values that could be realized quickly in a situation of financial distress or termination of company operations. Liabilities are subtracted so that only the equity portion of the firm's value is being estimated.

Example: Portfolio company comparables approach

A private equity fund is valuing a French private manufacturing company. EBITDA and market values for four publicly traded European companies in the same industry are shown in the following table (in millions of euros):

	EBITDA	Market Value
Company 1:	€100	€1,000
Company 2:	€250	€2,000
Company 3:	€250	€1,500
Company 4:	€275	€2,200

The estimated EBITDA for the French company is €175 million. Using an average of the four companies as the industry multiple, estimate the market value for the French company.

Answer:

	EBITDA Multiple
Company 1:	€1,000 / €100 = 10×
Company 2:	€2,000 / €250 = 8×
Company 3:	€1,500 / €250 = 6×
Company 4:	€2,200 / €275 = 8×

The average multiple for these four companies is 8×. Based on the French company's expected EBITDA of €175 million, its estimated value is €175 million × 8 = €1,400 million or €1.4 billion.

Private Equity Due Diligence

Because of the high leverage typically used for private equity funds, investors should consider how interest rates and the availability of capital may affect any required refinancing of portfolio company debt. The choice of manager (general partner) is quite important and many of the factors we listed for hedge fund due diligence also apply to private equity fund investments. Specifically, the operating and financial experience of the manager, the valuation methods used, the incentive fee structures, and drawdown procedures are all important areas to investigate prior to investing.

REAL ESTATE

Investment in real estate can provide income in the form of rents as well as the potential for capital gains. Real estate as an asset class can provide diversification benefits to an investor's portfolio and a potential inflation hedge because rents and real estate values tend to increase with inflation. Real estate investments can be differentiated according to their underlying assets. Assets included under the heading of real estate investments include:

- Residential property—single-family homes.

- Commercial property—produces income.
- Loans with residential or commercial property as collateral—mortgages ("whole loans"), construction loans.

Forms of Real Estate Investment

Residential property is considered a direct investment in real estate. Some buyers pay cash but most take on a mortgage (borrow) to purchase. The issuer (lender) of the mortgage has a direct investment in a whole loan and is said to "hold the mortgage." Issuers often sell the mortgages they originate and the mortgages are then pooled (securitized) as publicly traded mortgage-backed securities (MBS), which represent an indirect investment in the mortgage loan pool. Property purchased with a mortgage is referred to as a *leveraged investment* and the owner's equity is the property value minus the outstanding loan amount. Changes in property value over time, therefore, affect the property owner's equity in the property.

Commercial real estate properties generate income from rents. Homes purchased for rental income are considered investment in commercial property. Large properties (e.g., an office building) are a form of direct investment for institutions or wealthy individuals, either purchased for cash or leveraged (a mortgage loan is taken for a portion of the purchase price). Long time horizons, illiquidity, the large size of investment needed, and the complexity of the investments make commercial real estate inappropriate for many investors. Commercial real estate properties can also be held by a limited partnership in which the partners have limited liability and the general partner manages the investment and the properties, or by a real estate investment trust (REIT).

As with residential mortgages, whole loans (commercial property mortgages) are considered a direct investment, but loans can be pooled into commercial mortgage-backed securities (CMBS) that represent an indirect investment.

Real estate investment trusts (REITs) issue shares that trade publicly like shares of stock. REITs are often identified by the type of real estate assets they hold: mortgages, hotel properties, malls, office buildings, or other commercial property. Income is used to pay dividends. Typically, 90% of income must be distributed to shareholders to avoid taxes on this income that would have to be paid by the REIT before distribution to shareholders.

Other Real Estate Assets

Two additional assets considered as real estate are timberland and farmland, for which one component of returns comes from sales of timber or agricultural products. Timberland returns also include price changes on timberland, which depend on expectations of lumber prices in the future and how much timber has been harvested. Farmland returns are based on land price changes, changes in farm commodity prices, and the quality and quantity of the crops produced.

Potential Benefits and Risks of Real Estate

Real estate performance is measured by three different types of indices. An **appraisal index**, such as those prepared by the National Council of Real Estate Investment Fiduciaries (NCREIF), is based on periodic estimates of property values. Appraisal index returns are smoother than those based on actual sales and have the lowest standard deviation of returns of the various index methods. A **repeat sales index** is based on price changes for properties that have sold multiple times. The sample of properties sold and thus included in the index is not necessarily random and may not be representative of the broad spectrum of properties available (an example of sample selection bias). **REIT indices** are based on the actual trading prices of REIT shares, similar to equity indices.

Historically, REIT index returns and global equity returns have had a relatively strong correlation (on the order of 0.6) because business cycles affect REITs and global equities similarly. The correlation between global bond returns and REIT returns has been very low historically. In either case diversification benefits can result from including real estate in an investor's portfolio. However, the methods of index construction (e.g., appraisal or repeat sales indices) may be a factor in the low reported correlations, in which case actual diversification benefits may be less than expected.

Real Estate Valuation

Three methods are commonly used to value real estate:

- The **comparable sales approach** bases valuation on recent sales of similar properties. Values for individual properties include adjustments for differences between the characteristics of the specific property and those of the properties for which recent sales prices are available, such as age, location, condition, and size.
- The **income approach** estimates property values by calculating the present value of expected future cash flows from property ownership or by dividing the net operating income (NOI) for a property by a capitalization (cap) rate. The cap rate is a discount rate minus a growth rate and is estimated based on factors such as general business conditions, property qualities, management effectiveness, and sales of comparable properties. Note that dividing by a cap rate of 12.5% is the same as using a multiple of 8 times NOI (1 / 0.125 = 8).
- The **cost approach** estimates the replacement cost of a property. The cost of land and the cost of rebuilding at current construction costs are added to estimate replacement cost.

Value estimates for real estate investment trusts can be income based or asset based. The income-based approach is similar to the income approach for a specific property and uses some measure of cash flow and a cap rate based on the factors we noted previously for the income approach. One measure of cash flow for a REIT is funds from operations (FFO). FFO is calculated from net income with depreciation added back (because depreciation is a non-cash charge) and with gains from property sales subtracted and losses on property sales added (because these gains and losses are assumed to be nonrecurring). A second measure of cash flow is adjusted funds from operations (AFFO), which is FFO with recurring capital expenditures subtracted. AFFO is similar to free cash flow. The asset-based approach provides an estimate of the net asset value of the REIT by subtracting total liabilities from the total value of the real estate assets and dividing by the number of shares outstanding.

Real Estate Investment Due Diligence

Property values fluctuate because of global and national economic factors, local market conditions, and interest rate levels. Other specific risks include variation in the abilities of managers to select and manage properties, and changes in regulations. Decisions regarding selecting, financing, and managing real estate projects directly affect performance. The degree of leverage used in a real estate investment is important because leverage amplifies losses as well as gains.

Distressed properties investing has additional risk factors compared to investing in properties with sound financials and stable operating histories. *Real estate development* has additional risk factors including regulatory issues such as zoning, permitting, and environmental considerations or remediation, and economic changes and financing decisions over the development period. The possible inability to get long-term financing at the appropriate time for properties initially developed with temporary (short-term) financing presents an additional risk.

COMMODITIES

While it is possible to invest directly in commodities such as grain and gold, the most commonly used instruments to gain exposure to commodity prices are derivatives. Commodities themselves are physical goods and thus incur costs for storage and transportation. Returns are based on price changes and not on income streams.

Futures, forwards, options, and swaps are all available forms of commodity derivatives. Futures trade on exchanges; some options trade on exchanges while others trade over the counter; and forwards and swaps are over-the-counter instruments originated by dealers. Futures and forwards are contractual obligations to buy or sell a commodity at a specified price and time. Options convey the right, but not the obligation, to buy or sell a commodity at a specified price and time. Other methods of exposures to commodities include the following:

- **Exchange-traded funds** (commodity ETFs) are suitable for investors who are limited to buying equity shares. ETFs can invest in commodities or commodity futures and can track prices or indices.
- **Equities that are directly linked to a commodity** include shares of a commodity producer, such as an oil producer or a gold mining firm, and give investors exposure to price changes of the produced commodity. One potential drawback to commodity-linked equities is that the price movements of the stock and the price movements of the commodity may not be perfectly correlated.
- **Managed futures funds** are actively managed. Some managers concentrate on specific sectors (e.g., agricultural commodities) while others are more diversified. Managed future funds can be structured as limited partnerships with fees like those of hedge funds (e.g., 2 and 20) and restrictions on the number, net worth, and liquidity of the investors. They can also be structured like mutual funds with shares that are publicly traded so that retail investors can also benefit from professional management. Additionally, such a structure allows a lower minimum investment and greater liquidity compared to a limited partnership structure.

- **Individual managed accounts** provide an alternative to pooled funds for high net worth individuals and institutions. Accounts are tailored to the needs of the specific investor.
- **Specialized funds in specific commodity sectors** can be organized under any of the structures we have discussed and focus on certain commodities, such as oil and gas, grains, precious metals, or industrial metals.

Potential Benefits and Risks of Commodities

Returns on commodities over time have been lower than returns on global stocks or bonds. Sharpe ratios for commodities as an asset class have been low due to these lower returns and the high volatility of commodities prices. As with other investments, speculators can earn high returns over short periods when their expectations about short-term commodity price movements are correct and they act on them.

Historically, correlations of commodity returns with those of global equities and global bonds have been low, typically less than 0.2, so that adding commodities to a traditional portfolio can provide diversification benefits. Because commodity prices tend to move with inflation rates, holding commodities can act as a hedge of inflation risk. To the extent that commodities prices move with inflation the real return over time would be zero, although futures contracts may offer positive real returns.

Commodity Prices and Investments

Spot prices for commodities are a function of supply and demand. Demand is affected by the value of the commodity to end-users and by global economic conditions and cycles. Supply is affected by production and storage costs and existing inventories. Both supply and demand are affected by the purchases and sales of non-hedging investors (speculators).

For many commodities, supply is inelastic in the short run because of long lead times to alter production levels (e.g., drill oil wells, plant crops, or decide to plant less of them). As a result, commodity prices can be volatile when demand changes significantly over the economic cycle. Production of some commodities, especially agricultural commodities, can be significantly affected by the weather, leading to high prices when production is low and low prices when production is high. Costs of extracting oil and minerals increase as more expensive methods or more remote areas are used. To estimate future needs, commodities producers analyze economic events, government policy, and forecasts of future supply. Investors analyze inventory levels, forecasts of production, changes in government policy, and expectations of economic growth in order to forecast commodity prices.

Commodity Futures Pricing

Wheat today and wheat six months from today are different products. Purchasing the commodity today will give the buyer the use of it if needed, while contracting for wheat to be delivered six months from today avoids storage costs and having cash tied up. An equation that considers these aspects is:

$$\text{futures price} \approx \text{spot price} (1 + \text{risk-free rate}) + \text{storage costs} - \text{convenience yield}$$

Convenience yield is the value of having the physical commodity for use over the period of the futures contract. If this equation does not hold, an arbitrage transaction is possible.

If there is little or no convenience yield, futures prices will be higher than spot prices, a situation termed **contango**. When the convenience yield is high, futures prices will be less than spot prices, a situation referred to as **backwardation**.

Three sources of commodities futures returns are:

1. **Roll yield**—The yield due to a difference between the spot price and futures price, or a difference between two futures prices with different expiration dates.

2. **Collateral yield**—The interest earned on collateral required to enter into a futures contract.

3. **Change in spot prices**—The total price return is a combination of the change in spot prices and the convergence of futures prices to spot prices over the term of the futures contract.

 Professor's Note: These three sources of return are described more fully in the Investing in Commodities topic review.

Other Alternative Investments

Various types of tangible collectibles are considered investments, including rare wines, art, rare coins and stamps, valuable jewelry and watches, and sports memorabilia. There is no income generation but owners do get enjoyment from use, as with a collectible automobile. Storage costs may be significant, especially with art and wine. Specialized knowledge is required, the markets for many collectibles are illiquid, and gains result only from increases in the prices of these assets.

LOS 66.f: Describe, calculate, and interpret management and incentive fees and net-of-fees returns to hedge funds.

CFA® Program Curriculum, Volume 6, page 185

Hedge Fund Fees

The total fee paid by investors in a hedge fund consists of a **management fee** and an **incentive fee**. The management fee is earned regardless of investment performance and incentive fees are a portion of profits. The most common fee structure for a hedge fund is "2 and 20" or "2 plus," 2% of the value of the assets under management plus an incentive fee of 20% of profits.

Profits can be (1) any gains in value, (2) any gains in value in excess of the management fee, or (3) gains in excess of a **hurdle rate**. A hurdle rate can be set either as a percentage (e.g., 4%) or a rate plus a premium (e.g., LIBOR + 2%). A *hard hurdle rate* means that incentive fees are earned only on returns in excess of the benchmark. A *soft hurdle rate* means that incentive fees are paid on all profits, but only if the hurdle rate is met.

Another feature that is often included is called a **high water mark**. This means that the incentive fee is not paid on gains that just offset prior losses. Thus incentive fees are only paid to the extent that the current value of an investor's account is above the highest value previously recorded. This feature ensures that investors will not be charged incentive fees twice on the same gains in their portfolio values.

Investors in funds of funds incur additional fees from the managers of the funds of funds. A common fee structure from funds of funds is "1 and 10." A 1% management fee and a 10% incentive fee are charged in addition to any fees charged by the individual hedge funds within the fund-of-funds structure.

Fee calculations for both management fees and incentive fees can differ not only by the schedule of rates but also method of fee determination. Management fees may be calculated on either the beginning-of-period or end-of-period values of assets under management. Incentive fees may be calculated net of management fees (value increase less management fees) or independent of management fees. Although the most common hedge fund fee rates tend to be the "2 and 20" and "1 and 10" for funds of funds, fee structures can vary. Price breaks to investors, competitive conditions, and historical performance can influence negotiated rates.

Fee structures and their impact on investors' results are illustrated in the following example.

Example: Hedge fund fees

BJI Funds is a hedge fund with a value of $100 million at the beginning of the year (an all-time high). BJI Funds charges a 2% management fee based on assets under management at the beginning of the year and a 20% incentive fee with a 5% hard hurdle rate and uses a high water mark. Incentive fees are calculated on gains net of management fees. The ending values before fees are:

Year 1: $125.75 million
Year 2: $127.40 million
Year 3: $138.44 million

Calculate the total fees and investor's net return for all three years.

Answer:

Year 1:
Management fee: $100 \times 2\% = 2$
Gross value end of year (given): $125.75 million
Incentive fee: $[125.75 - 100 - 2 - (100 \times 5\%)] \times 20\% = \$3.75$ million
Total fee: $2 + 3.75 = \$5.75$ million
Ending value net of fees: $125.75 - 5.75 = \$120.00$ million
Net return to investors: $(120 / 100) - 1 = 20.00\%$

Year 2:
Management fee: $120 \times 2\% = \$2.40$ million
Gross value end of year (given): $127.40 million
Incentive fee: $[127.40 - 120 - 2.40 - (120 \times 5.0\%)] \times 20\% = -\$0.20$ million. Since this result is negative there is no incentive fee. The return did not exceed the hurdle rate.
Total fee: $2.40 million
Ending value net of fee: $127.40 - 2.40 = \$125.00$ million
Net return: $(125 / 120) - 1 = 4.17\%$
The net return of less than 5% is consistent with no incentive fee.

Year 3:
Management fee: $125 \times 2.0\% = \$2.50$ million
Gross value end of year (given): $138.44 million
Incentive fee: $[138.44 - 125.00 - 2.50 - (125.00 \times 5.0\%)] \times 20\% = \$0.94$ million
Total fee: $2.50 + 0.94 = \$3.44$ million
Ending value net of fee: $138.44 - 3.44 = \$135.00$ million
Net return: $(135 / 125) - 1 = 8.00\%$

The high water mark was never an issue because this hedge fund had positive returns over each of the three years.

LOS 66.g: Describe risk management of alternative investments.

CFA® Program Curriculum, Volume 6, page 219

Risk management of alternative investments requires additional understanding of the unique set of circumstances for each category. We can summarize some of the more important risk considerations as follows:

- Standard deviation of returns may be a misleading measure of risk for two reasons. First, returns distributions are not approximately normal; they tend to be leptokurtic (fat tails) and negatively skewed (possibility of extreme negative outcomes). Second, for alternative assets that use appraisal or models to estimate values, returns are smoothed so that standard deviation of returns (and correlations with returns of traditional investments) will be understated. Even market-based returns can have these same limitations when transactions are infrequent. These problems can bias

Sharpe measures upward and make estimates of beta misleading as well. Investors should consider downside risk measures such as **value at risk (VaR)**, which is an estimate of the size of a potential decline over a period that will occur, for example, less than 5% of the time; or the **Sortino ratio**, which measures risk as downside deviation rather than standard deviation. For publicly traded securities, such as REITs and ETFs, market returns are used and standard definitions of risk are more applicable.

- Use of derivatives introduces operational, financial, counterparty, and liquidity risk.
- Performance for some alternative investment categories is primarily determined by management expertise and execution, so risk is not just that of holding an asset class but also risk of management underperformance.
- Hedge funds and private equity funds are much less transparent than traditional investments as they release less information and may consider their strategies to be proprietary information.
- Many alternative investments are illiquid. Returns should reflect a premium for lack of liquidity to compensate investors for liquidity risk or the inability to redeem securities at all during lockup periods.
- When calculating optimal allocations, indices of historical returns and standard deviations may not be good indicators of future returns and volatility.
- Correlations vary across periods and are affected by events.

Due Diligence

A listing of key items for due diligence for alternative investments includes six major categories: organization, portfolio management, operations and controls, risk management, legal review, and fund terms.

1. **Organization:** Experience, quality, and compensation of management and staff; analysis of all their prior and current fund results; alignment of manager and investor interests; and reputation and quality of third-party service providers used.

2. **Portfolio management:** Management of the investment process; target markets, asset types, and strategies; investment sources; operating partners' roles; underwriting; environmental and engineering review; integration of asset management, acquisitions, and dispositions; and the process for dispositions.

3. **Operations and controls:** Reporting and accounting methods; audited financial statements; internal controls; frequency of valuations; valuation approaches; insurance; and contingency plans.

4. **Risk management:** Fund policies and limits; portfolio risk and key factors; and constraints on leverage and currencies and hedging of related risks.

5. **Legal review:** Fund legal structure; registrations; and current and past litigation.

6. **Fund terms:** Fees, both management and incentive, and expenses; contractual terms; investment period; fund term and extensions; carried interest; distributions; conflicts; rights of limited partners; and termination procedures for key personnel.

KEY CONCEPTS

LOS 66.a

"Traditional investments" refers to long-only positions in stocks, bonds, and cash. "Alternative investments" refers to some types of assets such as real estate, commodities, and various collectables, as well as some specific structures of investment vehicles. Hedge funds and private equity funds (including venture capital funds) are often structured as limited partnerships; real estate investment trusts (REITs) are similar to mutual funds; and ETFs can contain alternative investments as well.

Compared to traditional investments, alternative investments typically have lower liquidity; less regulation and disclosure; higher management fees and more specialized management; potential diversification benefits; more use of leverage, use of derivatives; potentially higher returns; limited and possibly biased historical returns data; problematic historical risk measures; and unique legal and tax considerations.

LOS 66.b

Hedge funds are investment companies that use a variety of strategies and may be highly leveraged, use long and short positions, and use derivatives.

Private equity funds usually invest in the equity of private companies or companies wanting to become private, financing their assets with high levels of debt. This category also includes venture capital funds, which provide capital to companies early in their development.

Real estate as an asset class includes residential and commercial real estate, individual mortgages, and pools of mortgages or properties. It includes direct investment in single properties or loans as well as indirect investment in limited partnerships, which are private securities, and mortgage-backed securities and real estate investment trusts, which are publicly traded.

Commodities refer to physical assets such as agricultural products, metals, oil and gas, and other raw materials used in production. Commodities market exposure can provide an inflation hedge and diversification benefits.

Various types of collectibles, such as cars, wines, and art, are considered alternative investments as well.

LOS 66.c

The primary motivation for adding alternative investments to a portfolio is to reduce portfolio risk based on the less-than-perfect correlation between alternative asset returns and traditional asset returns. For many alternative investments, the expertise of the manager can be an important determinant of returns.

LOS 66.d

Hedge Funds

- *Event-driven* strategies include merger arbitrage, distressed/restructuring, activist shareholder and special situations.
- *Relative value* strategies seek profits from unusual pricing issues.
- *Macro hedge* strategies are "top down" strategies based on global economic trends.
- *Equity hedge* strategies are "bottom up" strategies that take long and short positions in equities and equity derivatives. Strategies include market neutral, fundamental growth, fundamental value, quantitative directional, short bias, and sector specific.

In periods of financial crisis, the correlation of returns between global equities and hedge funds tends to increase, which limits hedge funds' effectiveness as a diversifying asset class.

Due diligence factors for hedge funds are investment strategy, investment process, competitive advantages, track record, longevity of fund, and size (assets under management). Other qualitative factors include management style, key person risk, reputation, investor relations, growth plans, and management of systematic risk.

Private Equity

Leveraged buyouts (LBOs) and *venture capital* are the two dominant strategies. Other strategies include developmental capital and distressed securities.

Types of LBOs include management buyouts, in which the existing management team is involved in the purchase, and management buy-ins, in which an external management team replaces the existing management.

Stages of venture capital investing include the formative stage (composed of the angel investing, seed, and early stages); the later stage (expansion); and the mezzanine stage (prepare for IPO).

Methods for exiting investments in portfolio companies include trade sale (sell to a competitor or another strategic buyer); IPO (sell some or all shares to investors); recapitalization (issue portfolio company debt); secondary sale (sell to another private equity firm or other investors); or write-off/liquidation.

Private equity has some historical record of potential diversification benefits. An investor must identify top performing private equity managers to benefit from private equity.

Due diligence factors for private equity include the manager's experience, valuation methods used, fee structure, and drawdown procedures for committed capital.

Real Estate

Reasons to invest in real estate include potential long-term total returns, income from rent payments, diversification benefits, and hedging against inflation.

Forms of real estate investing:

	Public (Indirect)	Private (Direct)
Debt	• Mortgage-backed securities • Collateralized mortgage obligations	• Mortgages • Construction loans
Equity	• Real estate corporation shares • Real estate investment trust shares	• Sole ownership • Joint ventures • Limited partnerships • Commingled funds

Real estate investment categories include residential properties, commercial real estate, REITs, mortgage-backed securities, and timberland and farmland.

Historically, real estate returns are highly correlated with global equity returns but less correlated with global bond returns. The construction method of real estate indexes may contribute to the low correlation with bond returns.

Due diligence factors for real estate include global and national economic factors, local market conditions, interest rates, and property-specific risks including regulations and abilities of managers. Distressed properties investing and real estate development have additional risk factors to consider.

Commodities

The most common way to invest in commodities is with derivatives. Other methods include exchange-traded funds, equities that are directly linked to a commodity, managed futures funds, individual managed accounts, and specialized funds in specific commodity sectors.

Beyond the potential for higher returns and lower volatility benefits to a portfolio, commodity as an asset class may offer inflation protection. Commodities can offset inflation, especially if commodity prices are used to determine inflation indices.

Spot prices for commodities are a function of supply and demand. Global economics, production costs, and storage costs, along with value to user, all factor into prices.

LOS 66.e
Hedge funds often invest in securities that are not actively traded and must estimate their values, and invest in securities that are illiquid relative to the size of a hedge fund's position. Hedge funds may calculate a trading NAV that adjusts for the illiquidity of these securities.

A private equity portfolio company may be valued using a market/comparables approach (multiple-based) approach, a discounted cash flow approach, or an asset-based approach.

Real estate property valuation approaches include the comparable sales approach, the income approach (multiples or discounted cash flows), and the cost approach. REITs can be valued using an income-based approach or an asset-based approach.

A commodity futures price is approximately equal to the spot price compounded at the risk-free rate, plus storage costs, minus the convenience yield.

LOS 66.f

The total fee for a hedge fund consists of a management fee and an incentive fee. Other fee structure specifications include hurdle rates and high water marks. Funds of funds incur an additional level of management fees. Fee calculations for both management fees and incentive fees can differ by the schedule and method of fee determination.

LOS 66.g

Risk management of alternative investments requires understanding of the unique circumstances for each category.

- Standard deviation of returns may be misleading as a measure of risk.
- Use of derivatives introduces operational, financial, counterparty, and liquidity risks.
- Performance for some alternative investment categories depends primarily on management expertise.
- Hedge funds and private equity funds are less transparent than traditional investments.
- Many alternative investments are illiquid.
- Indices of historical returns and standard deviations may not be good indicators of future returns and volatility.
- Correlations vary across periods and are affected by events.

Key items for due diligence include organization, portfolio management, operations and controls, risk management, legal review, and fund terms.

CONCEPT CHECKERS

1. Compared to managers of traditional investments, managers of alternative investments are likely to have fewer restrictions on:
    A. holding cash.
    B. buying stocks.
    C. using derivatives.

2. Compared to alternative investments, traditional investments tend to:
    A. be less liquid.
    B. be less regulated.
    C. require lower fees.

3. In which category of alternative investments is an investor *most likely* to use derivatives?
    A. Real estate.
    B. Commodities.
    C. Collectibles.

4. An investor who chooses a fund of funds as an alternative to a single hedge fund is *most likely* to benefit from:
    A. lower fees.
    B. higher returns.
    C. more due diligence.

5. In a leveraged buyout, covenants in leveraged loans can:
    A. restrict additional borrowing.
    B. require lenders to provide transparency.
    C. provide protection for the general partners.

6. Direct commercial real estate ownership *least likely* requires investing in:
    A. large amounts.
    B. illiquid assets.
    C. a short time horizon.

7. Diversification benefits from adding hedge funds to an equity portfolio may be limited because:
    A. correlations tend to increase during periods of financial crisis.
    B. hedge fund returns are less than perfectly correlated with global equities.
    C. hedge funds tend to perform better when global equity prices are declining.

8. A private equity valuation approach that uses estimated multiples of cash flows to value a portfolio company is the:
    A. asset-based approach.
    B. discount cash flow approach.
    C. market/comparables approach.

9. A real estate property valuation would *least likely* use a(n):
   A. income approach.
   B. asset-based approach.
   C. comparable sales approach.

10. A high water mark of £150 million was established two years ago for a British hedge fund. The end-of-year value before fees for last year was £140 million. This year's end-of-year value before fees is £155 million. The fund charges "2 and 20." Management fees are paid independently of incentive fees and are calculated on end-of-year values. What is the total fee paid this year?
    A. £3.1 million.
    B. £4.1 million.
    C. £6.1 million.

11. Standard deviation is *least likely* an appropriate measure of risk for:
    A. hedge funds.
    B. publicly traded REITs.
    C. exchange-traded funds.

ANSWERS – CONCEPT CHECKERS

1. **C** Traditional managers can hold cash and buy stocks but may be restricted from using derivatives.

2. **C** Traditional investments typically require lower fees, are more regulated, and are more liquid than alternative investments.

3. **B** Commodities investing frequently involves the use of futures contracts. Derivatives are less often employed in real estate or collectibles investing.

4. **C** A fund of funds manager is expected to provide more due diligence and better redemption terms. Funds of funds charge an additional layer of fees. Investing in fund of funds may provide more diversification but may not necessarily provide higher returns.

5. **A** Debt covenants in leveraged buyout loans may restrict additional borrowing by the acquired firm. Covenants restrict and require borrowers' actions, not lenders' actions. Covenants in leveraged loans provide protection for the lenders, not the general partners.

6. **C** Commercial real estate ownership requires long time horizons and purchasing illiquid assets that require large investment amounts.

7. **A** Adding hedge funds to traditional portfolios may not provide the expected diversification to an equity portfolio because return correlations tend to increase during periods of financial crisis.

8. **C** The market/comparables approach uses market or private transaction values of similar companies to estimate multiples of EBITDA, net income, or revenue to use in estimating the portfolio company's value.

9. **B** The three approaches to valuing a property are income, comparable sales, and cost. An asset-based approach can be used for real estate investment trusts, but not for valuing individual real estate properties.

10. **B** Management fee is £155 million × 0.02 = £3.1 million.

    Incentive fee is (£155 million – £150 million) × 0.20 = £1.0 million.

    Total fee is £3.1 million + £1.0 million = £4.1 million.

11. **A** Hedge funds may hold illiquid assets that may use estimated values to calculate returns. Risk as measured by standard deviation could be understated. For publicly traded securities, such as REITs and ETFs, standard definitions of risk are more applicable.

INVESTING IN COMMODITIES

EXAM FOCUS

There are only three LOS here. The concepts of backwardation and contango are based on the relation between current (spot) prices and futures prices and are important for understanding the component of returns called the roll yield, which stems from the necessity to re-establish long commodity positions as they reach their settlement (delivery) dates. The fact that positions must be periodically closed out and re-established makes even a commodity indexing strategy active compared to a long equity or bond indexing strategy.

LOS 67.a: Explain the relationship between spot prices and expected future prices in terms of contango and backwardation.

CFA® Program Curriculum, Volume 6, page 232

Contango refers to a situation in commodities futures contracts where the futures price is above the spot price, the price for current purchase and delivery of the physical commodity. This is the current situation (as of the time of writing) in the oil futures market. One way to view the explanation for this is based on the needs of either long or short hedgers. With oil prices rising sharply over the last year, users of oil and oil-related commodities are concerned with the risk they face from rising oil prices. Airlines, for example, sell tickets at prices based on expected fuel prices and are exposed to the financial consequences of increases in fuel prices above those expected to prevail in the future.

When an end user of a commodity buys futures contracts to protect against unexpected future price increases, we refer to that futures buyer as a *long hedger*, as they are hedging commodity price risk with long positions. If the predominant reason for futures positions in a commodity is to hedge the risk of price increases, long hedgers will be paying for the protection of long futures positions, which will produce gains as the futures price increases. In a situation of contango, long hedgers are bidding up the price of commodity futures and, in effect, paying a premium for the hedging benefit they get from taking long futures positions.

Backwardation refers to a situation in commodities futures contracts where the futures price is below the spot price. If the dominant traders in a commodity future are producers of the commodity hedging their exposure to financial losses arising from unexpected price declines in the future, the result will be backwardation. In this situation, producers are paying for protection against price declines and that is reflected in futures prices which are lower than current market prices (spot prices). Historically, producers hedging the price risk of future production have been dominant in futures markets, so that backwardation was the typical situation and sometimes referred to as **normal backwardation**.

LOS 67.b: Describe the sources of return and risk for a commodity investment and the effect on a portfolio of adding an allocation to commodities.

CFA® Program Curriculum, Volume 6, page 234

An investor who desires long exposure to a commodity price will typically achieve this exposure through a derivative investment in forwards or futures. Some physical commodities cannot be effectively purchased and stored long term, and for others, such as precious metals, derivative positions may be a more efficient means of gaining long exposure than purchasing the commodities outright and storing them long term.

To take a position in forwards or futures, a speculator or hedger must post collateral. If U.S. Treasury bills are deposited as collateral, the **collateral yield** is simply the yield on the T-bills. Active management of the collateral, within the bounds of what is acceptable collateral, can increase the collateral yield above the 90-day T-bill rate.

The **price return** on a long-only investment in commodities derivatives can be positive or negative depending on the direction of change in the spot price for the commodity over the life of the derivatives contract employed.

Since commodity derivative contracts expire, a speculator or hedger who wants to maintain a position over time must close out the expiring derivative position and re-establish a new position with a settlement date further in the future. This process is referred to as *rolling over* the position and leads to gains or losses which are termed the **roll yield**. The roll yield can be positive or negative depending on whether the derivative contract used to establish the long exposure is in backwardation or contango. You can view this roll yield as the gains or losses that would be realized on the position if the spot price remained unchanged over the life of the contract.

As a futures contract gets closer to expiration, the futures price converges toward the spot price. At expiration, the futures price must equal the spot price. For a future or forward in backwardation (i.e., the futures/forward price is less than the current spot price) the roll yield is positive, since an unchanged spot price at contract settlement would mean the futures/forward price increased over the life of the contract, and the investor would have gains at settlement. For a future or forward in contango, the roll yield is negative. Since contango means the forward/futures price is greater than the spot price, an unchanged spot price over the life of the contract means the futures price will have fallen and losses will result when the position is closed out.

When commodity derivative markets were dominated by short hedgers (commodity producers) and markets were typically in backwardation, the roll yield was positive. In current market conditions, with futures and forwards typically in contango, the roll yield is negative. It may be the case that structural changes in the markets for commodities derivatives mean that a zero or negative roll yield has become the new norm for these markets.

Adding a long commodities index position to a portfolio can provide several benefits, particularly for pension fund portfolios. Commodities provide diversification benefits because their prices tend to be uncorrelated with securities prices, and they can serve as a hedge against inflation.

LOS 67.c: Explain why a commodity index strategy is generally considered an active investment.

CFA® Program Curriculum, Volume 6, page 239

An index strategy in equities is considered a passive strategy. While changes may be necessary if one of the component stocks of the index is changed, in the absence of any change in the component stocks, no active management of an index portfolio is required. Because of the necessity of closing out and re-establishing long derivative positions to maintain long exposure to changes in commodity prices, a commodity index strategy is considered an active strategy. Managers can add value to the long-only commodity index strategy by choosing the maturities of the derivative contracts they buy and by their decisions about when to roll over their positions. To the extent that many long-only commodity derivative managers attempt to roll their positions over at the same time, they pay a premium in transactions costs, which reduces both the roll yield and overall yield of their commodity index strategy.

There are two other aspects of commodity index investing that require active management. The weightings of various commodities and commodity blocks (such as metals or energy) in indexes do not necessarily change with the values of the derivative positions in the portfolio. Since commodities index weightings, whether based on commodity production or consumption, change over time, a manager who seeks to match an index must actively manage the size of the exposure to various commodity markets as positions are rolled over. Additionally, as mentioned earlier, the short-term debt used to collateralize derivative positions must be managed as well. The collateral debt securities mature and new ones must be purchased, and the collateral yield can be enhanced by taking advantage of market conditions as maturing collateral debt securities are replaced.

KEY CONCEPTS

LOS 67.a

A commodity futures market is in contango if futures prices are greater than the spot price. The market is in backwardation if futures prices are less than the spot price.

Futures markets that are dominated by long hedgers (users of the commodity who buy futures to protect against price increases) tend to be in contango. Futures markets that are dominated by short hedgers (producers of the commodity who short futures to protect against price decreases) tend to be in backwardation.

LOS 67.b

The return on a commodity investment includes:

- Collateral yield: the return on the collateral posted to satisfy margin requirements.
- Price return: the gain or loss due to changes in the spot price.
- Roll yield: the gain or loss resulting from re-establishing positions as contracts expire.

Roll yield is positive if the futures market is in backwardation and negative if the market is in contango.

Commodities can provide diversification benefits to a portfolio of securities because commodity returns tend not to be highly positively correlated with securities returns.

LOS 67.c

A commodity index strategy is considered an active investment because the manager has to decide what maturities to use for the forward or futures contracts and determine when to roll them over into new contracts. Active management is also required to manage portfolio weights to match those of the benchmark index selected and to determine the best choice of securities to post as collateral and how these should be rolled over as they mature.

CONCEPT CHECKERS

1. A commodities market tends to be in backwardation if:
    A. it is dominated by end users of the commodity.
    B. the spot price is greater than futures prices.
    C. futures prices are greater than the spot price.

2. The source of return on a long-only commodity investment that represents the change in the spot price over the life of the forward or futures contract used is the:
    A. roll yield.
    B. price return.
    C. spot yield.

3. For a commodity market that is in contango, an unchanged spot price over the life of a contract will result in a roll yield that is:
    A. zero.
    B. positive.
    C. negative.

4. A manager following a long-only commodity index strategy is *least likely* to adjust the portfolio:
    A. to reduce exposure to a declining commodity market.
    B. for changes in the composition of the commodity index.
    C. by closing out expiring contracts and re-establishing positions in new contracts.

ANSWERS – CONCEPT CHECKERS

1. **B**   Backwardation refers to the situation in which futures prices are less than the spot price. Commodity markets tend to be in backwardation when they are dominated by producers of the commodity.

2. **B**   The price return results from the change in the spot price. The roll yield is the gain or loss that results from closing a position in an expiring contract and re-establishing it in a new contract. The collateral yield is the return on the collateral deposited to establish the position.

3. **C**   For a commodities market in contango, if the spot price remains unchanged, the futures price will decrease over its life and the investor will realize a loss at expiration. Thus, the roll yield is negative.

4. **A**   A long-only commodity index strategy is always long the commodities in the index and the weights are not adjusted based on the performance of the positions. The manager must actively manage the roll out of expiring contracts, as well as matching any changes in the commodity index weightings.

10 questions, 15 minutes

1. Which of the following is *least likely* a similarity between a forward rate agreement based on LIBOR + 1.5% and an interest rate option on LIBOR?
    A. A long position in either one will result in a positive payment if interest rates increase above the contract rate.
    B. The payments to either are based on the difference between a contract rate and a market (reference) rate.
    C. If both have the same contract rate, notional principal, expiration date, and reference rate, they will make equal payments to their (long) owners.

2. Adam Vernon took a long position in four 100-ounce July gold futures contracts at 685 when spot gold was 670. Initial margin is $4,000 per contract and maintenance margin is $3,200 per contract. If the account is marked to market when spot gold is 660 and the futures price is 672, the additional margin the investor must deposit to keep the position open is *closest* to:
    A. $2,000.
    B. $4,000.
    C. $5,000.

3. The value of a call option on a stock is *least likely* to increase as a result of:
    A. an increase in asset price volatility.
    B. a decrease in the risk-free rate of interest.
    C. a decrease in the strike price of the option.

4. Kurt Crawford purchased shares of Acme, Inc., for $38 and sold call options at $40, covering all his shares for $2 each. The sum of the maximum per-share gain and maximum per-share loss (as an absolute value) on the covered call position is:
    A. $36.
    B. $40.
    C. unlimited.

5. Craig Grant has entered into a $10 million quarterly-pay equity swap based on the NASDAQ stock index as the 8% fixed rate payer when the index is at 2,750. Which of the following is *most accurate*?
    A. He will make a payment of $200,000 on the second payment date if the index is 2,750.
    B. He will neither make nor receive a payment on the first settlement date if the index is 2,805.
    C. If the index at the first settlement date is 2,782, he must make a payment at the second settlement date.

6. It is *least likely* that a forward contract on a zero-coupon bond:
    A. has counterparty risk.
    B. can be settled in cash.
    C. requires a margin deposit.

7. Survivorship bias in reported hedge fund index returns will *most likely* result in index:
   A. returns and risk that are biased upward.
   B. returns and risk that are biased downward.
   C. risk that is biased downward and returns that are biased upward.

8. A hedge fund with a 2 and 20 fee structure has a hard hurdle rate of 5%. If the incentive fee and management fee are calculated independently and the management fee is based on beginning-of-period asset values, an investor's net return over a period during which the gross value of the fund has increased 22% is *closest to*:
   A. 16.4%
   B. 16.6%
   C. 17.0%

9. Measures of downside risk for asset classes with asymmetric return distributions are *least likely* to include:
   A. value at risk (VaR).
   B. the Sortino ratio.
   C. kurtosis-adjusted standard deviation.

10. The type of real estate index that *most likely* exhibits sample selection bias is a(n):
    A. REIT index.
    B. appraisal index.
    C. repeat sales index.

SELF-TEST ANSWERS: DERIVATIVES AND ALTERNATIVE INVESTMENTS

1. **C** Because the FRA pays at the expiration of the forward contract, it pays the present value of the interest savings that would be realized at the end of the (hypothetical) loan term. The interest rate option will pay the interest savings on the (hypothetical) loan after expiration at the end of the loan term and its payment will be greater (since it's not discounted back to the expiration date).

2. **C** The initial margin is $4 \times \$4,000 = \$16,000$ and the maintenance margin is $4 \times \$3,200 = \$12,800$. The loss on the position is $(672 - 685) \times 4 \times 100 = -\$5,200$, leaving a balance of $\$16,000 - \$5,200 = \$10,800$. Because the account has fallen below the maintenance margin, a deposit of $5,200 is required to bring the balance back up to the initial margin.

3. **B** A decrease in the risk-free rate of interest will decrease call values. The other changes will tend to increase the value of a call option.

4. **B** The net cost of the covered call position is $38 - 2 = 36$, so the maximum loss (if the stock price goes to zero) is $36. The maximum gain (if the stock price goes to 40 or more) is $4. The sum is $36 + 4 = 40$.

5. **B** If the index has risen to 2,805 (+2%), the index payer's liability (2% × $10 million) just offsets the fixed rate payer's liability (8% / 4 × $10 million). The payment at the second settlement date cannot be determined without knowing the change in the index level between the first and second settlement dates. The index level at the first settlement date does not determine the payment at the second settlement date.

6. **C** Forward contracts typically do not require a margin deposit. They are custom instruments that may require settlement in cash or delivery of the underlying asset, and they have counterparty risk.

7. **C** Surviving firms are more likely to have had good past returns and have taken on less risk than the average fund, leading to upward bias in index returns and downward bias in index risk measures.

8. **B** The management fee is 2% of the beginning asset value, which reduces an investor's gross return by 2% to $22 - 2 = 20\%$. The incentive fee is 20% of the excess gross return over the hurdle rate, or $0.20(0.22 - 0.05) = 3.4\%$. The investor return net of fees is $22\% - 2\% - 3.4\% = 16.6\%$.

9. **C** Value at risk (VaR) and the Sortino ratio based on downside deviations from the mean are measures of downside risk. Kurtosis-adjusted standard deviation is not a concept presented in the curriculum.

10. **C** A repeat sales index includes prices of properties that have recently sold. Because these properties may not be representative of overall property values (may be biased toward properties that have declined or increased the most in value of the period), there is the risk of sample selection bias. An appraisal index or a REIT index is generally constructed for a sample of representative properties or REIT property pools.

FORMULAS

full price = clean price + accrued interest

$$\text{duration} = -\frac{\text{percentage change in bond price}}{\text{yield change in percent}}$$

value of a callable bond = value of an option-free bond − value of the call

$$\text{TIPS coupon payment} = \text{inflation-adjusted par value} \times \frac{\text{stated coupon rate}}{2}$$

absolute yield spread = yield on the higher-yield bond − yield on the lower-yield bond

$$\text{relative yield spread} = \frac{\text{absolute yield spread}}{\text{yield on the benchmark bond}}$$

$$\text{yield ratio} = \frac{\text{subject bond yield}}{\text{benchmark bond yield}}$$

after-tax yield = taxable yield × (1 − marginal tax rate)

$$\text{taxable-equivalent yield} = \frac{\text{tax-free yield}}{(1 - \text{marginal tax rate})}$$

$$\text{zero-coupon bond value} = \frac{\text{maturity value}}{(1+i)^{\text{number of years} \times 2}}$$

$$\text{current yield} = \frac{\text{annual cash coupon payment}}{\text{bond price}}$$

$$\text{bond equivalent yield} = \left[\left(1 + \text{monthly CFY}\right)^6 - 1\right] \times 2$$
$$= \left[\sqrt{1 + \text{annual-pay YTM}} - 1\right] \times 2$$

$$\text{effective annual yield} = \left(1 + \frac{\text{semiannual-pay YTM}}{2}\right)^2 - 1$$

spot rate from forward rates:

$$S_3 = \left[(1 + {_1f_0})(1 + {_1f_1})(1 + {_1f_2})\right]^{1/3} - 1$$

forward rate from spot rates:

$$_1f_2 = \frac{\left(1 + S_3\right)^3}{\left(1 + S_2\right)^2} - 1$$

$$\text{effective duration} = \frac{(\text{bond price when yields fall} - \text{bond price when yields rise})}{2 \times (\text{initial price}) \times (\text{change in yield in decimal form})} = \frac{V_- - V_+}{2V_0(\Delta y)}$$

percentage change in bond price = $-$effective duration $\times$ change in yield in percent

portfolio duration = $w_1 D_1 + w_2 D_2 + \ldots + w_N D_N$

percentage change in price = duration effect + convexity effect

$$= \{[-\text{duration} \times (\Delta y)] + [\text{convexity} \times (\Delta y)^2]\} \times 100$$

price value of a basis point = duration $\times$ 0.0001 $\times$ bond value

return impact of a change in spread $\approx -\text{duration} \times \Delta\text{spread} + \frac{1}{2}\text{convexity} \times (\Delta\text{spread})^2$

value of a long FRA at settlement: $(\text{notional principal}) \dfrac{(\text{floating} - \text{forward})\left(\dfrac{\text{days}}{360}\right)}{1 + \left[(\text{floating})\left(\dfrac{\text{days}}{360}\right)\right]}$

intrinsic value of a call: $C = \text{Max}[0, S - X]$

intrinsic value of a put: $P = \text{Max}[0, X - S]$

option value = intrinsic value + time value

lower and upper bounds for options:

Option	Minimum Value	Maximum Value
European call	$c_t \geq \text{Max}[0, S_t - X / (1 + RFR)^{T-t}]$	S_t
American call	$C_T \geq \text{Max}[0, S_t - X / (1 + RFR)^{T-t}]]$	S_t
European put	$p_t \geq \text{Max}[0, X / (1 + RFR)^{T-t} - S_t]$	$X / (1 + RFR)^{T-t}$
American put	$P_t \geq \text{Max}[0, X - S_t]$	X

put-call parity: $c + X / (1 + RFR)^T = S + p$

put-call parity with asset cash flows: $C + X / (1 + RFR)^T = (S_0 - PV_{CF}) + P$

plain-vanilla interest rate swap:

$$(\text{net fixed-rate payment})_t = (\text{swap fixed rate} - LIBOR_{t-1})\left(\frac{\text{number of days}}{360}\right)$$
$$\times \text{notional principal}$$

INDEX

©2012 Kaplan, Inc.

©2012 Kaplan, Inc.